Understanding
Technical Graphics

Co-operating authors:

John O'Sullivan, Tadhg O'Sullivan, Gabriel Wade

Gill & Macmillan

Gill & Macmillan Ltd
Hume Avenue
Park West
Dublin 12
with associated companies throughout the world
www.gillmacmillan.ie

ISBN-13: 978 0 7171 3829 6

Print origination in Ireland by Carole Lynch

Photo-realistic images in this book were generated using
Autodesk Inventor and reproduced courtesy of Autodesk

*The paper used in this book is made from the wood pulp of
managed forests. For every tree felled, at least one tree is planted,
thereby renewing natural resources.*

Picture Credits
For permission to reproduce photographs and other material the authors and publisher gratefully acknowledge the following:

ALDI Stores Ltd, A-Plant, Atlantic Homecare, Black and Decker Ireland, BLACKTIE, Bosch, Bus Eireann, Celtic Linen,
Joe Conway/Digicast, Daimler Chrysler, Delta Air Lines, Department of Transport, Dublin Bus, Four Star Pizza, Galway
County Council, Guaranteed Irish, Hewlett Packard, Iarnród Éireann, IDA Ireland, Kawasaki, Manchester United,
Marks & Spencer, Massey Ferguson, McDonalds, McMahon Group, Motorola, Nintendo, NRA, Pizza Hut, Procad Group,
Remax, Renault Ireland, Rosslare Europort, Shell, Siptu, Superquinn, Texaco (Ireland) Limited, Credit Union, The National
Lottery, Vodafone Ireland, Volkswagen, Whiskas, Wolverhampton Wanderers FC

69, 74 © The Advertising Archives; 6, 7, 18, 26, 96, 111, 159, 164, 166, 168, 175, 187, 199, 201, 230 © Alamy; 62, 99,
112 © Inpho; 10 © Photocall Ireland

The authors and publisher have made every effort to trace all copyright holders, but if any has been inadvertently overlooked
we would be pleased to make the necessary arrangement at the first opportunity.

Contents

Contents

Chapter 1
Learning to Draw

The Tee Square

The **tee square** is always positioned on the left-hand side of the drawing board. It is moved up and down the board as shown in the figure over. It consists of two parts, the **stock** and the **blade**.

The stock must always be held firmly against the edge of the drawing board.

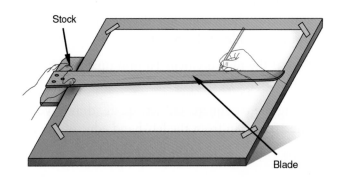

Paper

The paper is attached near the top left-hand corner of the drawing board. To get the paper straight on the board, move the tee square to the bottom of the board and line the paper up against it. The paper can be attached with **masking tape** or **drawing clips**. It is good practice to place one or two drawing sheets under the sheet being used to give a softer drawing surface.

Paper for technical graphics is available in various sizes. The A2 and A3 sizes are popular for school use.

Horizontal and Vertical Lines

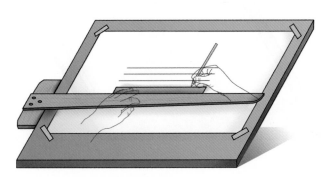
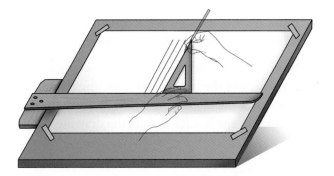

- To draw **horizontal lines**, place the **ruler** on the blade of the tee square as shown in the figure above (left). Holding the stock against the edge of the drawing board, slide the tee square and ruler up and down to draw **horizontal lines**.
- To draw **vertical lines**, place either of your **set squares** on the edge of the tee square as shown in the figure above (right). Sliding the set square along the tee square enables you to draw **vertical lines**.

Hold the pencil close to the point, always 'pulling' and never 'pushing' it. Rotate it slowly between your thumb and fingers, and go over each line two or three times.

Drawing the Border

A **border** is a line drawn around the edge of the sheet. It helps to improve the appearance of a drawing. It should be the darkest line on the paper, and is normally 10 mm in from the edge of the sheet. It is drawn with a **H pencil**. All four lines of the border should be the same darkness and thickness.

1. Measure down from the top edge of the paper a distance of 10 mm and mark a dot.

2. Slide the tee square and ruler up to touch the dot and draw a horizontal line through it 10 mm in from each side of the paper.

3. Repeat the measurement 10 mm up from the bottom edge of the paper.

4. Using the tee square and set square, draw a vertical line 10 mm in from the left-hand edge of the paper.

5. Repeat this on the right-hand side.

Technical drawings are always framed within a border.

Activity Attach a sheet of paper to your drawing board and draw in the border.

Sheet Layout and Balance

The **layout** is the arrangement of the drawing on the sheet. All technical drawings should be **balanced**. This means that each drawing should be positioned in the middle of the paper. To balance a drawing, do the following:

1. Subtract the overall length of the drawing from the overall length of the border and divide the result by two. This gives the distance to come in from the border to start the drawing.

2. Subtract the overall height of the drawing from the width of the border and halve the result. This gives the distance to come up from the bottom of the border to start the drawing.

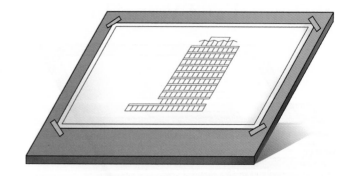

Outlines

These are thick, continuous lines used to show the outline of the object. They are drawn crisp, clear and dark with a **2H pencil**. All outlines should be the same darkness and thickness.

Take great care to ensure that the lines touch at all corners, never stopping short to leave a gap, nor drawing too far to show a projecting 'whisker'.

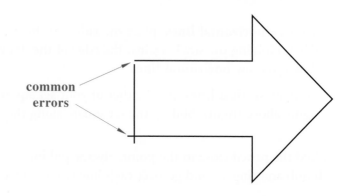

common errors

Exercises

1. Draw the view of the **fireplace** shown in the figure below to the given dimensions. Make sure to **balance** the drawing.

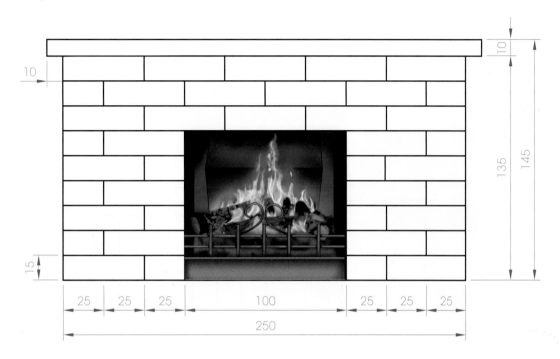

2. (a) Copy the view of the **gate** shown in the figure below, making sure your drawing is **balanced** on the sheet.

   (b) Draw a gate of your own design. You will find a sketch helpful to start with.

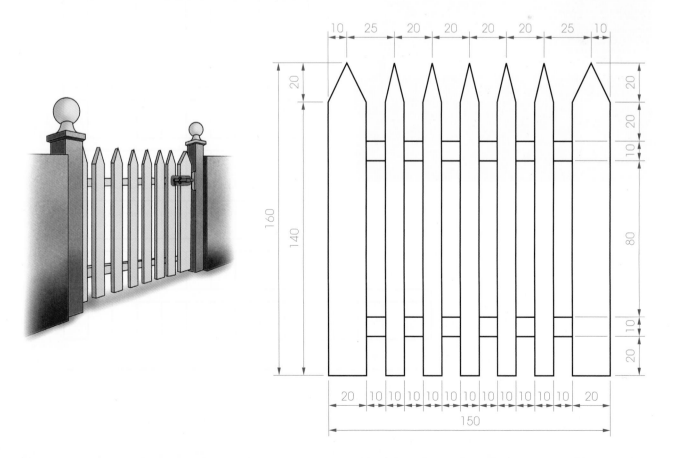

3. (a) The drawing of the **office block** in the figure below has been made using mainly horizontal and vertical lines. Draw the office block to the given dimensions. Don't forget to balance the drawing on the sheet!

(b) Design a **multistorey** building of your own, using mainly horizontal and vertical lines.

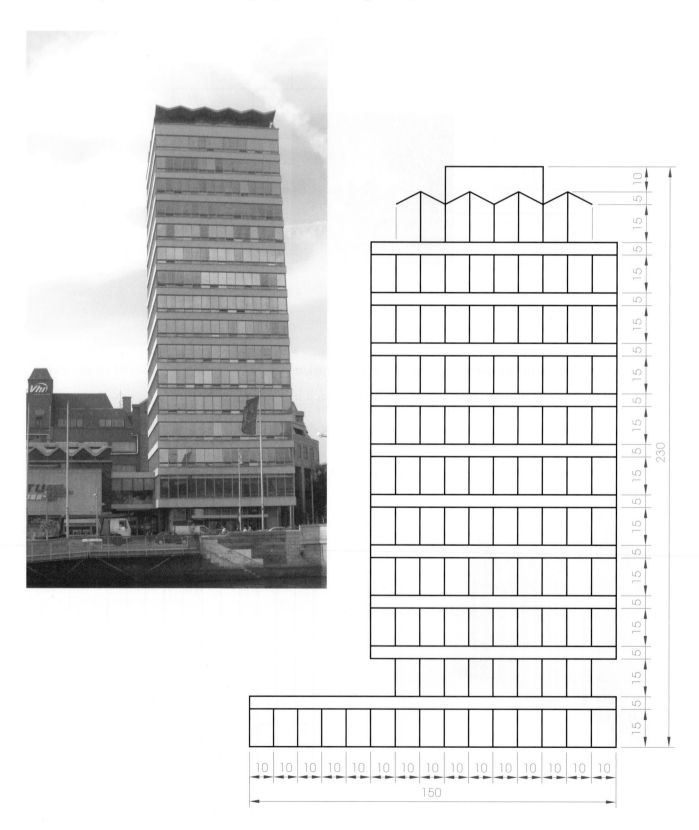

Construction Lines

These are thin continuous lines that form the basis upon which we build up rectangular drawings. They should be drawn faint, but clear. They can be drawn with a **3H** or **4H pencil**. Use very little pressure on the pencil for construction lines.

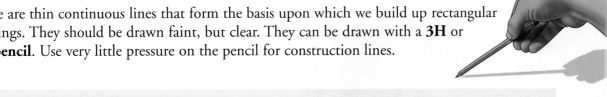

Hold the pencil close to its end, tilt it in the direction of travel and trail it by its own weight.

Logograms

A **logogram** or **logo** is a graphical symbol used to stand for a company or its product.

As a form of graphic communication it is a company's trademark or shorthand symbol. The figures below show drawings of the logos for the **Speedo** and **Pizza Hut** companies respectively.

Exercises

1. The logo for the **Speedo** sportswear manufacturer is shown in the figure below. It is drawn on a grid made up of *equally spaced* horizontal and vertical **construction lines**. Draw the logo on a grid as shown.

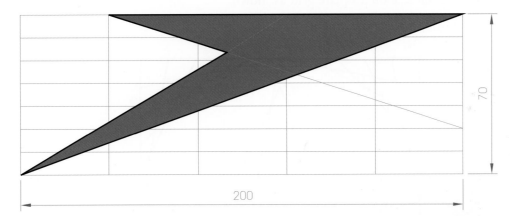

2. The logo for **Pizza Hut** in the figure below is drawn using a grid of equally spaced horizontal and vertical lines.

   Draw the logo on a grid as shown.

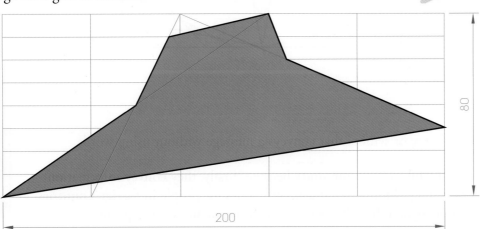

3. Draw the **National Housebuilding Guarantee Scheme** logo, using a grid as shown in the figure below. The grid is made up of 15 mm squares.

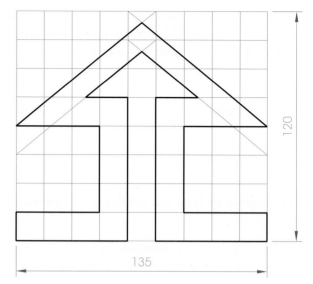

4. The figure below is a design drawn on a square grid of 15 mm squares. Notice how the straight lines give the impression of a circular curve.

(a) Draw this design full-size on a square grid as shown.

(b) Using a similar grid, make a drawing of your own design.

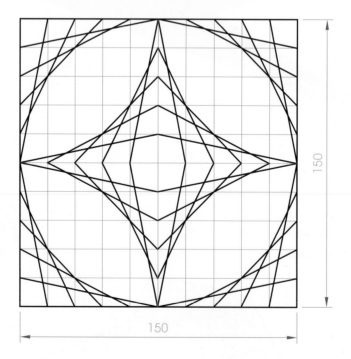

Pictograms

A **pictogram** is a picture or symbol that conveys a message without using words.

Pictograms are very useful to the community because, firstly, they convey information quickly, and secondly, they eliminate language difficulties for people in foreign countries. The figure over is a pictogram directing tourists to a caravan and camping site.

Exercises

1. **(a)** The figure shown below is a pictogram for a **ski resort**.

Draw the design using a 10 mm square grid as shown to build up your drawing.

(b) Use your imagination to design a pictogram for a **running track**.

Draw the design on a square grid similar to the one shown below.

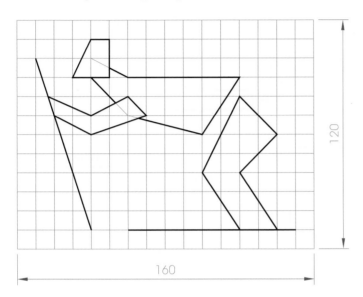

160

120

Lettering

Lettering helps to communicate information on drawings. All lettering should be done freehand without the aid of instruments. It must be **neat**, **clear** and **easy to read**. There are many different approaches to lettering, but the one shown below is standard for school use.

The letters and numbers are formed between light construction lines called **guidelines**, which are drawn 4 or 5 mm apart. **Capital letters** are usually used, but lower-case letters may be used. Note the following:

• The letters **A C D E G H K M O Q R W** fill a square space.

• The letters **O** and **Q** are based on a circle.

• The remainder (except **I**) fill about two-thirds of a square.

• Space between words should be equal to the width of one letter, and the distance between letters and numbers must be uniform. Keep the letters in each word close together.

Answer Worksheet 1A

Exercises

1. (a) The **flow chart** shown below is for the knockout stages of the **All-Ireland Football Championship**. Draw the chart as shown.

(b) Practise your lettering by entering the teams you predict will make it through from the Quarter Final stage to the Final of this years' All-Ireland Football Championship.

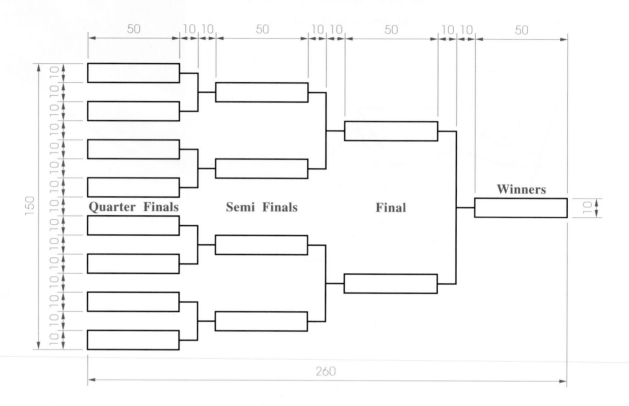

Title Block

Every drawing needs a **title block** to show the title of the drawing, your name and the date. There are many different styles. Two possibilities for title blocks are shown in the figure over.

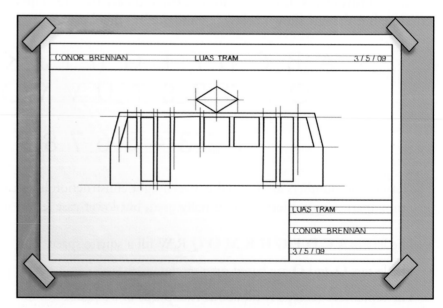

Lettering in the title block space is done between the guidelines. The **title** of the drawing, the **name** of the student and the **date** are usually included.

Monograms

A **monogram** is a logo that uses only text to convey a message.

Exercises

1. Shown in the figure below is a drawing of the **CAO** monogram. Reproduce the drawing full-size on an A3 sheet. Use **construction lines** to build up your drawing and don't forget to include a **title block**!

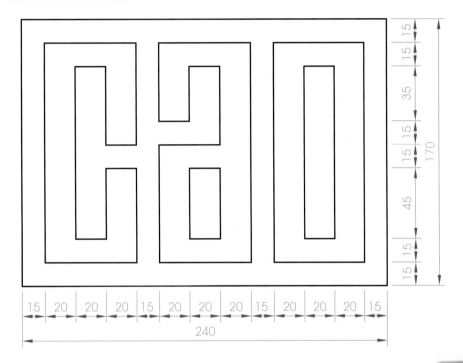

2. A drawing of an **EXIT** sign is shown in the figure below.
   Draw the sign to the sizes given on an A3 sheet, using **construction lines** to build up your drawing.

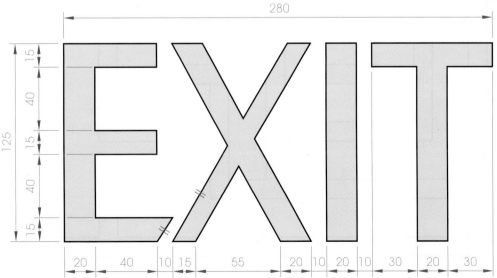

3. Draw the given view of a **Luas** tram shown in the figure below using **construction lines** to build up your drawing.

Insert a **title block** on the sheet.

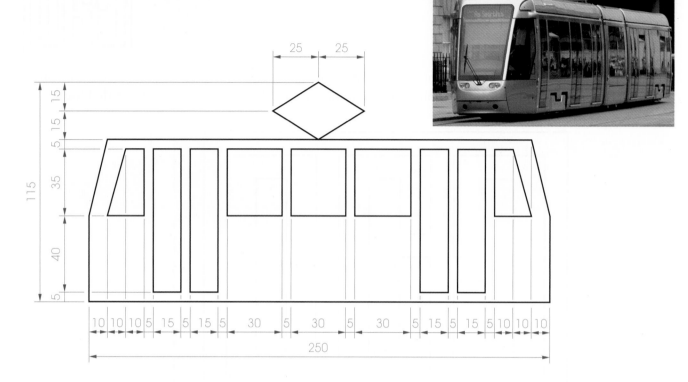

4. The drawing in the figure below shows a **maze** made up of a series of horizontal and vertical lines. The walls are 10 mm thick and the pathways are 20 mm wide.

Reproduce the drawing full-size on an A3 sheet. Using **construction lines** to build up your drawing will make the work easier to do!

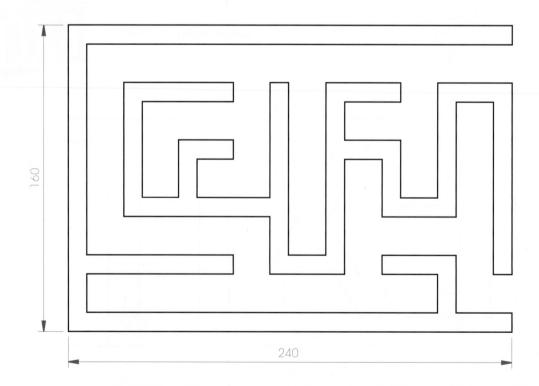

Chapter 2
Inclined Lines

Set Squares

Set squares are used to draw lines at 30, 45, 60 and 90 degrees. They are made of clear plastic so that you can see the drawing underneath. You will need two: a **45°** and a **30°/60° set square**.

By holding a set square against the tee square as shown in the figure below you can draw lines at 45°, 60° and 30° to the horizontal. The production of a technical drawing can be speeded up considerably by using set squares to obtain these angles.

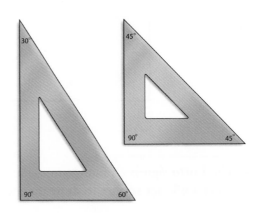

Lines at 45°

Lines at 60°

Lines at 30°

Exercises

1. The **Level Crossing Ahead** road sign is shown across. A drawing of a portion of this sign is shown in the figure below.

   Reproduce this drawing to the given dimensions, using a **45° set square** to draw the inclined lines.

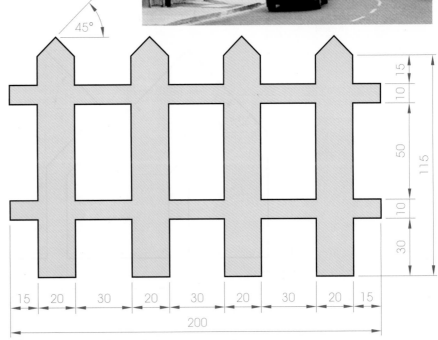

2. Make a full-size drawing of the **road direction sign** shown in the figure below. Use a **45° set square** to draw the inclined lines.

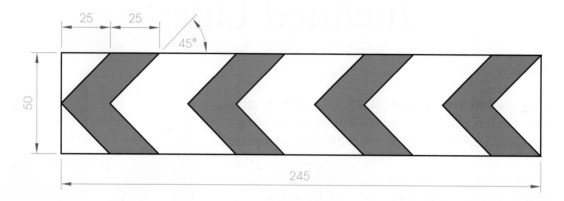

3. The **Lotto** sign is a monogram made up of a series of horizontal, vertical and 45° lines. Copy this sign using a **45° set square** to draw the inclined lines.

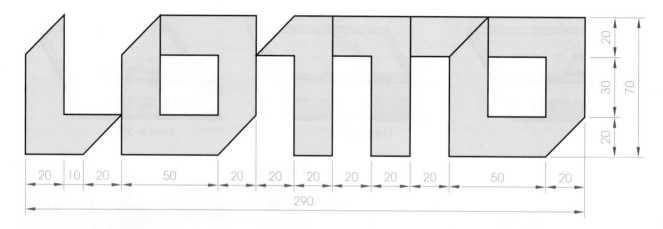

4. Shown below is a drawing of part of the logo for **McMahon's** builders suppliers. *All the inclined lines are drawn at an angle of 45°.*

Reproduce the drawing to the given dimensions.

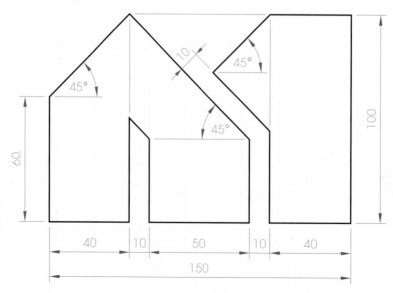

5. The **Ulster Bank** logo shown below is drawn on a grid where all angles are 60°. Using the measurement given and your **60° set square** to draw inclined lines, draw the logo.

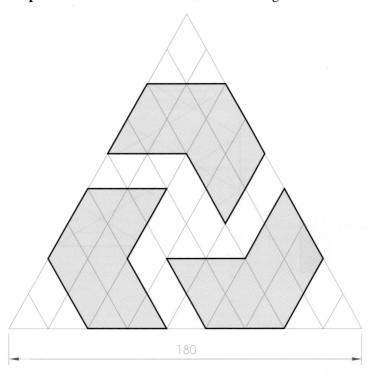

6. The figure below shows a drawing of the logo used by **EA Games**.

Make a drawing of this design, showing all construction lines.

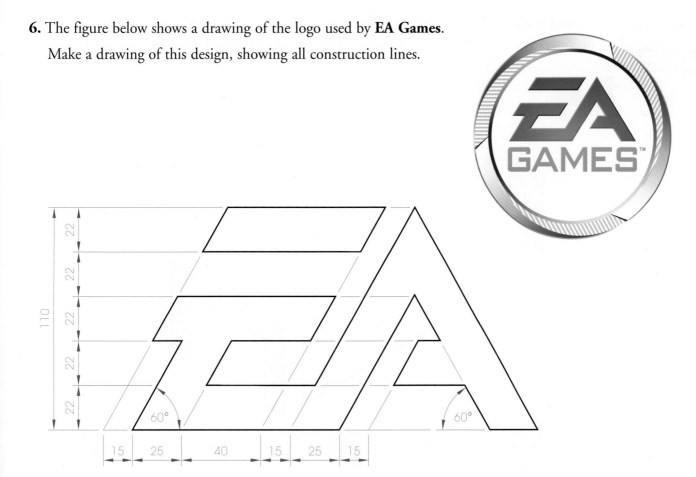

7. A drawing of a **box junction** is shown below. Reproduce the drawing to the given dimensions, using your **30° set square** to draw the inclined lines.

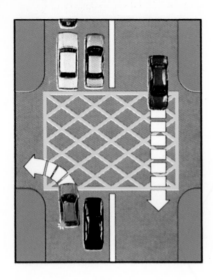

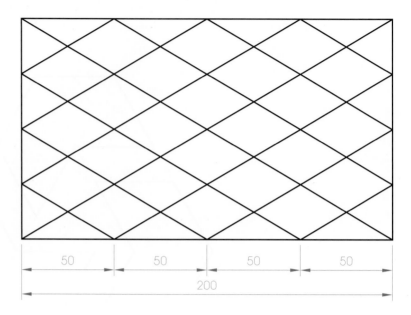

| 50 | 50 | 50 | 50 |

200

8. A sign for an **hotel** is shown in the figure below. It is drawn on a grid where all angles are 30°. Reproduce the drawing to the given dimensions. Use your **30° set square** to draw the inclined lines.

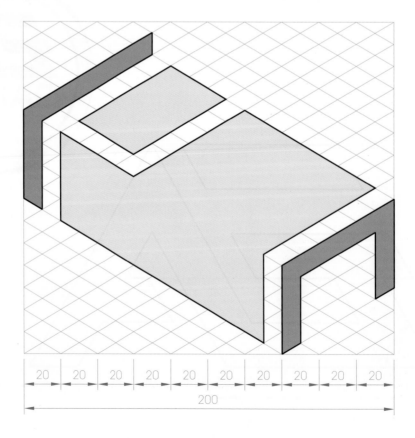

| 20 | 20 | 20 | 20 | 20 | 20 | 20 | 20 | 20 | 20 |

200

Drawing Angles with Set Squares

The 30°/60° and 45° set squares can be used to obtain certain inclined lines other than those at 30°, 60° and 45°. The drawings below show how the two set squares can be combined to obtain angles of 75° and 15°.

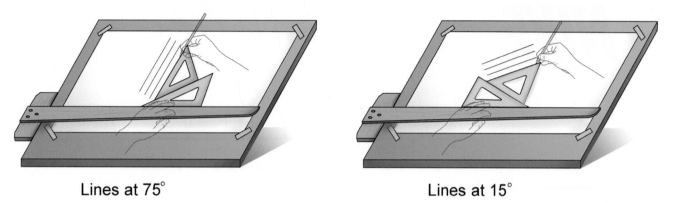

Lines at 75°   Lines at 15°

Exercises

1. Shown below are three drawings that contain lines drawn at 15° and 75° respectively. Reproduce each of the drawings to the given dimensions. For each drawing, combine the two set squares to draw the sloping lines at 75° and 15°.

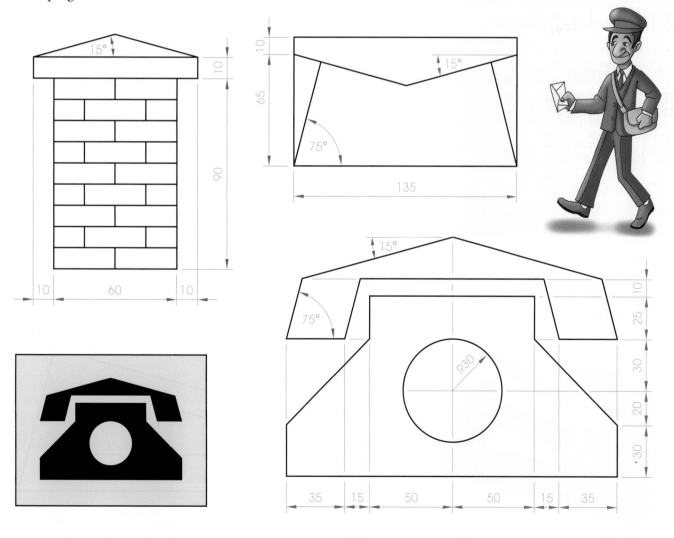

2. Reproduce full-size the drawing of the **Nike** monogram shown below. Combine the 45° and 30°/60° set squares to draw the lines at 75°.

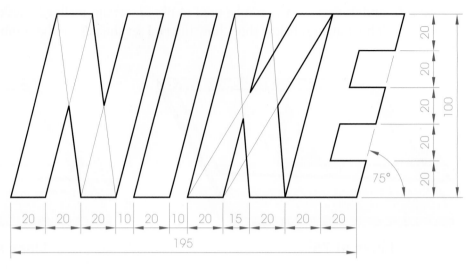

3. Reproduce the drawing of the **shopping trolley bay sign** shown in the figure below.

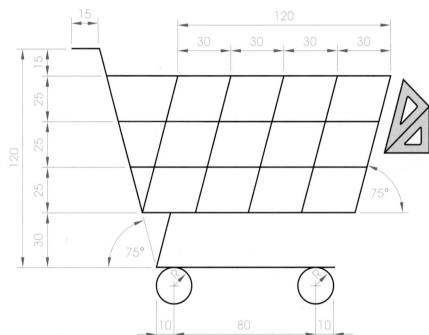

4. Reproduce the drawing of the **staple gun** shown in the figure below to the given dimensions.

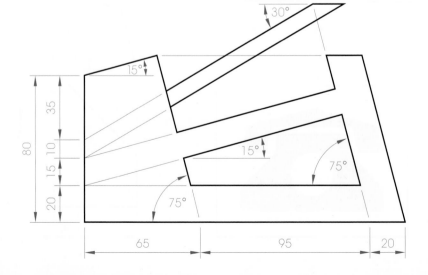

Chapter 3

Angles

Two straight lines meeting at a point form an angle. The lines are
called the **arms** of the angle, and the point is called the **vertex**.
The symbol for angle is ∠. Angles are measured in **degrees**.

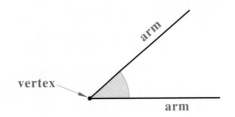

There are 360° in a full circle.

Protractor

A **protractor** is used to measure angles. The figure below shows a protractor that can be used to measure angles
between 0° and 180°. It has two scales – an **inner scale** and an **outer scale**. These go in opposite directions.

The **outer scale** goes from zero on the left in a clockwise
direction around to 180.

The **inner scale** goes from zero on the right in an anti-
clockwise direction around to 180.

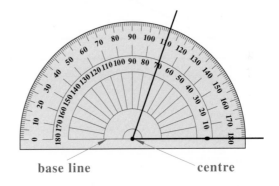

The diagram over shows how to draw an angle of 70°.

The **centre** of the protractor is positioned at the vertex of the angle.

The **base line** of the protractor is placed exactly on one arm of the angle.

Answer Worksheet 3A

Exercises

1. Draw full-size the view of a
picnic bench shown in the
figure over.

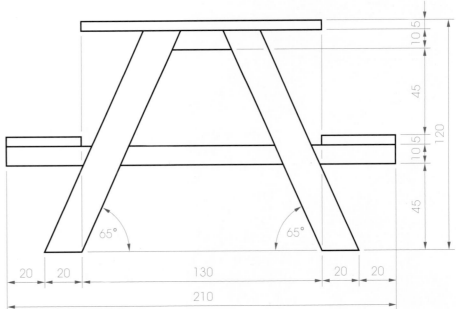

2. Shown below are a photograph and drawing of the **Boyne cable bridge**. Reproduce the given drawing.

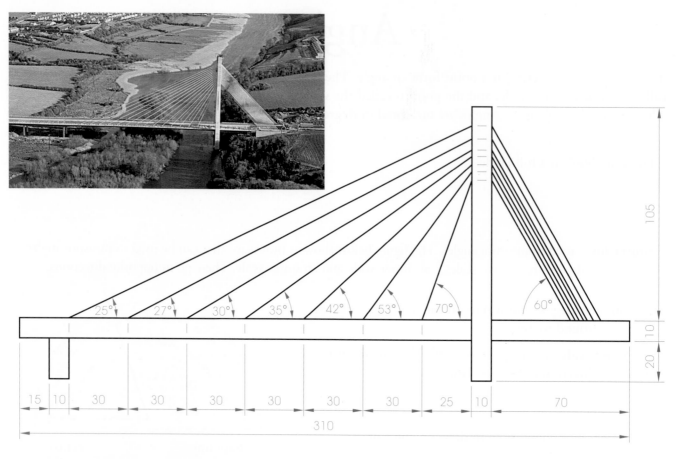

3. Make a drawing of the **pylon** to the given dimensions.

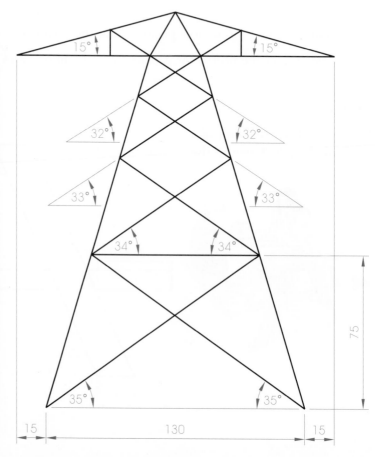

4. The drawing below shows a view of a **tent**. The window is in the shape of a **square**. Reproduce this drawing to the given dimensions.

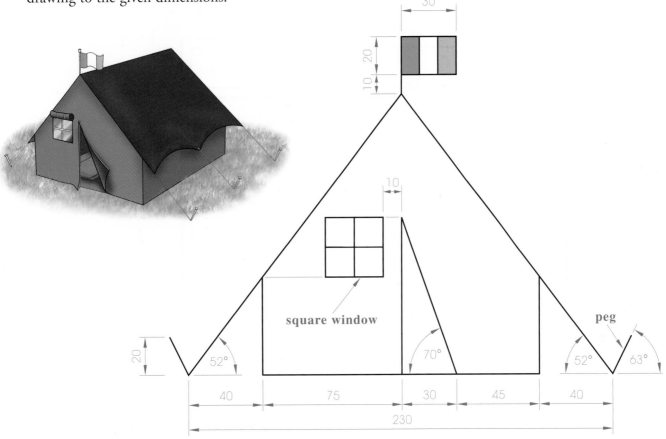

5. This is the logo used by **Iarnród Éireann**. This sign gives the impression of movement and fast transportation. Make a drawing of this design showing all construction lines.

Start the drawing at point A. Don't forget to combine the two set squares to draw the lines at 75°.

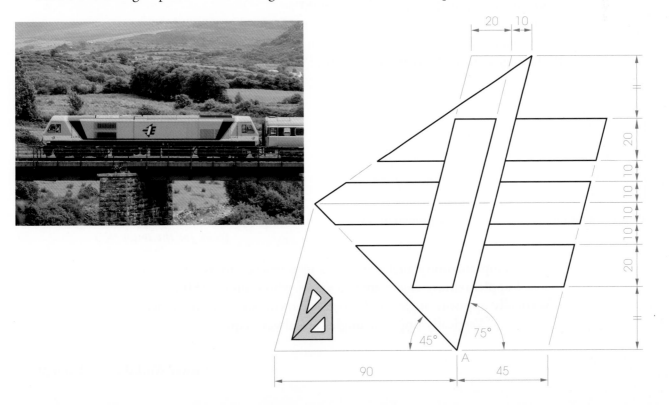

6. Make a full-size drawing of the **rectangular gate** shown below, showing all construction lines.

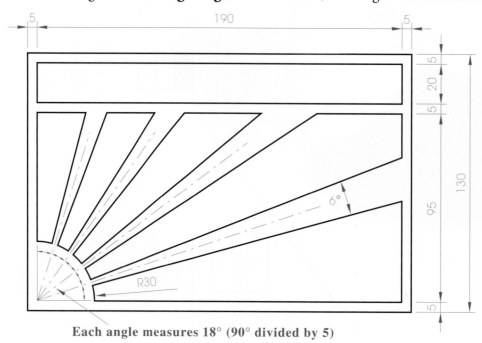

Each angle measures 18° (90° divided by 5)

Types of Angles

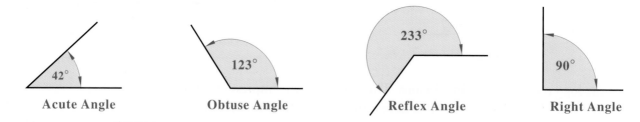

42°	123°	233°	90°
Acute Angle	**Obtuse Angle**	**Reflex Angle**	**Right Angle**

Acute angles are angles that are less than 90°.
Obtuse angles are angles that are more than 90° and less than 180°.
Reflex angles are angles that are more than 180°.
Right angles are angles that measure 90°.

Pairs of Angles

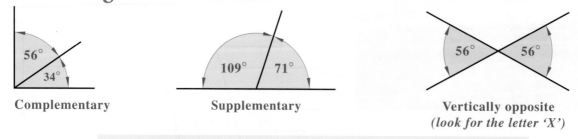

56° 34°	109° 71°	56° 56°
Complementary	**Supplementary**	**Vertically opposite** *(look for the letter 'X')*

Complementary angles are two angles whose sum is 90°.
Supplementary angles are two angles whose sum is 180°.
Vertically opposite angles are formed when two straight lines cross.
Vertically opposite angles are always equal.

Answer Worksheets 3B and 3C

Perpendicular Lines

Perpendicular lines are lines that meet at right angles.

The figure over shows two perpendicular lines. The symbol shows that the angle between the two lines is 90°.

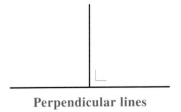

Perpendicular lines

Example
Draw a line from A perpendicular to the line BC.

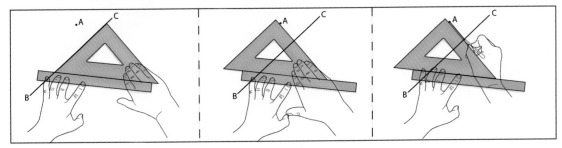

1. Place one of the shorter edges of the 45° set square so that it lines up with BC. Place the ruler against the set square as illustrated (above, left).

2. Hold the ruler firmly on the paper so that it remains stationary. Slide the set square along the ruler until the other edge of the set square is in line with A as illustrated (above, middle). Draw a line through A to meet the line BC. This line is perpendicular to BC (above, right).

Parallel Lines

Parallel lines are lines in a plane that never meet.

The figure across shows two parallel lines. These lines will never meet no matter how far they are extended.

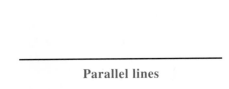

Parallel lines

Example
Draw a line parallel to PQ and a distance of 20 mm from it.

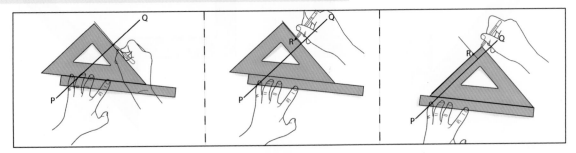

1. Place one of the shorter edges of the 45° set square so that it lines up with PQ. Hold the ruler firmly against the set square so that it remains stationary and slide the set square along the ruler for any distance. Draw a line perpendicular to PQ as illustrated (above, left).

2. Mark a point R on this line 20 mm from PQ (above, middle). Slide the set square along the ruler until the other edge of the set square is in line with R. Draw a line through R parallel to PQ (above, right).

Answer Worksheet 3D

Exercises

1. Can you find a pair of **vertically opposite angles** in the drawing of the **Umbro** emblem shown in the figure below? Notice that the emblem is **symmetrical** i.e. the same shape on either side of the two centre lines.

    Make a full-size drawing of the emblem. Apply shading or colour to enhance your drawing.

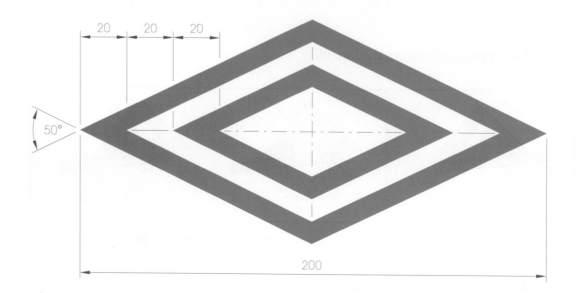

2. The figure below shows a drawing of **turn signals**. Reproduce this drawing full-size, showing all construction lines.

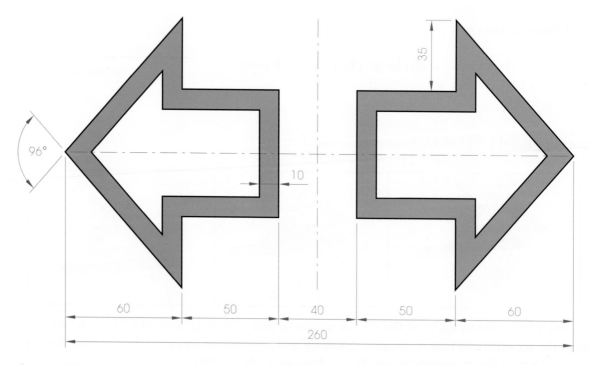

All margins are 10 mm

3. (a) Draw the **Dublin Bus** logo to the sizes given.

  (b) Draw, to your own design, the side view of a double-decker bus. Incorporate the **Dublin Bus** logo in your drawing.

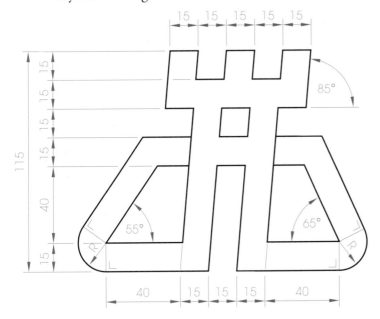

Corresponding and Alternate Angles

The figure below shows a straight line T and a pair of parallel lines, L and K. The line T cuts the parallel lines at two separate points. When a line cuts two parallel lines, pairs of **corresponding angles** and **alternate angles** are formed. The figure shows an example of a pair of **corresponding angles** (below, left) and a pair of **alternate angles** (below, right).

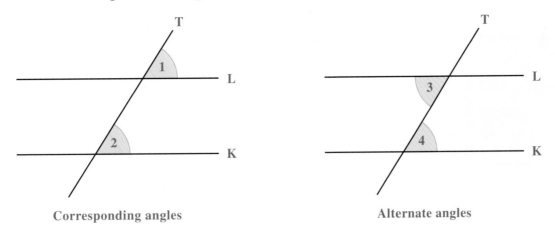

Corresponding angles   Alternate angles

∠1 and ∠2 are called **corresponding angles** because the position of ∠1 with respect to T and L is the same as the position of ∠2 with respect to T and K. ∠3 and ∠4 are called **alternate angles** because they are positioned on alternate sides of the line T.

When a straight line cuts two parallel lines:

• Corresponding angles are equal.

• Alternate angles are equal.

Answer Worksheet 3E

Exercises

1. The figure below shows a sign for an **All-weather pitch**. Can you find two pairs of **alternate angles** in the drawing?

Reproduce the drawing of the sign to the given dimensions.

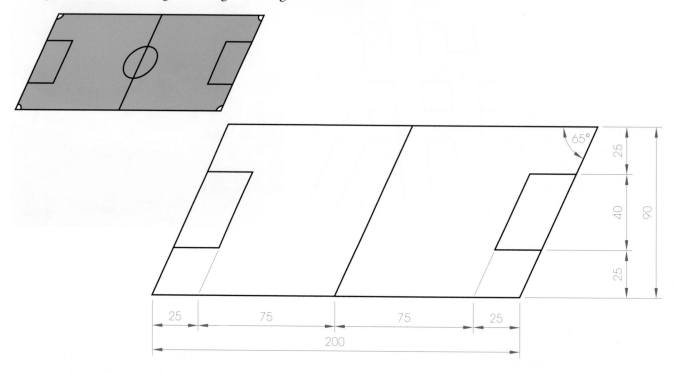

2. Reproduce the drawing of the **Aldi** sign to the given dimensions. Use a coloured pencil to enhance your drawing.

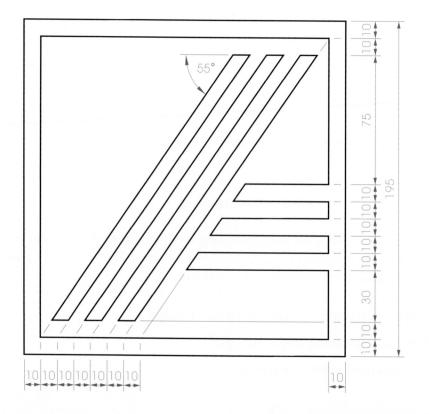

3. Make a full-size drawing of the **Woodie's** logo shown in the figure below.

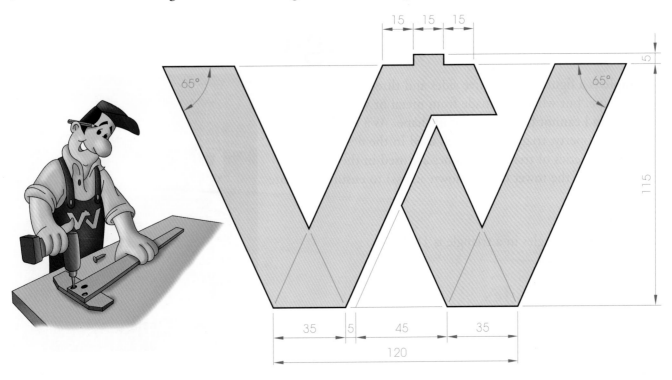

4. Reproduce the drawing of the **Massey Ferguson** logo to the given dimensions. The three triangles in the design are **congruent**.

> **Congruent** shapes are shapes that have the same shape and size.

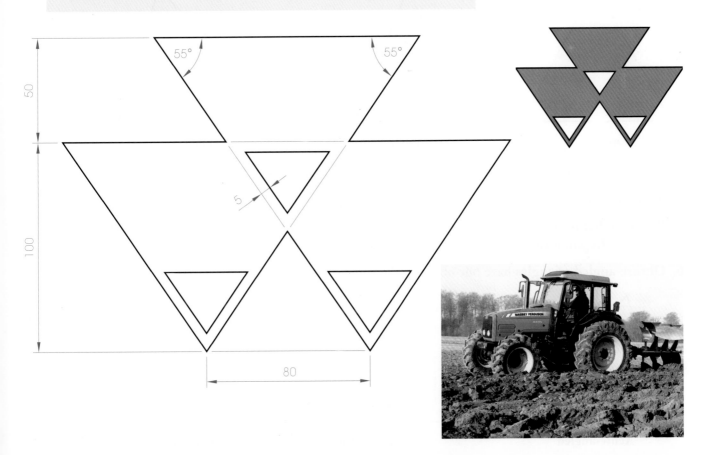

Chapter 4

Triangles

A **triangle** is a figure having three sides and three angles. It is a simple shape, but when it is made from metal or wood it is strong and rigid and cannot be pushed out of shape. As a result of this structural property, triangles are often used in the design of structures. A series of triangular frames are used in the construction of the tower crane (shown across) to ensure adequate strength.

The sum of the angles in a triangle is 180°.

Types of Triangles

There are six different types of triangles; three of these are named by the length of their sides:

1. **Equilateral triangles** have three equal sides and three equal angles. Each angle measures **60°**.
2. **Isosceles triangles** have two equal sides and two equal angles. The equal angles are opposite the equal sides.
3. **Scalene triangles** have no equal sides and no equal angles.

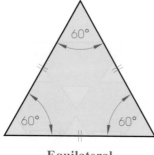

Equilateral

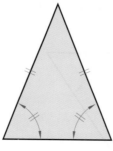

Isosceles

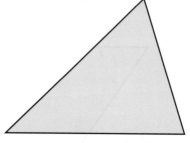

Scalene

The other three types of triangles are named by the size of their angles:

4. **Acute-angled triangles** have three acute angles.
5. **Right-angled triangles** have one right angle and two acute angles. The side opposite the right angle is called the **hypotenuse**.
6. **Obtuse-angled triangles** have one obtuse angle and two acute angles.

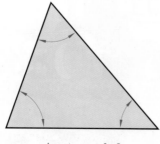

Acute-angled

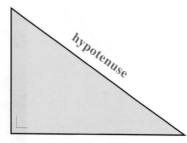

hypotenuse

Right-angled

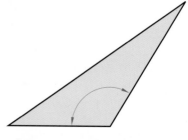

Obtuse-angled

Exterior Angles of a Triangle

An **exterior angle** of a triangle is formed when one side is extended through a vertex. In the figure over, the base of the triangle is extended to form an **exterior angle**.

> The exterior angle at any vertex in a triangle is equal to the sum of the two interior opposite angles.

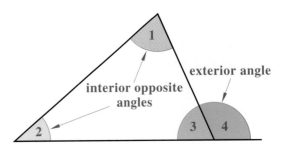

In the figure across, $\angle 4 = \angle 1 + \angle 2$.

The following activity is an informal proof of the theorem:

1. Cut out a triangle of any shape and size from a sheet of paper.
2. Cut off the two angles opposite the exterior angle and arrange these at the exterior angle as shown across.
3. Notice that the two interior opposite angles together form the exterior angle.

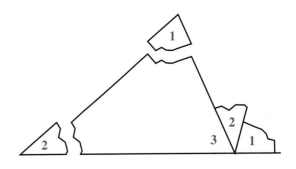

Answer Worksheet 4A

Properties of Triangles

The **vertex** or **apex** is the point of the angle opposite the **base**.

The **altitude** is the perpendicular distance from the apex to the base.

The angles at the base are called the **base angles**.

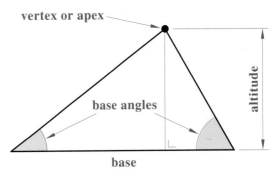

Example 1
Construct a **triangle** having a base of length 80 mm and **base angles** of 60° and 40°.

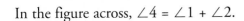

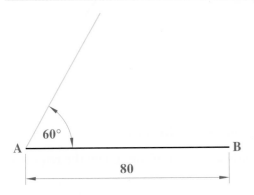

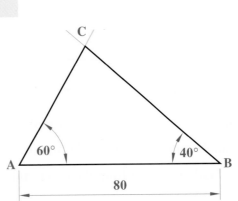

1. Draw the **base** AB 80 mm in length.
2. Using the 60°/30° set square, construct a 60° angle at A.
3. Using a protractor, construct a 40° angle at B, cutting the 60° line at C. Then ABC is the required triangle.

Example 2
Construct a **triangle** having sides of length 70 mm, 65 mm and 55 mm.

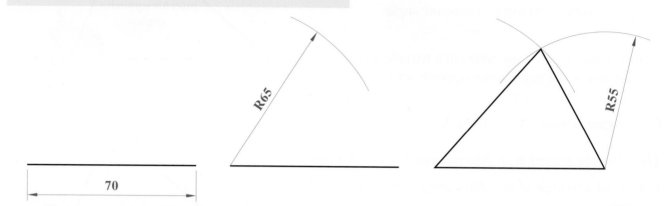

1. Draw the **base** of the triangle of length 70 mm.

2. With the point of the compass at one end of the base, swing an arc of radius 65 mm.

3. Swing an arc of radius 55 mm from the other end of the base to intersect the first arc. Draw the required triangle.

Example 3
Construct a **triangle** having a **base** of length 90 mm, a side of length 75 mm and an **altitude** of 60 mm.

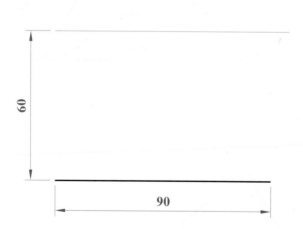

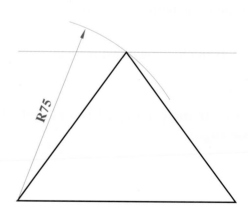

1. Draw the **base** of the triangle, 90 mm in length.

2. Draw a line parallel to the base and a distance of 60 mm from it. This is the **altitude**.

3. Swing an arc of radius 75 mm from the other end of the base to intersect the altitude. Draw the required triangle.

Always use this parallel line method when the altitude is given.

Answer Worksheet 4B

Exercises

1. The **Mitsubishi** logo shown below has become one of the most widely used logos in the world. The basic shape is an **equilateral triangle** of side 150 mm.

   Draw the logo. Using a coloured pencil, apply shading to your drawing.

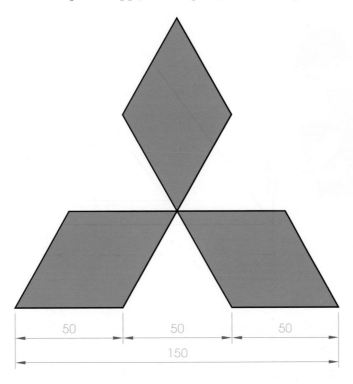

2. The drawing shown in the figure below is the symbol for a **hazard light** switch in a car. It is composed of a series of **equilateral triangles**. The **altitude** of the outer triangle is 140 mm.

   Reproduce the drawing full-size. Apply shading to your drawing with a coloured pencil.

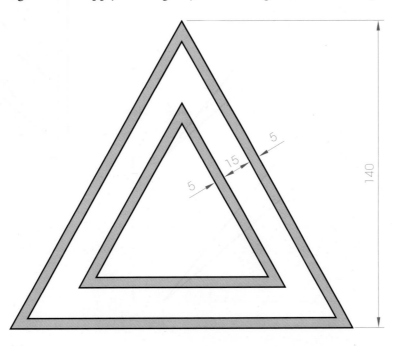

3. A sign for a **camp site** is shown in the figure below. It contains two **isosceles triangles** which are **similar** (see page 33). The base of the larger triangle is 140 mm long and the two equal sides are each of length 115 mm.

Make a full-size drawing of the sign showing all construction lines.

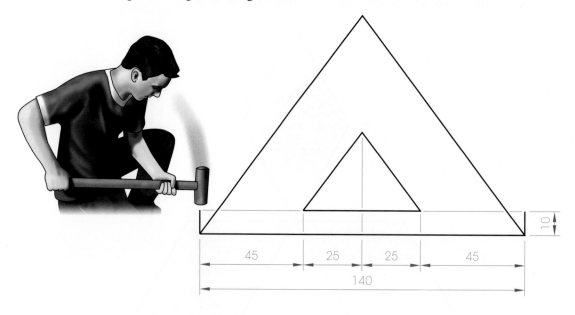

4. A drawing of the symbol for the **Citroen** car company is shown below. Notice that the symbol contains two sets of **isosceles triangles**.

Using the measurements given, make a full-size drawing of the symbol.

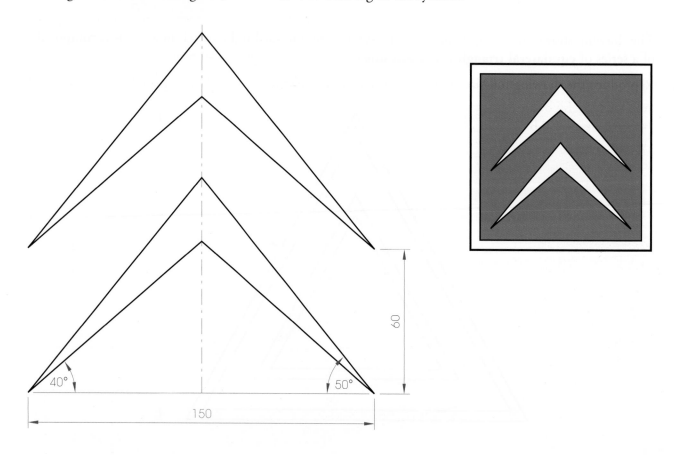

5. The drawing of the **Irish Insurance Federation** symbol shown across is based on an **isosceles triangle**.

Make a copy of this drawing.

Irish Insurance Federation

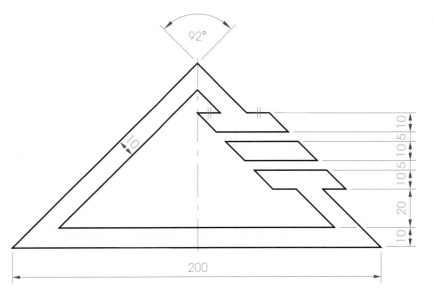

6. A drawing of the **Delta Airlines** emblem is shown across. You will notice that the emblem contains two interlocking **isosceles triangles**.

Draw the emblem.

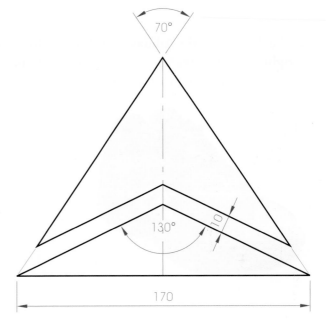

7. Make a full-size drawing of the **Blacktie** logo shown below. The sides AB and BC of the **scalene** triangle ABC are of lengths 70 mm and 100 mm, respectively.

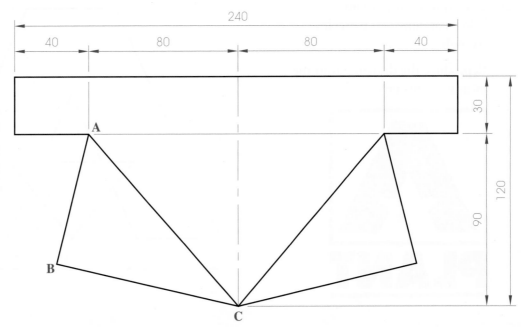

8. A drawing of the **Autoglass** sign is shown below. It is made up of **right-angled triangles** and **rectangles**. All margins are 5 mm. Copy the drawing.

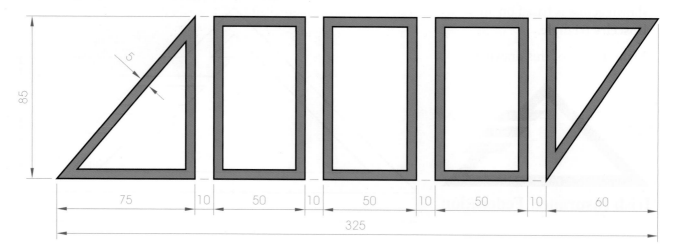

9. The drawing of the **Adidas** logo shown below is based around **three right-angled triangles**. The length of the **hypotenuse** of the largest triangle is given. Copy the drawing.

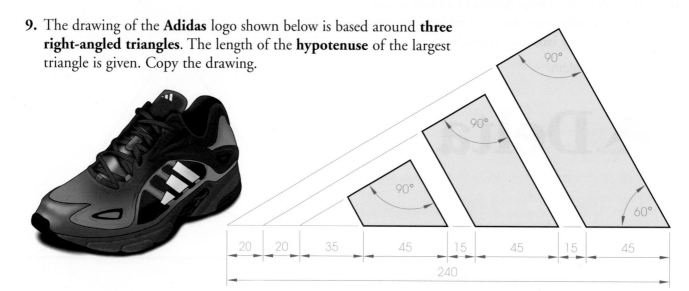

10. The symbol for **A Plant** shown below contains two **isosceles triangles**.

Reproduce the drawing from the measurements given.

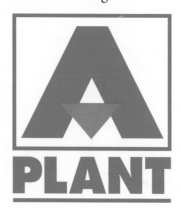

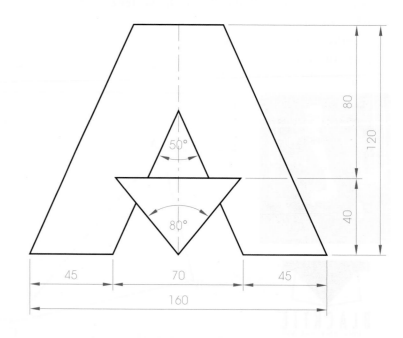

Ratios in Geometry

Ratios are used to compare quantities. For example, if the lengths of two line segments are 10 mm and 30 mm respectively, the ratio of the lengths is 1:3. We can be asked to divide a line in a given ratio.

Dividing a Line in a Given Ratio

Example
Divide the given line PQ in the ratio 3:2.

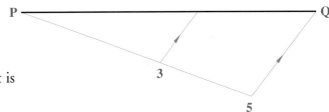

1. Draw a line at an angle to PQ and of a length that is exactly divisible by five (3 + 2) – say 50 mm.

2. Mark off the line in the ratio 30:20 which is the same as the ratio 3:2. Join the end of the line to Q.

3. Draw a line parallel to this line through point 3, cutting PQ in the ratio 3:2.

Dividing a Line into a Number of Equal Parts

Example
Divide the given line AB into five equal parts.

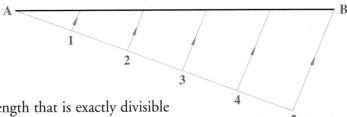

1. Draw a line at an acute angle to AB and of a length that is exactly divisible by five (say 100 mm).

2. Mark off the line into five equal parts (100 ÷ 5 = 20 mm). Join the end of the line to B.

3. Draw lines parallel to this line through points 4, 3, 2 and 1, dividing AB into five equal parts.

Answer Worksheet 4C

Similar Triangles

Similar triangles are triangles that are the same shape, but not the same size.

When two triangles are similar, the angles of one are the same size as the angles of the other. In similar triangles, the sides of each triangle are in the same ratio. In the figure below, the sides of the similar triangles are in the same ratio 3:4:5.

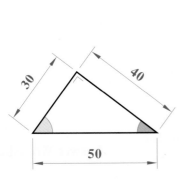
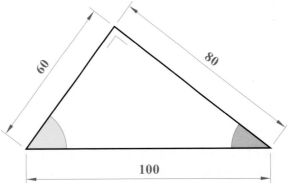

Perimeter of a Triangle

The perimeter of a triangle is the sum of the lengths of the three sides.

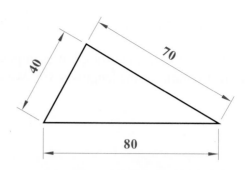

Thus, the **perimeter** of the triangle over
= 80 + 70 + 40
= 190 mm

Example 1

Construct a triangle having a perimeter of 125 mm and having sides in the ratio 2:3:4.

1. Draw the line AB 125 mm long. Draw a line at an acute angle to AB and of a length that is divisible by 9 (2 + 3 + 4) – say 90 mm.

2. Mark off the line in the ratio 20:30:40, which is the same as the ratio 2:3:4. Join the end of the line to B.

3. Draw lines parallel to this line through the points 2 and 5, cutting AB at the points C and D. Draw the base CD of the triangle.

4. Using C and D as centres and CA and DB as radii respectively, draw the two arcs intersecting at E. Join CE and DE. CDE is the required triangle.

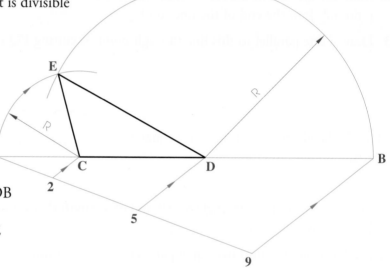

Example 2

Construct a triangle similar to ABC having a perimeter of 115 mm.

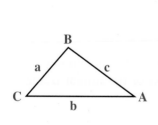

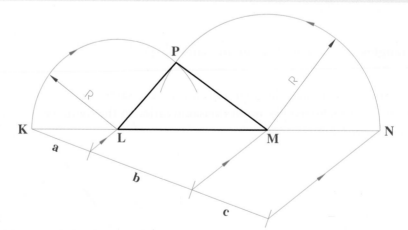

1. Draw the line KN 115 mm long and divide it in the ratio a:b:c.

2. Draw the base LM of the triangle.

3. Using L and M as centres and LK and MN as radii respectively, draw the two arcs intersecting at P. Join LP and MP. LMP is the required triangle.

Answer Worksheet 4D

Chapter 5
Quadrilaterals

A **quadrilateral** is a plane figure having four sides and four angles. The sum of the angles in a quadrilateral is 360°, as every quadrilateral can be divided into two triangles.

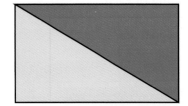

> The sum of the angles in a quadrilateral is 360°.

Types of Quadrilaterals

There are six different shapes of quadrilateral, each having a special name.

1. A **parallelogram** is a quadrilateral having opposite sides parallel and opposite angles equal.

2. A **square** is a parallelogram having four equal sides and four right angles.

3. A **rectangle** is a parallelogram having two pairs of equal sides and four right angles. The longer side is called the **length** and the shorter side is called the **width**.

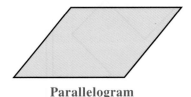

| Parallelogram | Square | Rectangle |

4. A **rhombus** is a parallelogram having four equal sides. It is like a square pushed out of shape.

5. A **trapezium** is a quadrilateral having two, and only two, parallel sides.

6. A **trapezoid** is a quadrilateral having no sides equal or parallel.

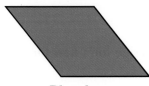
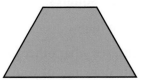

| Rhombus | Trapezium | Trapezoid |

Exercises

1. The **Fiat** sign consists of four **parallelograms**. A letter of the company name is inscribed in each of the **parallelograms**. Make a drawing of the sign. Use shading to enhance your drawing.

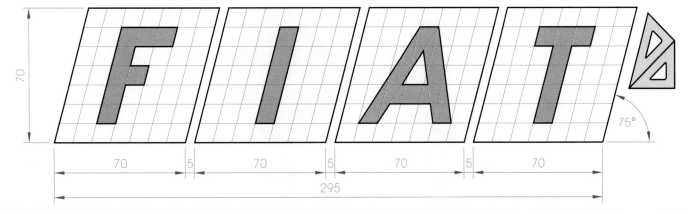

2. The **First Aid** sign (below) and the **Level Crossing Ahead** road sign (across) are straightforward, bold designs based around a square.

Make a drawing of each.

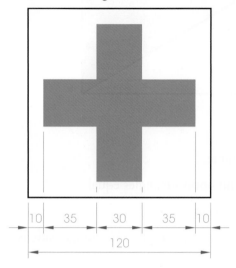

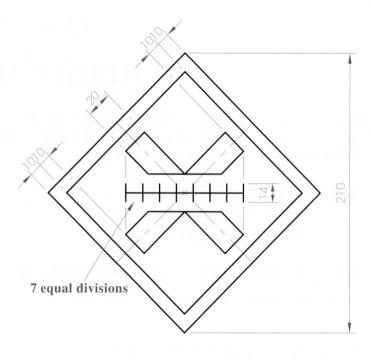

7 equal divisions

3. Shown across is a drawing of the **hazard warning** graphical symbol found on containers of hazardous substances. It is a simple and effective design based on a **square**.

  (a) Make a drawing of this graphical symbol.

  (b) You have been asked to design a new graphical symbol for hazardous materials, still based on a **square**. Sketch out a series of ideas, and then make a drawing of your best one.

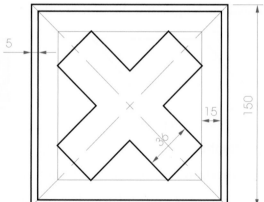

4. The **Tile Savers** logo is made up of three identical **squares**.

  (a) Reproduce the logo showing all construction lines.

  (b) Using a square as the basis for your designs, see what other logos you can design for a new tile store that is opening in your area. Make accurate drawings of your ideas.

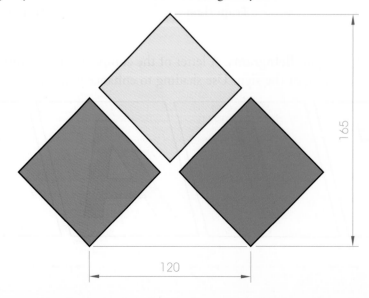

5. The **ERA** real estate agency logo is a design based on a house. It is composed of three **squares**, two **parallelograms** and an **isosceles triangle**.

Make a full-size drawing of the logo to the given dimensions.

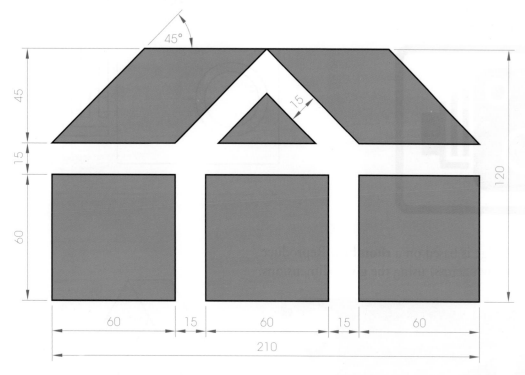

6. The drawing in the figure below is a logogram for a **jewellery store**. The logo uses **quadrilaterals** and **triangles** to indicate the diamond shape.

Draw the logogram to the given dimensions.

Hint: Start your work by drawing the two **parallelograms** and the **trapezium**.

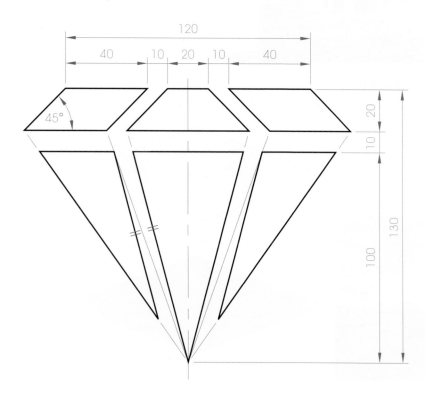

7. A drawing of a road sign for a **speed camera** is shown in the figure below. The diagonal of the rectangle is 150 mm long.

Copy the drawing showing clearly how the width of the rectangle is determined.

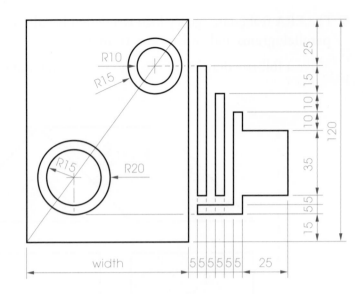

8. The **Renault** badge is based on a **rhombus**. Reproduce the drawing (shown across) using the given dimensions.

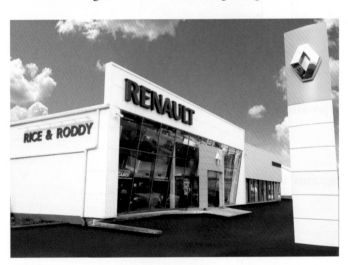

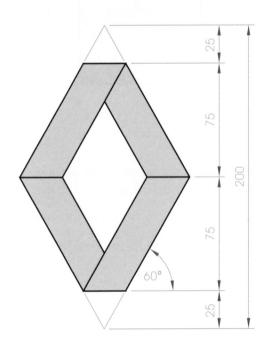

9. A drawing of the **Celtic Linen** symbol is shown in the figure below. It is composed of three identical **rhombi** that are equally spaced. Copy the drawing using the given dimensions.

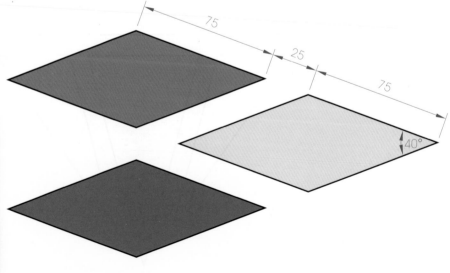

A Special Parallelogram

The **rhombus** is a special parallelogram. If you arrange four 30°/60° set squares to form a rhombus as shown in the figure across, you will notice that the diagonals bisect each other at 90°. This enables us to bisect a line and an angle.

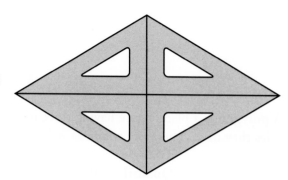

The diagonals of a rhombus bisect each other at 90°.

Bisecting a Line

Example
Bisect the given line AB.

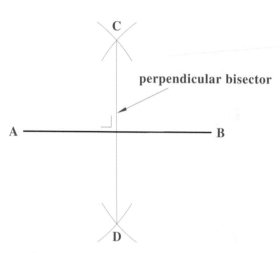

1. Place the compass point at A, open it to a distance greater than half the length of the line and draw arcs on either side of the line.

2. Place the compass point at B. Using the same radius, draw two more arcs cutting the first set of arcs at C and D respectively.

3. Join C and D. The line CD is called the perpendicular bisector of AB.

A **perpendicular bisector** of a line is always at right angles to the line.
Any point on the perpendicular bisector of a line segment AB is equidistant from A and B.

Bisecting an Angle

Example
Bisect the given angle LMN.

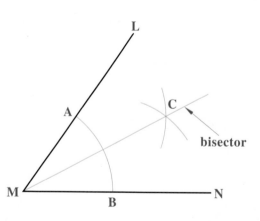

1. Place the compass point at the vertex M of the angle and draw an arc of any convenient radius to intersect the two arms of the angle at A and B.

2. Using A and B as centres and a convenient radius, draw two intersecting arcs at C.

3. Join M to C. The line MC is the bisector of the angle LMN.

Any point on the bisector of an angle is equidistant from the arms of the angle.
The bisector of any acute or obtuse angle also bisects its reflex angle.

Answer Worksheet 5A

Chapter 6

Polygons

A **polygon** is a plane figure having three or more sides. Polygons are named according to the number of sides they have. The more common polygons have their own names:

Triangle	3 sides	**Heptagon**	7 sides
Quadrilateral	4 sides	**Octagon**	8 sides
Pentagon	5 sides	**Nonagon**	9 sides
Hexagon	6 sides	**Decagon**	10 sides

Regular Polygons

When all the sides and all the angles of a polygon are equal, it is called a **regular polygon**. The figure below shows the first eight **regular polygons**. In this chapter, we will study the **regular pentagon**, the **regular hexagon**, the **regular octagon**, the **regular nonagon** and the **regular decagon**.

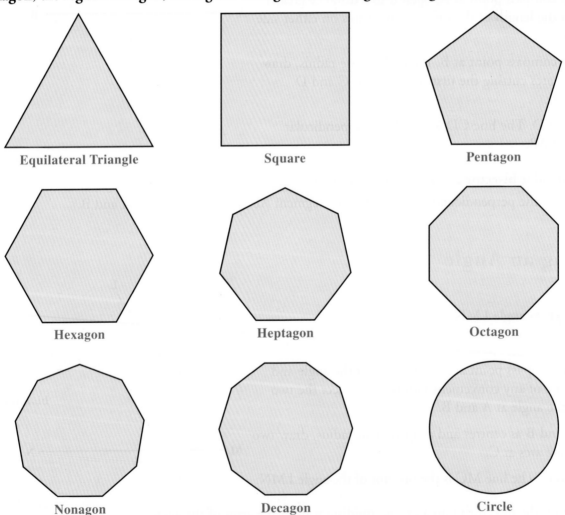

Equilateral Triangle	**Square**	**Pentagon**
Hexagon	**Heptagon**	**Octagon**
Nonagon	**Decagon**	**Circle**

A circle is also included. This is the limiting case, which results if we imagine that the number of sides of the regular polygon is increased to infinity. The polygon is now circular and the sides are points.

A **regular polygon** has equal sides and equal angles.

Exterior Angle of a Polygon

An **exterior angle** of a polygon is formed when one of its sides is extended through a vertex. The figure over shows a pentagon with an exterior angle at each of its five vertices. The five turns add up to 360°.

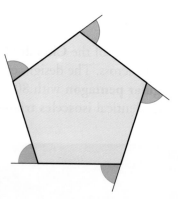

The sum of the exterior angles of any polygon is 360°. To calculate the exterior angle of any regular polygon, we use the following formula:

Exterior Angle = 360° ÷ number of sides.

The figure below shows how to calculate the **exterior angle** for a **regular pentagon**, a **regular hexagon** and a **regular octagon**.

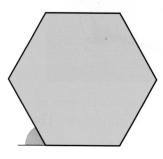

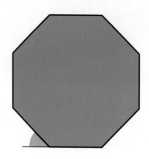

360° ÷ 5 = 72°   360° ÷ 6 = 60°   360° ÷ 8 = 45°

Constructing a Regular Pentagon

Example
Construct a **regular pentagon** of side 90 mm.

A **regular pentagon** has five equal sides and five equal angles.

The **exterior angle** for a regular pentagon is 360° ÷ 5 = 72°.

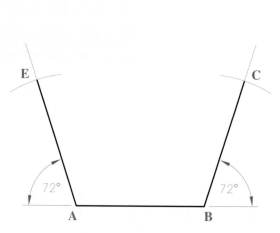

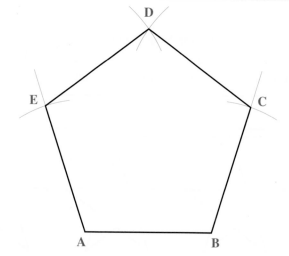

1. Draw the base AB of length 90 mm.

2. Using a protractor, draw 72° lines at A and B. Mark off the two sides AE and BC of length 90 mm from A and B, respectively.

3. Swing arcs of radius 90 mm from C and E to locate the fifth vertex D. Join CD and ED to give the remaining two sides of the regular pentagon.

Exercises

1. A drawing of the **Chrysler Corporation** logo is shown in the figure across. The design, called a **pentastar**, is based on a **regular pentagon** with 80 mm sides. The badge also contains five identical **isosceles triangles**. Copy the drawing.

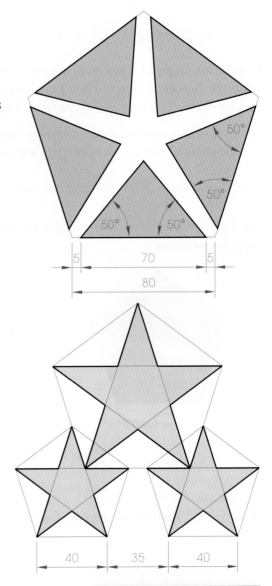

2. The five-pointed stars shown in the figure across are part of an advertising sign for the **Winning Streak** game show. They are based on **regular pentagons**.

Draw the design showing all construction lines.

3. A drawing of the **Four Star Pizza** emblem is shown in the figure below. The design is based around a **regular pentagon** of side 40 mm. Draw the sign as shown.

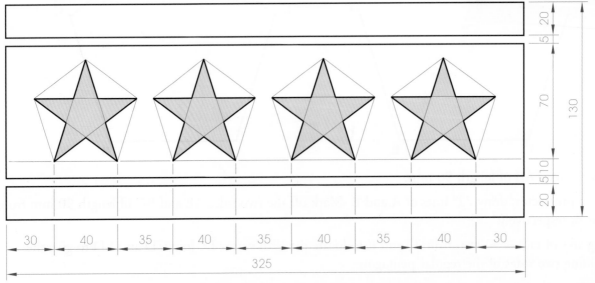

Constructing a Regular Hexagon and a Regular Octagon

Example 1
Construct a **regular hexagon** of side 70 mm.

A **regular hexagon** has six equal sides and six equal angles.
The **exterior angle** for a regular hexagon is 360° ÷ 6 = 60°.

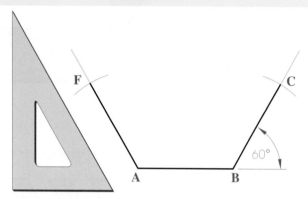
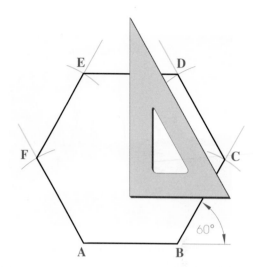

1. Draw the base AB of length 70 mm.

2. Using the 30°/60° set square, draw 60° lines from A and B. Mark off the two sides of length 70 mm from A and B, respectively.

3. Complete the hexagon using the 30°/60° set square to draw the two inclined sides of length 70 mm and the ruler to draw the horizontal side.

Example 2
Construct a **regular octagon** of side 55 mm.

A **regular octagon** has eight equal sides and eight equal angles.
The **exterior angle** for a regular octagon is 360° ÷ 8 = 45°.

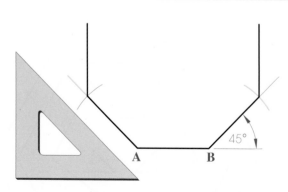
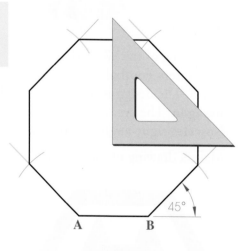

1. Draw the base AB of length 55 mm.
2. Using the 45° set square, draw 45° lines from A and B. Mark off the two sides of length 55 mm.
3. Draw the two vertical sides of length 55 mm.
4. Complete the octagon using the 45° set square to draw the two inclined sides of length 55 mm and the ruler to draw the horizontal side.

Exercises

1. Reproduce the drawing of the **Construction Industry Federation** symbol shown across. It is based on a **regular hexagon** of 75 mm side. An **equilateral triangle** is also included in the symbol.

2. The figure over shows a drawing of the **Black and Decker** logo, which is based on a **regular hexagon** of 78 mm side.

   Draw this logo to the sizes given.

3. A drawing of the **Wolverhampton Wanderers Football Club** logo is shown across. The design is based on a **regular hexagon**. The eyes are in the shape of **isosceles right-angled triangles**.

   Make a drawing of the design.

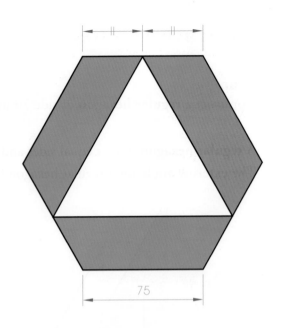

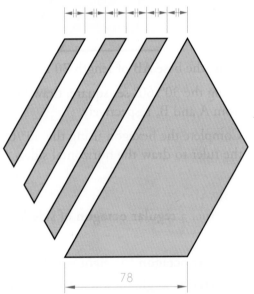

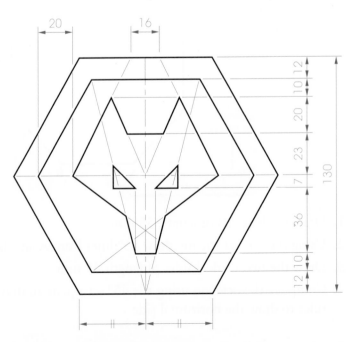

4. The outline of the **Stop road sign** is a **regular octagon**. A drawing of the road sign is shown in the figure below. The inner octagon has a side of length 65 mm and the outer octagon is offset a distance of 10 mm.

Make a copy of this drawing to the sizes given. Include the letters, which are drawn on a grid of 5 mm squares, in your drawing. Position the letters in the centre of the octagon.

5. The **MG Motors** emblem is based on a **regular octagon**. Draw the emblem to the sizes given.

Begin your work by drawing the octagon of side 55 mm in which the letters M and G are inscribed. Start the drawing at point A.

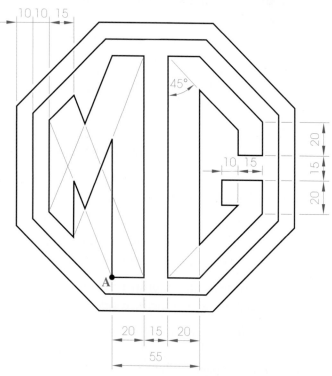

Constructing a Regular Octagon in a Given Square

Example
Construct a **regular octagon** in a square of side 90 mm.

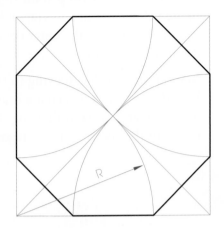

1. Construct the square of side 90 mm and draw the diagonals.

2. Using each vertex of the square as centre and half the diagonal as radius, draw the four arcs as shown in the figure over.

3. Join the points where the arcs intersect the sides of the square to obtain the required octagon.

Constructing a Regular Nonagon and a Regular Decagon

Example 1
Construct a **regular nonagon** of side 35 mm.

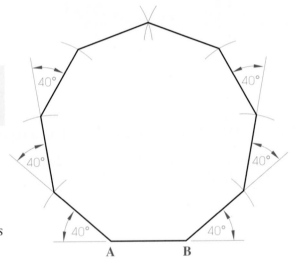

1. Draw the base AB of length 35 mm.

2. The **exterior angle** of a regular nonagon is 360° ÷ 9 = 40°. Using the protractor, draw 40° lines from A and B. Mark off the two sides of length 35 mm.

3. Extend these two sides. Construct exterior angles of 40° as shown. Draw these two inclined sides of length 35 mm.

4. Complete the nonagon using the protractor to draw the next two inclined sides, and the compass to locate the final vertex.

Example 2
Construct a **regular decagon** of side 32 mm.

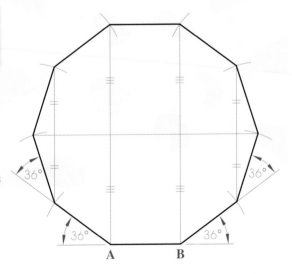

1. Draw the base AB of length 32 mm.

2. The exterior angle of a regular decagon is 360° ÷ 10 = 36°. Using the protractor, draw 36° lines from A and B. Mark off the two sides of length 32 mm.

3. Extend these two sides. Construct exterior angles of 36° as shown. Draw these two inclined sides of length 32 mm.

4. Complete the decagon using the protractor to draw the remaining inclined sides, or by means of an **axial symmetry** (see page 151).

Answer Worksheet 6A

Regular Polygons in a Circle

Example 1
Inscribe a **regular pentagon** in a given circle.

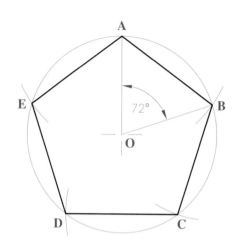

1. Draw any radius OA of the circle. The angle at the centre (called the **central angle**) equals 360° ÷ 5 = 72°. Draw radius OB at 72° to the radius OA. Join AB. This is one side of the required pentagon.

2. With radius AB mark off the remaining vertices of the pentagon around the circumference of the circle as shown. Draw the required pentagon ABCDE.

Exercises

1. The **Texaco** logo is based on a **regular pentagon** inscribed in a circle. Reproduce this drawing to the given dimensions, showing all construction lines.

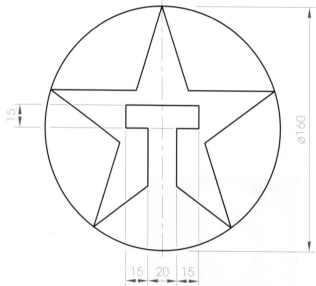

2. The **United States Air Force** sign is shown in the figure below. It is based on a **regular pentagon** inscribed in a circle. Draw the sign.

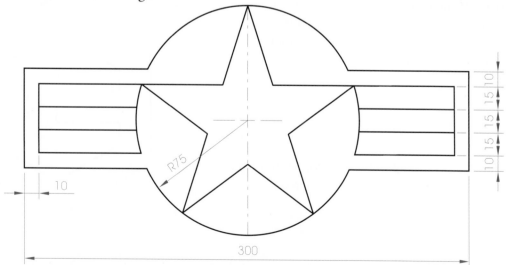

Example 2
Inscribe a **regular hexagon** in a given circle.

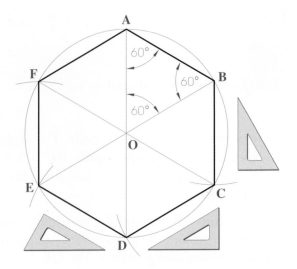

1. Draw any radius OA of the circle. The **central angle** equals 360° ÷ 6 = 60°. Draw radius OB at 60° to the radius OA. Join AB. This is one side of the hexagon.

2. With radius AB mark off the remaining vertices of the hexagon around the circumference of the circle as shown. Draw the required hexagon ABCDEF using the 30°/60° set square as shown.

When a regular hexagon is inscribed in a circle:
- the diagonals divide the hexagon into 6 equilateral triangles.
- the radius of the circle is equal to the side of the hexagon.

Exercises

1. A drawing of the **Nintendo Gamecube** emblem is shown in the figure over. It is based on a **regular hexagon** of side 80 mm.

   Reproduce this drawing to the given dimensions.

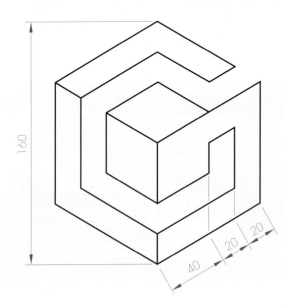

2. The **Electro Automation Ltd** card for a multistorey car park contains a symbol based on a **regular hexagon**. Reproduce the drawing of this symbol showing all construction lines.

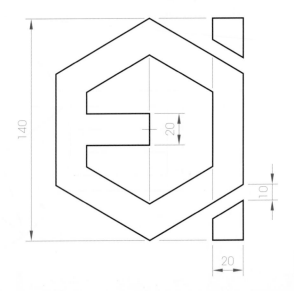

3. The **IDA** logo contains three equally spaced **regular hexagons**. Each hexagon is inscribed in a circle of radius 50 mm. Draw the logo showing all construction lines.

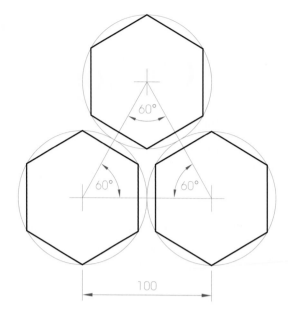

Example 3
Inscribe a **regular octagon** in a given circle.

1. Draw any radius OA of the circle. The **central angle** equals 360° ÷ 8 = 45°. Draw radius OB at 45° to the radius OA. Join AB. This is one side of the required octagon.

2. Draw lines using the 45° set square as shown to locate the remaining vertices of the octagon around the circumference of the circle. Draw the required octagon ABCDEFGH.

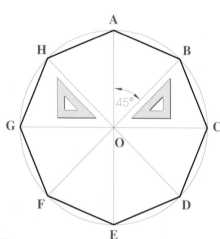

Example 4
Inscribe a **regular nonagon** and a **regular decagon** in a given circle.

1. The central angle for the regular nonagon is 360° ÷ 9 = 40°. The solution is based on drawing nine equal sectors (see page 94) in the circle as shown in the figure (above, left).

2. The central angle for the regular decagon is 360° ÷ 10 = 36°. The solution is based on drawing ten equal sectors (see page 94) in the circle as shown in the figure (above, right).

Answer Worksheet 6B

Chapter 7
Orthographic Projection 1

Orthographic projection is a method of representing a three-dimensional object on a plane surface.

It is based on projecting points on the object perpendicularly onto planes of projection and joining them in order, as shown below. Three different views are obtained:

> (i) The view looking in the direction of arrow **A** is called a **front elevation**.
> (ii) The view looking in the direction of arrow **B** is called an **end elevation**.
> (iii) The view looking in the direction of arrow **C** is called a **plan**.

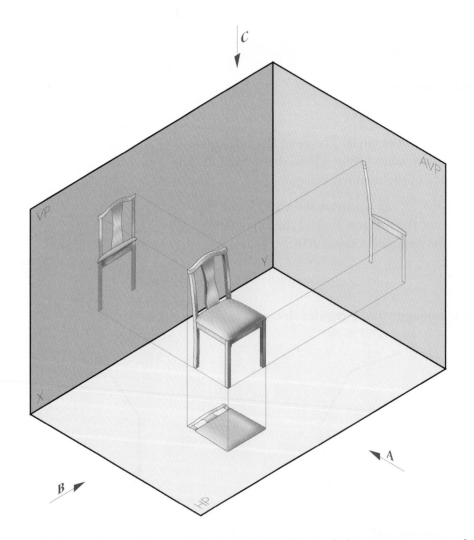

The front elevation is projected onto the **vertical plane** (VP). The end elevation is projected onto an **auxiliary vertical plane** (AVP). The plan is projected onto the **horizontal plane** (HP).

> The line of intersection between the vertical plane and the horizontal plane is called the XY line.

The three views shown above are still three-dimensional.

The planes of projection are then rotated into one plane, as shown over and below, allowing the three views to be transferred to a sheet of paper.

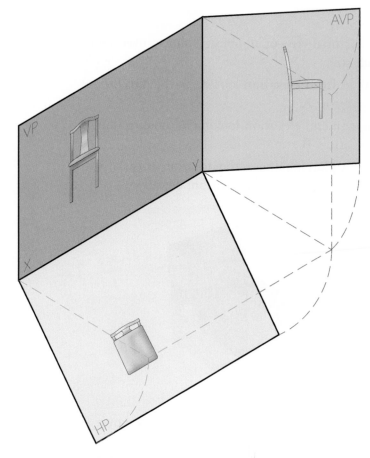

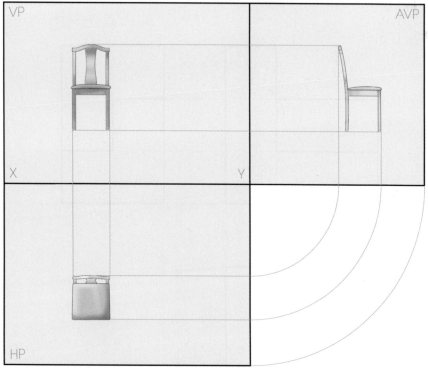

The end elevation looking from the left lies directly to the right of the front elevation.
The plan lies directly below the front elevation.
In this arrangement, the three views are said to be in projection.

Example

A pictorial view of an object is shown over. Draw full-size:

(a) A **front elevation** looking in the direction of arrow **A**.

(b) An **end elevation** looking in the direction of arrow **B**.

(c) A **plan** looking in the direction of the arrow **C**, projected from the front elevation.

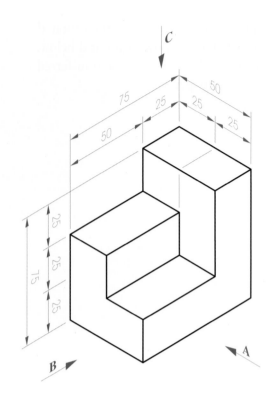

Build the object from 25 mm cubes as shown above. Use the model to help you visualise the solution.

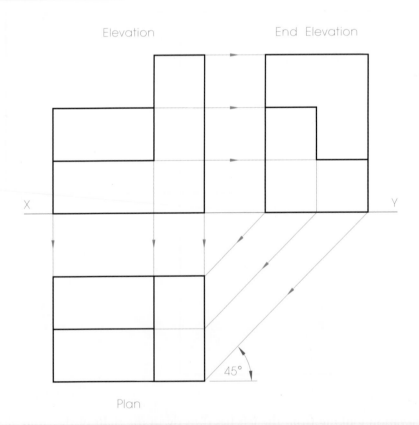

The end elevation looking from the left lies directly to the right of the front elevation.
The plan lies directly below the front elevation.

Exercises

Represent each of the objects shown below using **orthographic projection** by drawing the following views:

(a) A **front elevation** looking in the direction of arrow **A**.

(b) An **end elevation** looking in the direction of arrow **B**.

(c) A **plan** looking in the direction of the arrow **C**, projected from the front elevation.

Build each of the objects from 25 mm cubes and use the models to help you visualise the solutions.

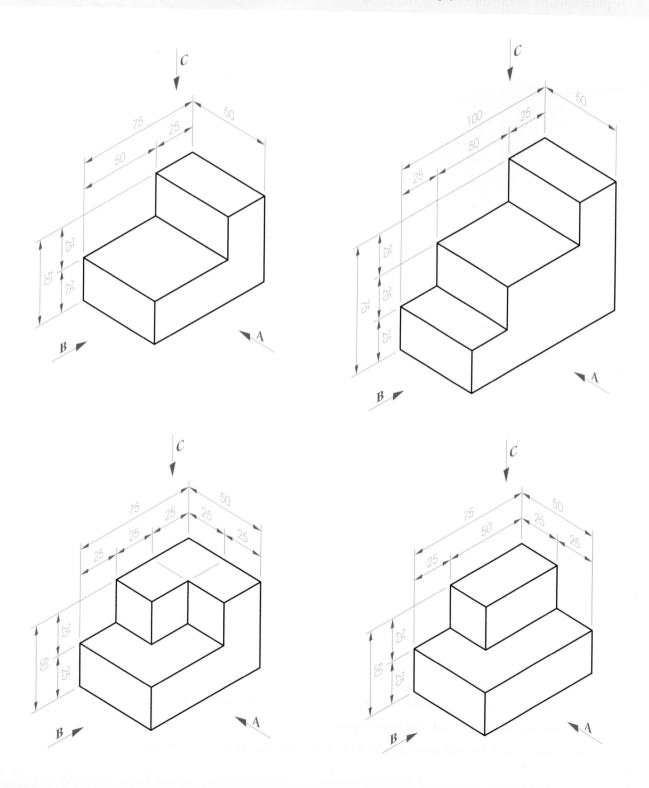

Example

A pictorial view of an object is shown across.
Draw full-size:

(a) A **front elevation** looking in the direction of arrow **A**.

(b) An **end elevation** looking in the direction of arrow **B**.

(c) A **plan** looking in the direction of the arrow **C**, projected from the front elevation.

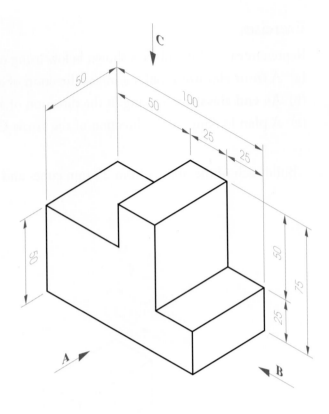

Build the object from 25 mm cubes as shown above. Use the model to help you visualise the solution.

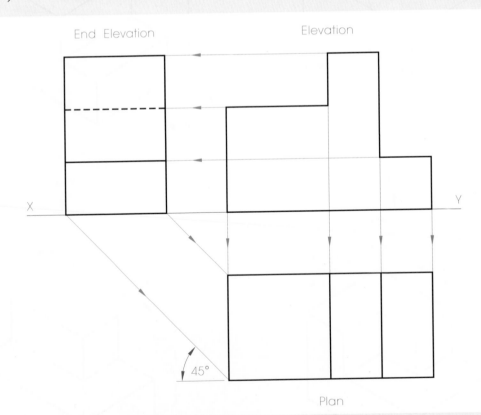

The end elevation looking from the right lies directly to the left of the front elevation.

The plan lies directly below the front elevation.

Lines that cannot be seen from the viewing direction are represented by dashed lines.

Exercises

1. Represent each of the objects shown below using **orthographic projection** by drawing the following views:

   (a) A **front elevation** looking in the direction of arrow **A**.

   (b) An **end elevation** looking in the direction of arrow **B**.

   (c) A **plan** looking in the direction of the arrow **C**, projected from the front elevation.

Build each of the objects from 25 mm cubes and use the models to help you visualise the solutions.

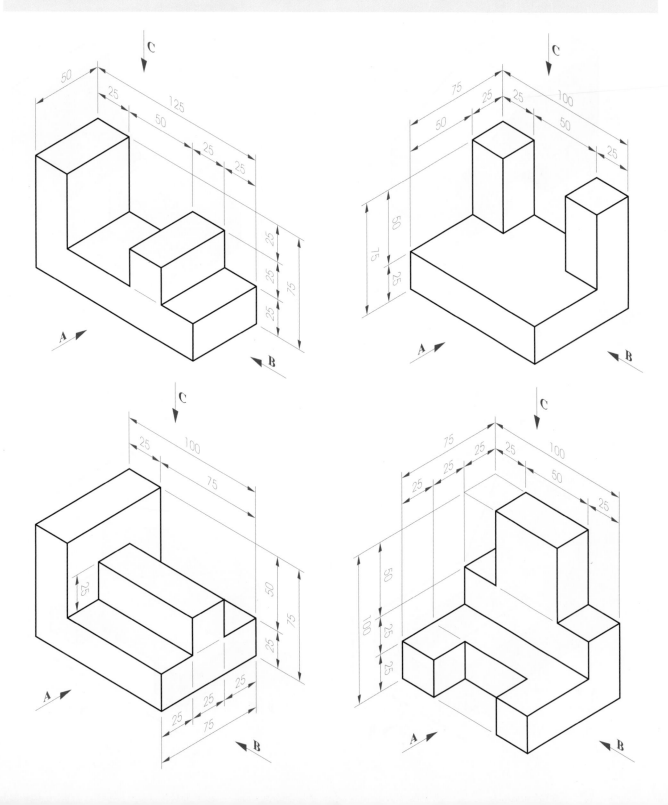

2. Represent each of the objects shown below using **orthographic projection** by drawing the following views:

    (a) A **front elevation** looking in the direction of arrow **A**.

    (b) An **end elevation** looking in the direction of arrow **B**.

    (c) A **plan** looking in the direction of the arrow **C**, projected from the front elevation.

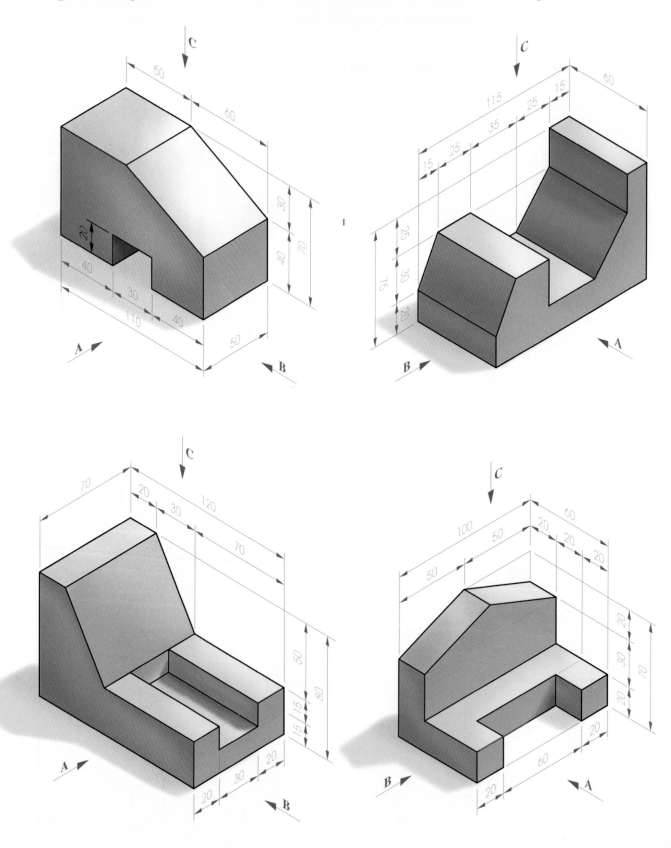

3. Represent each of the objects shown below using **orthographic projection** by drawing the following views:
   (a) A **front elevation** looking in the direction of arrow **A**.
   (b) An **end elevation** looking in the direction of arrow **B**.
   (c) A **plan** looking in the direction of the arrow **C**, projected from the front elevation.

Building the objects from 25 mm cubes will help you visualise the solutions to these questions.
It will also develop your ability to visualise more complex objects without the aid of a model.

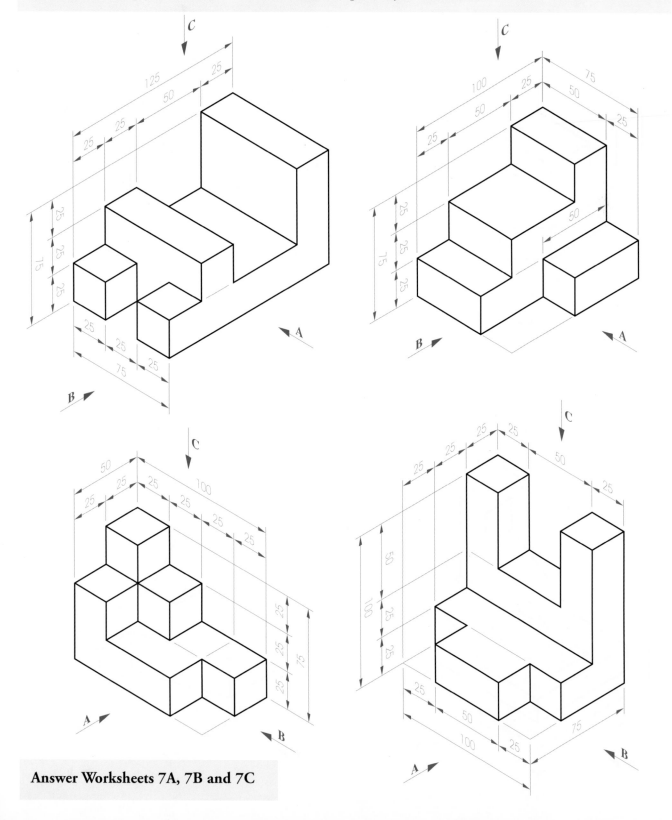

Answer Worksheets 7A, 7B and 7C

4. Represent each of the objects shown below using **orthographic projection** by drawing the following views:

(a) A **front elevation** looking in the direction of arrow **A**.

(b) An **end elevation** looking in the direction of arrow **B**.

(c) A **plan** looking in the direction of the arrow **C**, projected from the front elevation.

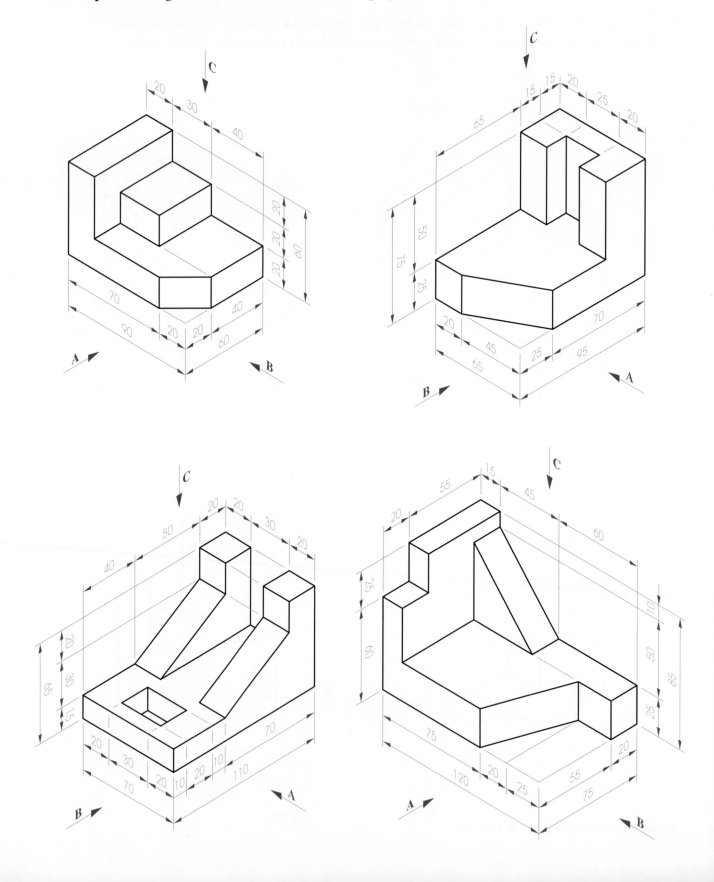

5. The figure over shows a pictorial view of a **microwave**. Draw:

(a) A **front elevation** looking in the direction of arrow **A**.

(b) An **end elevation** looking in the direction of arrow **B**.

(c) A **plan** projected from the front elevation.

6. A pictorial view of a **cooker** is shown over. The radius of each circle is *ten millimetres*. Draw:

(a) A **front elevation** looking in the direction of arrow **A**.

(b) An **end elevation** looking in the direction of arrow **B**.

(c) A **plan** projected from the front elevation.

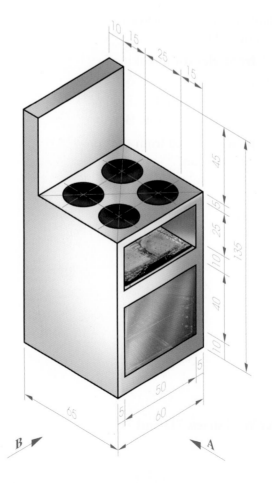

7. The figure over shows a pictorial view of a **toy boat**. Draw:

   (a) A **front elevation** looking in the direction of arrow **A**.

   (b) An **end elevation** looking in the direction of arrow **B**.

   (c) A **plan** projected from the front elevation.

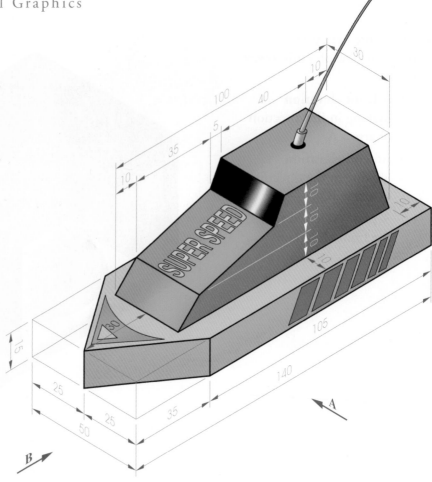

8. A pictorial view of a **locker** is shown over. Draw:

   (a) A **front elevation** looking in the direction of arrow **A**.

   (b) An **end elevation** looking in the direction of arrow **B**.

   (c) A **plan** projected from the front elevation.

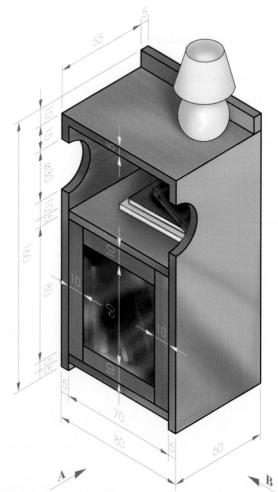

Answer Worksheets 7D and 7E

Chapter 8

Pictorial Drawing 1

We saw in chapter 7 that elevations and plans are useful for communicating precise details about the shape and size of an object. However, such drawings can be difficult to interpret. A **pictorial drawing** gives an overall impression of what an object looks like which is easy to visualise.

There are many different types of pictorial drawing. In this chapter we shall consider:

- Common oblique drawing.
- Isometric drawing.

Common Oblique Drawing

In **oblique drawing** the front face of the object is drawn full-size. Receding lines are drawn at 45° to the horizontal.

> **Example**
> The elevation and plan of a letter **F** are shown over. Draw an **oblique view** of the letter.

1. Draw the front face of the given letter **F** full-size.

2. Draw light lines at 45° from the corners as shown below, left. These lines may be drawn to the left or to the right depending on which will convey more information.

3. Mark the true depth of 20 mm off along the 45° lines as shown below, middle.

4. Complete the drawing as shown below, right.

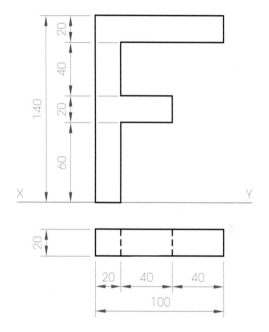

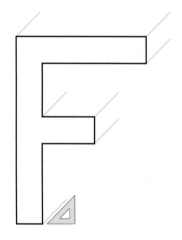 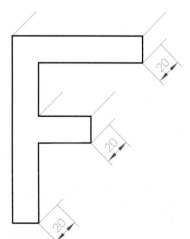 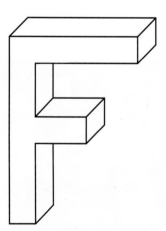

The front face is a **true shape** in an oblique drawing. This means that it appears in its actual shape and size. **Hidden lines** are normally omitted from pictorial drawings.

Exercises

1. The figure below shows the elevation and plan of a logo for **Eldon Transport Limited**.

Draw an **oblique view** of the logo.

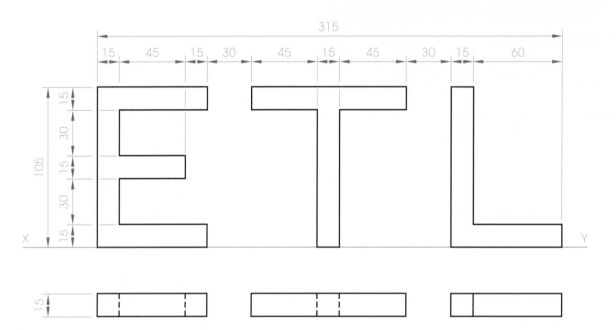

2. The elevation and plan of a **number 14** are shown below. A pictorial view of the number is to be placed on a **football jersey**.

Draw an **oblique view** of the number.

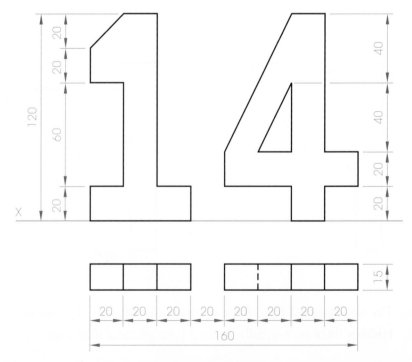

3. The figure below shows the elevation and plan of a **Robot's face**. The grid is made up of 10 mm squares.

Draw an **oblique view** of the face.

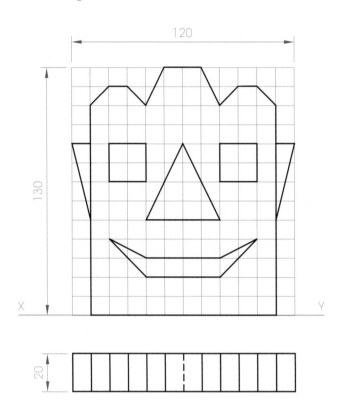

4. The elevation and plan of a logo, which is to be used as a **Parking Sign** are shown below. The grid is made up of 10 mm squares.

Draw an **oblique view** of the logo.

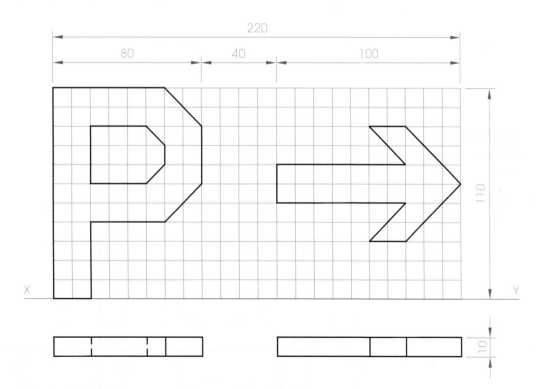

Example
The elevation and plan of a **clock** are shown over.

Draw an **oblique view** of the clock.

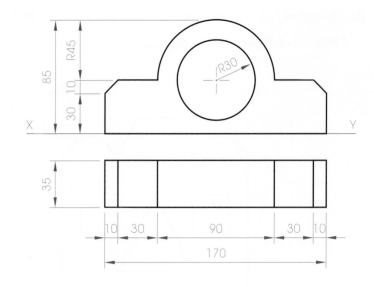

1. Draw the front face of the clock full-size and draw light lines at 45° from the corners.

2. Mark the true depth of 35 mm off along a 45° line and complete the base of the clock as shown below, left.

3. The semicircle on the back surface of the clock will appear as a semicircle because it is parallel to the front face of the clock. Its centre C_1 can be located by drawing a line at 45° from C as shown below, right.

4. Draw the visible part of the rear semicircle with a compass and complete the drawing as shown.

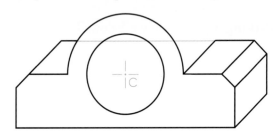

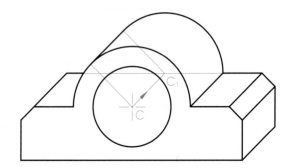

Exercise

1. The elevation and plan of the **Carter Printers** company monogram are shown over. .

   Draw an **oblique view** of the monogram.

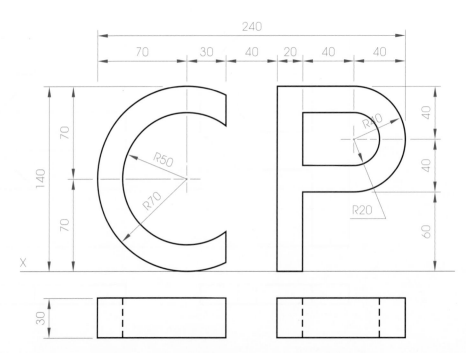

Isometric Drawing

Isometric drawing is a form of pictorial drawing in which vertical lines remain vertical and horizontal lines that are parallel to the principal axes are inclined at 30° as illustrated across. Note that the **principal axes** have been highlighted.

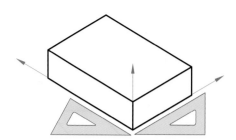

Example
Make an **isometric drawing** of the poly-cubical solid shown over. The solid is composed of 25 mm cubes.

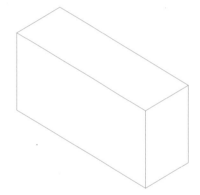

1. Draw the principal axes at 30° to the left, 30° to the right and vertically as shown below, left.

2. Mark off the overall length, width and height of the solid along the axes as shown.

3. Complete the box into which the solid fits by drawing lines vertically and at 30° in either direction as shown below, right.

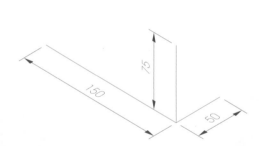

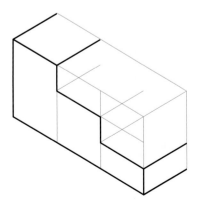

4. Mark off the intermediate lengths of 50 mm and heights of 25 mm and line in the side face as shown below, left.

5. Draw lines at 30° to the right from the corners of the front face as shown below, middle.

6. Complete the isometric view by drawing vertical lines and lines at 30° in either direction as shown below, right.

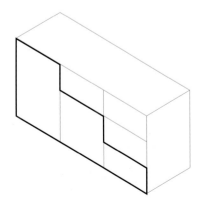

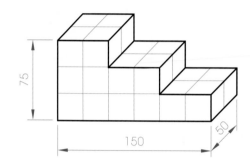

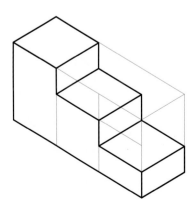

In isometric drawing distances can only be measured on, or parallel to, the principal axes.

Activities

1. The figure below shows pictorial views of some poly-cubical solids composed of 25 mm cubes. In each case:

(a) **Build** the solid from cubes.

(b) Draw an **isometric view** of the solid.

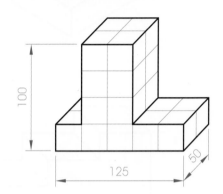

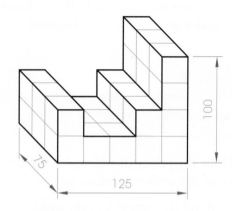

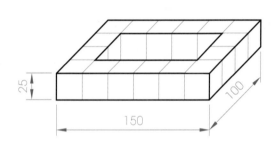

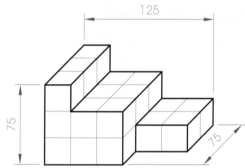

2. Build a solid of your own from cubes and make an **isometric drawing** of it.

3. Make an **isometric drawing** of the poly-cubical solids shown below. Note that they are composed of 15 mm cubes.

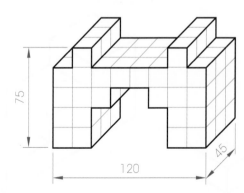

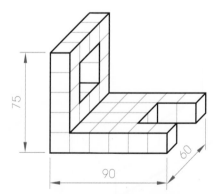

Answer Worksheet 8A

Example

The elevation and plan of a logo for the **U2** rock group are shown over. The grid is made up of 10 mm squares. Draw an **isometric view** of the logo.

1. Draw the principal axes.

2. Mark off the overall length, width and height of the logo along the appropriate axes.

3. Complete the box into which the logo fits by drawing lines vertically and at 30° in either direction.

4. Mark off 10 mm intervals along the axes and complete the grid as shown across.

5. Line in the letter **U** and the number **2** on the grid.

6. Draw the depth lines as shown below, left.

7. Complete the drawing as shown below, right.

Parallel lines on an object appear parallel in an isometric view.

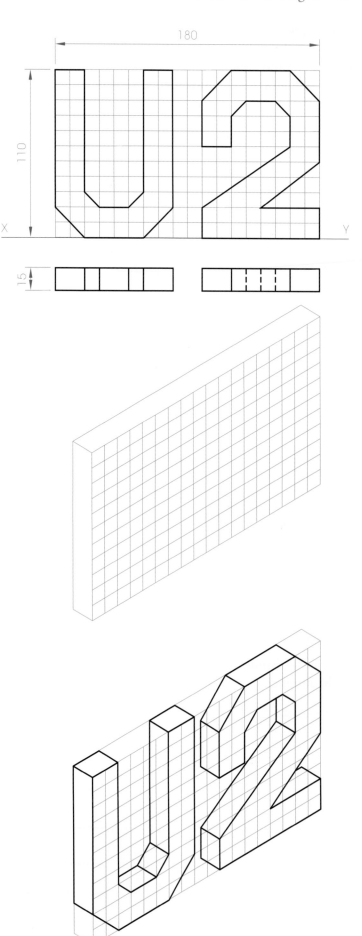

Exercises

1. The elevation and plan of a **toy fish** are shown below. The fish is based on a grid which is made up of 20 mm squares. Draw an **isometric view** of the fish.

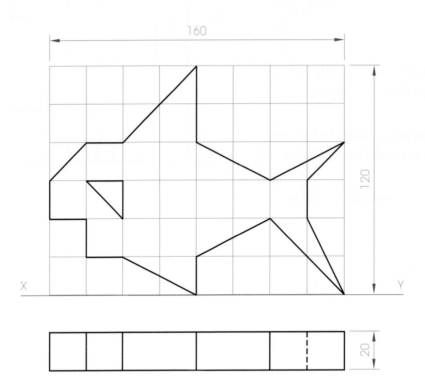

2. The figure over shows the elevation and plan of a **number** for a jersey. The grid is made up of 10 mm squares.

Draw an **isometric view** of the number.

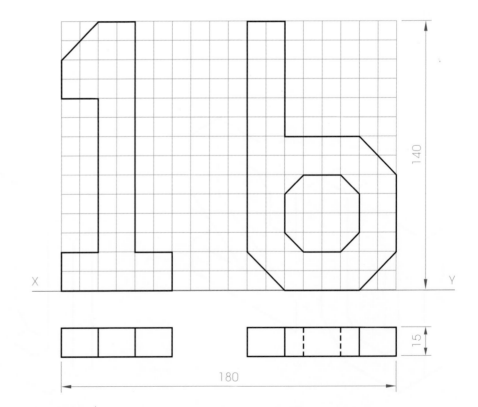

3. The elevation and plan of a sign for a **Pharmacy** are shown below. The grid is made up of 20 mm squares.

Draw an **isometric view** of the sign.

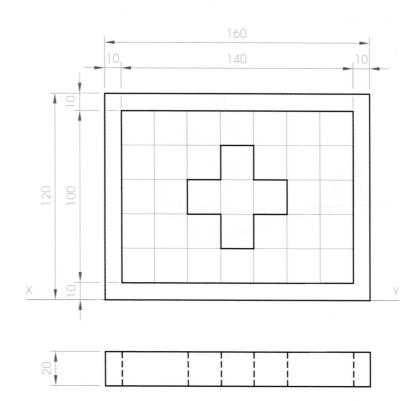

4. The letters **RL** are to be used to identify the **Ralph Lauren** section of a clothes shop. The elevation and plan of the letters, based on a 10 mm grid, are shown below.

Draw an **isometric view** of the letters.

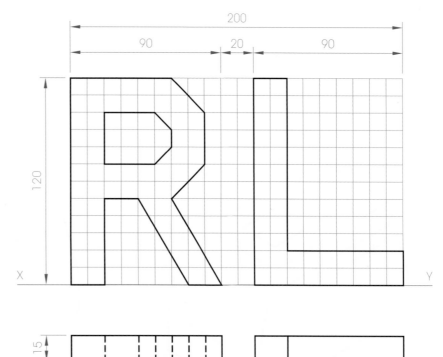

Example

The elevation and plan of a **toaster** are shown over. Draw an **isometric view** of the toaster.

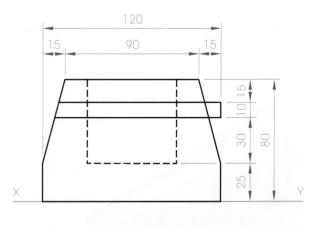

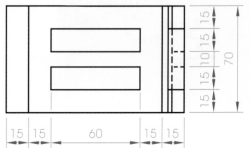

1. Draw the principal axes and mark off the overall length, width and height of the toaster.

2. Complete the box into which the toaster fits.

3. Mark off the intermediate heights and lengths and line in the front face of the toaster as shown over.

4. Draw the lines at 30° to the right as shown below, left. Complete the outline of the toaster.

5. Mark off the lengths (15, 60) and widths (15, 15, 10, 15) for the holes and complete the top of the toaster.

6. Mark off the widths of 15 mm and 40 mm for the handle and complete the isometric view as shown below, right.

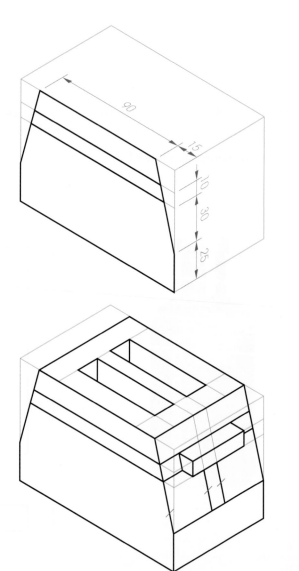

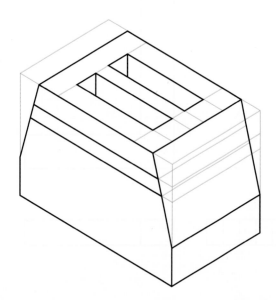

Exercises

1. The elevation and end view of a **garden shed** are shown below.

Draw an **isometric view** of the shed.

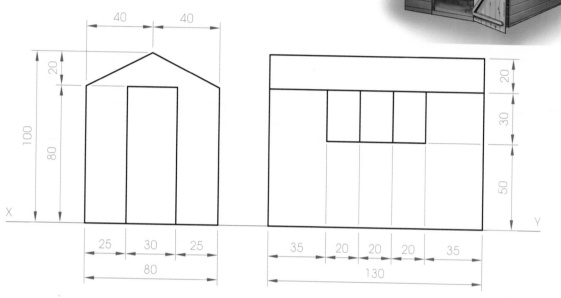

2. The elevation, plan and end view of a **first aid box** are shown below. The grid for the cross is made up of 10 mm squares.

Draw an **isometric view** of the box.

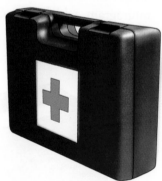

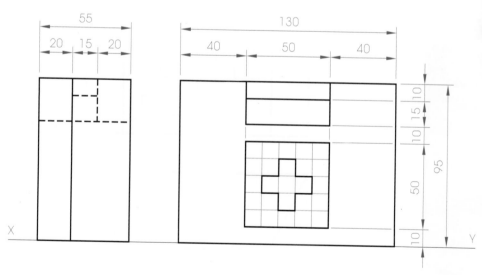

3. The figure over shows the elevation and plan of a **calculator**.

Draw an **isometric view** of the calculator.

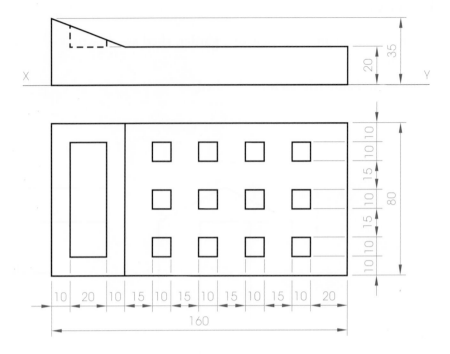

4. The elevation and plan of a box for an **ink cartridge** manufactured by **Holden Limited** are shown across. The front face of the box contains the company monogram, which is based on a 10 mm square grid.

Draw an **isometric view** of the box.

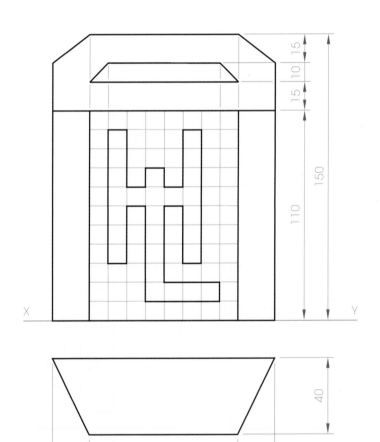

Answer Worksheets 8B and 8C

5. The elevation and plan of a logo for **Logan Film Production** is shown below. The grid is made up of 10 mm squares.

Draw an **isometric view** of the logo. Use an A2 sheet.

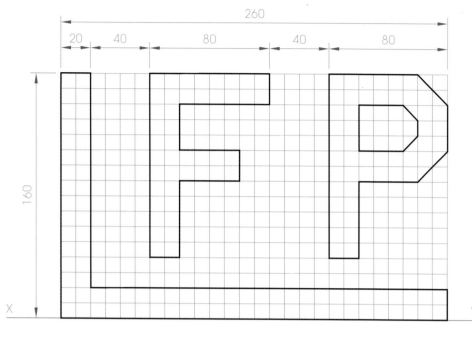

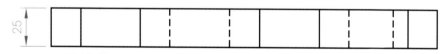

6. The figure below shows the elevation and plan of a sign for the **DIY** department in a store. The grid for the letters is made up of 10 mm squares.

Draw an **isometric view** of the sign.

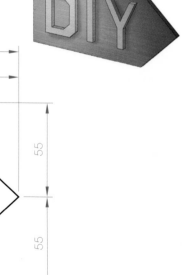

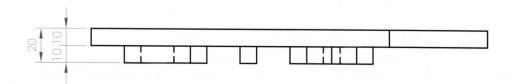

7. The elevation and plan of a **CK** monogram are shown over. The grid for the letter C is made up of 10 mm squares. Use an A2 sheet to draw one of the following views of the monogram:

(a) An **isometric view**
   OR

(b) An **oblique view**.

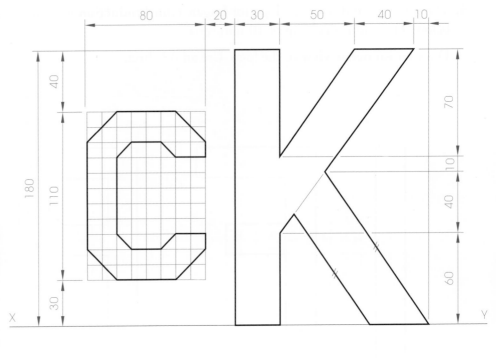

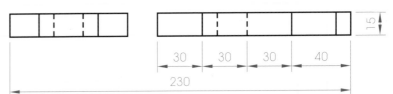

8. The elevation and plan of a monogram for **Manchester United Football Club** are shown below. The grid is made up of 10 mm squares. Using an A2 sheet draw one of the following views of the monogram:

(a) An **isometric view**
   OR

(b) An **oblique view**.

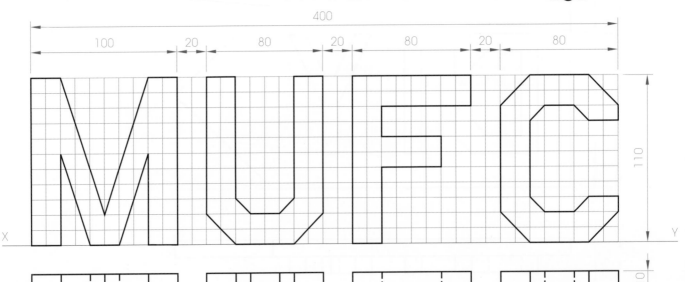

Chapter 9
Freehand Drawing

Freehand drawing is where you don't use any drawing equipment apart from a pencil. It is a very important stage in the design of new products such as mobile phones, cars and buildings. When professional designers have an idea for a design, the first step is often to make some quick freehand sketches. Through these sketches, a design can be changed and improved as new ideas arise. In addition, the sketches enable the designers to present a clear picture of what they want an object to look like.

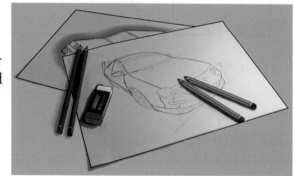

Becoming skilled in sketching requires hard work. However, all the necessary skills can be learned with practice.

Drawing with a Pencil

The following key points should be remembered when sketching:

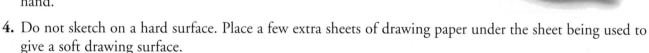

1. Hold the pencil between your thumb and first two fingers about 20 to 30 mm from the point.

2. Use a soft pencil such as a **HB**, **B** or **2B**. These are excellent for sketching.

3. Do not attach the paper to the drawing board when sketching. Have it free to move around, keeping it steady with your free hand.

4. Do not sketch on a hard surface. Place a few extra sheets of drawing paper under the sheet being used to give a soft drawing surface.

Lines

Draw lines with one continuous stroke. Begin your practice by drawing short, equally spaced horizontal lines, keeping them straight and the same length. Then, draw a series of equally spaced vertical lines.

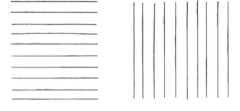

Keep your wrist firm and move your whole arm across the paper as you draw.

Now try drawing lines in different directions. Use different pressures on the pencil. Draw away from your body as shown in the figure over.

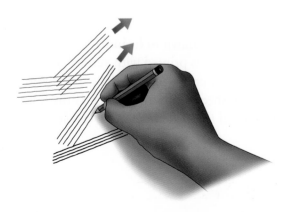

Next, try drawing a few different geometric shapes like the ones shown in the figure below.

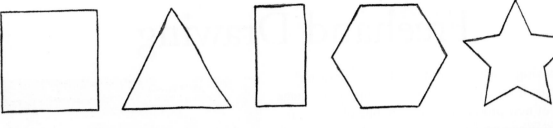

Circles

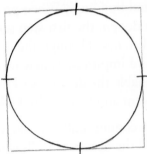

Circles can be drawn in squares. Mark points half way along each side and join the points with a curve to form the circle.

Begin by drawing a series of circles all the same size. Relax the pressure on the pencil as you draw. Next practice drawing circles of varying sizes. Do it over and over again until you get it perfect.

Three Dimensions

Your sketching can be improved by practicing drawing real objects. It is easier to draw objects if you first draw a box (or 'crate') enclosing the object. This is called **crating**. This box (or crate) should be sketched lightly first. The following method shows you how to draw a 3-D view of a box:

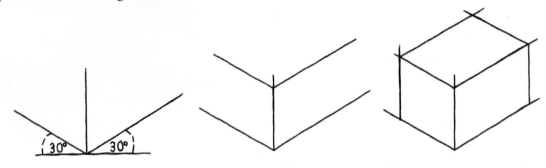

1. Start by drawing a vertical line to represent the **leading edge** of the box. This is the edge that appears to be closest to the viewer. Draw the two base lines at an angle of 30° to the horizontal.

2. Mark off the height for the box along the leading edge. Draw the top two edges from this point parallel to the base lines as shown in the figure above, middle.

3. Mark off the length and width of the box along the base lines. Draw in the left and right side vertical edges. Finally, draw in the top of the box by drawing the top edges parallel to their opposite edges.

Horizontal lines are parallel to the base lines and vertical lines are parallel to the leading edge.

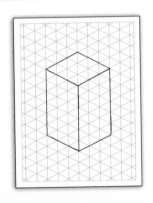

Once you can draw 3-D boxes, you will be able to build up many shapes as most objects can be drawn to fit into a box. A sheet of **isometric grid paper** (shown across), which is printed with vertical and 30° lines, can be used as an aid to help you draw the crate. You can draw directly on the grid paper or you can place it under the sheet of drawing paper. If the lines on the grid paper are a little faint, use a pencil to make them more visible.

The Thick and Thin Line Technique

Artists and illustrators use the **thick and thin line technique** to make 3-D drawings stand out from the crate in which they are drawn. The rules for deciding whether a line should be thick or thin are outlined in the box below. The rules are used for curved as well as straight lines. There are three types of line.

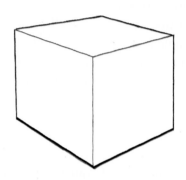

1. If you can see **both surfaces** at a line, draw a **thin line**.
2. If you can only see **one surface** at a line, draw a **thick line**.
3. Use an even heavier line where an object meets the surface on which it is resting.

Exercise

Make a **freehand pictorial sketch** of each of the objects shown in the figure below, making your sketches about three times the printed size. Start by drawing a **crate** to enclose the object.

Look carefully at each drawing in order to help you work out proportion, position and size all at once. Keep checking the proportions and only add details when you're sure they are the correct shape and size.

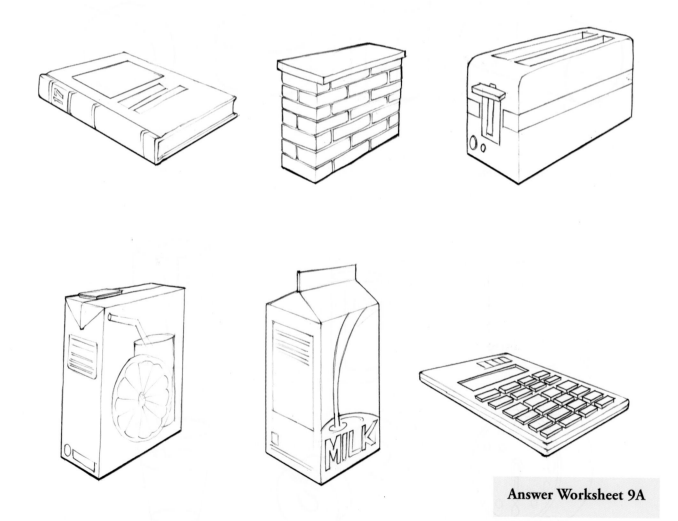

Answer Worksheet 9A

Cylinders

In order to be able to sketch **cylinders** or cylindrical objects, you must first learn to draw **ellipses**. Every time you see a circle from an angle it appears as an ellipse. Every ellipse has a major axis and a minor axis. You can draw an ellipse by sketching the rectangle into which it fits. The dimensions of this rectangle equal the major and minor axes as shown in the figure over. Mark points halfway along each side and sketch the ellipse ensuring the curve touches the midpoints of the sides of the rectangle.

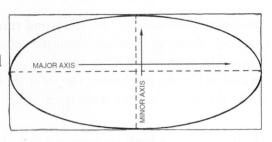

Rest the edge of your hand on the sheet when drawing ellipses:
- Move your whole arm when drawing large ellipses.
- Move only your fingers when drawing small ellipses.

When sketching cylinders, start by drawing the square-ended box into which the cylinder fits. Mark the centres of each side of the square ends. Sketch in ellipses to touch these points. Complete by drawing the sides and drawing in the outline of the cylinder as shown in the figure below.

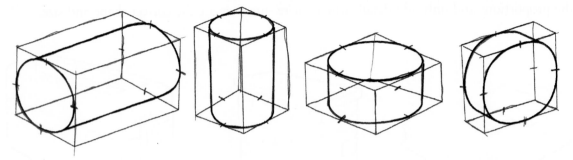

Exercise

Make **freehand pictorial sketches** of each of the objects shown in the figure below.

Pencil Shading

Pencil shading is used to improve the impact of a drawing. When shading, the pencil should be held about 50 mm from the lead between your thumb and first finger. This keeps the lead at a low angle, which means the edge of the lead is in contact with the paper. This means the area to be shaded can be covered quickly and evenly. Different pencils can be used to create different tones. Soft pencils such as HB, B or 2B allow a wide variety of tones from light grey to dense black by varying the pressure on the pencil.

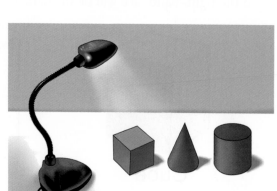

Pencil shading is a means of showing the effect of light falling on an object. When light falls on an object, different parts of the object receive differing amounts of light depending on their location with respect to the light source, as shown in the figure over. The surfaces facing the light receive the greatest amount of light and should be the lightest in tone. Any surface that is not illuminated by the light is 'in shade' and should be the darkest in tone. Other surfaces will be intermediate in tone.

A drawing is shaded as if the light source is coming over your left shoulder. This is because it is easier for the majority who are right-handed.

Exercises

1. Draw a long rectangular strip similar to the one in the figure below. Shade in the strip as heavily as you can on the left-hand side. Gradually lighten the pressure on the pencil as you move from dark to light across the rectangle.

2. Try the following two shading exercises with your pencil:

   (i) Lightly shade an area with a soft pencil and then smudge the area with your finger (below, left).

   (ii) Draw lots of small dots with the point of your pencil as close together as you can (below, right). When shading using this method, you need to use a different concentration of dots on each surface. The dot intensity is increased as you go from the lightest part of an object to the darkest. This method of shading is time-consuming to do.

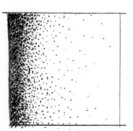

Shading Solids

Exercises

1. Draw each of the solids shown in the figure below. Assume the light source is coming over your left shoulder, and use a soft pencil to shade your drawings realistically to suit the effect of this light.

   A drawing of a **cube** has three faces. Each face will be shaded in a different tone. Since the light is coming from over your left shoulder, the top face will be the lightest, the left-hand face the next lightest and the right–hand face will be the darkest.

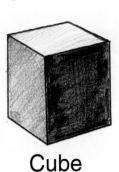
Cube

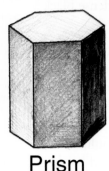
Prism

Pyramid

   Notice also in the case of the **prism** and the **pyramid** that the faces become darker as they turn away from the light.

2. Draw each of the curved objects shown in the figure below. Assume the light source is coming over your left shoulder and use a soft pencil to shade your drawings realistically to suit the effect of this light.

   Notice how the lightest part is the left-hand side and not in the centre of the **cylinder**. This is because the light is coming over your left shoulder. The shading becomes darker at the edges where less light is reflected.

Cylinder

Cone

Sphere

   Shading a **cone** is like shading a cylinder, except that the light area towards the left-hand side is triangular.

   The outline of a **sphere** will appear as a circle in every type of drawing. A circle is easily made to appear as a sphere when shading is applied. Notice the position of the lightest part. The surface becomes darker as it moves away from this light spot. Shading should follow the curve of the sphere.

Answer Worksheet 9B

Line Shading

Another means of shading involves using lines to show the effect of light and shade on an object. The lines differ in thickness and spacing on each side. When the lines follow the form of the object, the shading is known as **form shading**. Form shading on objects that have flat surfaces goes along in the same direction as one of the edges of the surface being shaded. Form shading on curved surfaces can go along a curved edge of the object.

Light lines widely spaced give a light tone.

Heavy lines closely spaced together give the darkest tone.

Portions of the object directly illuminated by the light are left with little or no shading.

Another type of line shading is **hatching**. Here, lines are drawn which do not go along the direction of any of the edges of the object. The figure over shows examples of **hatching** and **cross-hatching**.

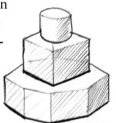

Colour Shading

Colour enhances a drawing by making it more attractive. The figure below (left) shows the effect of colour shading on a pencil sharpener. **Coloured pencils** provide an effective means of applying colour quickly without any mess. They should be held in the near-horizontal position. Be careful not to spoil your drawing with overuse of coloured pencils.

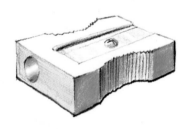

You can use a coloured pencil to make a drawing stand out by shading around it as shown in the figure above (right). This shading should be darker close to the object and becoming lighter away from it.

Exercise

Try drawing some shapes such as a cube, cylinder, cone and sphere. Use just one pencil for each object.

Exercise

(a) Make a **freehand pictorial sketch** of each of the objects shown in the figure below.

(b) Apply **shading** to enhance the sketches.

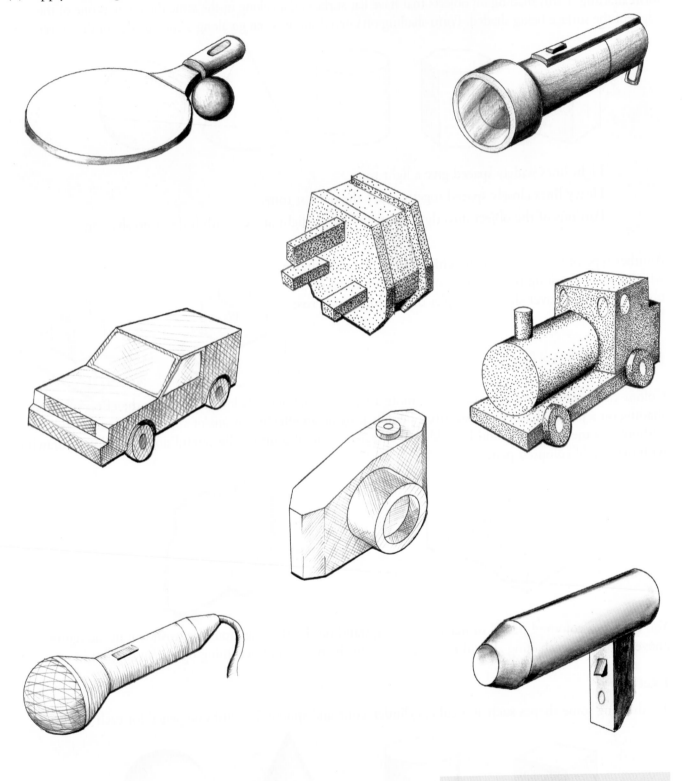

Answer Worksheets 9C and 9D

Shadow

The addition of shadow to a drawing makes a sketch more realistic. Shadows are projected onto another surface by an object that blocks the light from that surface. The surfaces that face away from the light source will cast a shadow (see over).

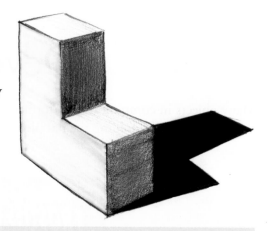

The shadow will have a shape similar to the object.

The light source fixes the position of the shadow.

The shadow is generally the darkest shading on the drawing.

Example

Sketch the **shadows** cast by the **solids** shown in the figure below when the light source is as shown by the arrows.

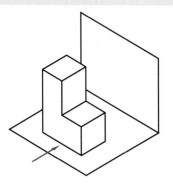 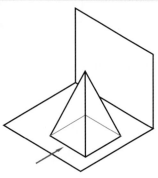

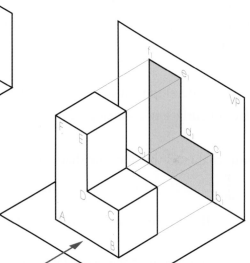

1. Index the corners of the solid as shown. Draw lines through the indexed points parallel to the direction of light.
2. Locate A_1 and B_1 on the XY line. Draw vertical lines from A_1 and B_1 to locate F_1 and C_1 respectively.
3. Draw lines parallel to DC (or FE) from C_1 and F_1 to locate D_1 and E_1 respectively.
4. Join the points in order. The shaded area is the shadow cast by the solid on the vertical plane.

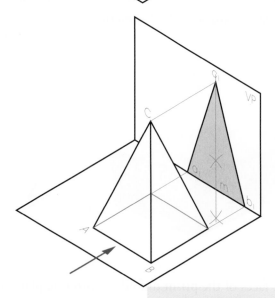

1. Index the corners of the solid as shown. Draw lines through the indexed points parallel to the direction of light.
2. Locate A_1 and B_1 on the XY line.
3. Bisect A_1B_1 at M. Draw a vertical line from M to locate C_1.
4. Join the points in order. The shaded area is the shadow cast by the solid on the vertical plane.

Answer Worksheet 9E

Chapter 10
Developments 1

Many objects in common use are formed from a flat sheet. Take for example the **Frosties box** shown below, left. It is formed by folding the flat piece of card shown below, right.

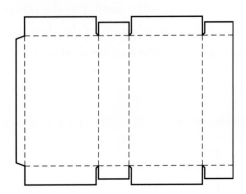

When the faces or surfaces of an object are unrolled or unfolded onto a plane, the result is known as a **development**.

> Every line in a development represents the **true length** of that line on the object.
>
> Every face or surface in a development represents the **true shape** of the face or surface of the object.

Recall from chapter 8 that the true shape simply refers to actual shape and size.

Example
The box for **Barry's Tea Bags** shown below, left, is based on a rectangular prism with dimensions as indicated.

(a) Draw an **elevation** of the prism looking in the direction of arrow **A**.

(b) Draw a **plan** of the prism looking in the direction of the arrow **B**, projected from the elevation.

(c) Draw a **surface development** of the prism.

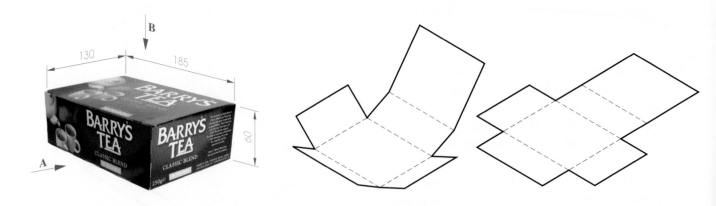

1. The faces of the prism unfolding into one plane are shown above. The development consists of six rectangles.

2. The elevation and plan are drawn as shown below.

3. The development can be drawn directly from the elevation and plan as all edges of the prism appear in true length in at least one of these views.

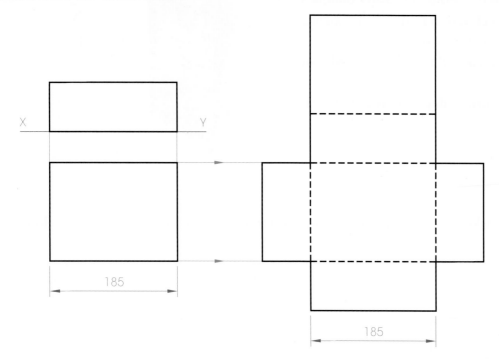

Dashed lines are used in a development to indicate lines along which folds are to occur.

Exercise

The **Chicken McNuggets** box shown below is based on a rectangular prism with dimensions as indicated.

(a) Draw an **elevation** of the prism looking in the direction of arrow **A**.

(b) Draw a **plan** of the prism looking in the direction of the arrow **B**, projected from the elevation.

(c) Draw a **surface development** of the prism.

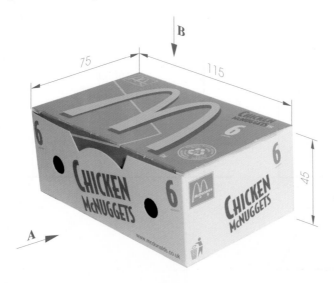

Example

The figure over shows a pictorial view of a prism, which is based on the **Scots Clan** box.

(a) Draw an **elevation** of the prism looking in the direction of arrow **A**.

(b) Draw a **plan** of the prism projected from the elevation.

(c) Draw a **surface development** of the prism.

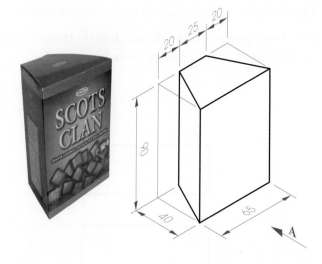

1. The figure below illustrates the faces of the prism unfolding into one plane. The development consists of four rectangles and two trapeziums.

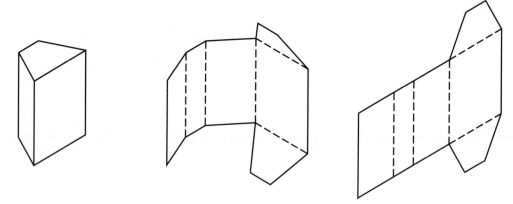

2. The elevation and plan are drawn as shown below.

3. The development can be drawn by transferring the relevant true lengths from the elevation and plan as indicated below.

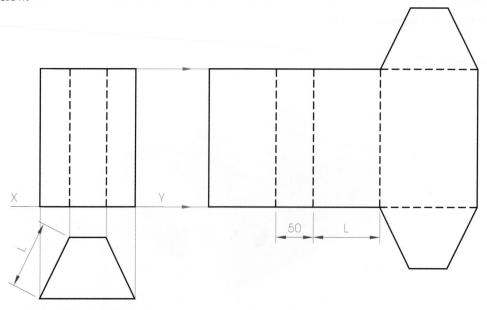

Exercises

1. The **Band-Aid®** box shown over is based on a **rectangular prism** with dimensions as indicated.

(a) Draw an **elevation** of the prism looking in the direction of arrow **A**.

(b) Draw a **plan** of the prism looking in the direction of the arrow **B**, projected from the elevation.

(c) Draw a **surface development** of the prism.

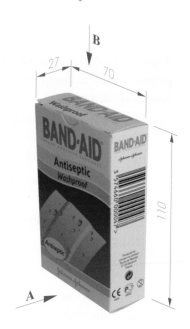

2. The **Amicelli** box shown across is based on a **regular hexagonal prism**. Using the dimensions shown:

(a) Draw an **elevation** of the prism looking in the direction of arrow **A**.

(b) Draw a **plan** of the prism looking in the direction of the arrow **B**, projected from the elevation.

(c) Draw a **surface development** of the prism.

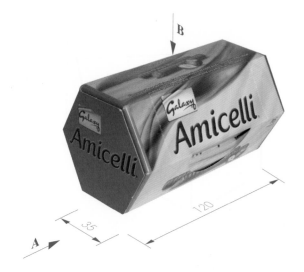

3. The **Walnut Whip** box shown across is based on an **equilateral triangular prism**. Using the dimensions indicated:

(a) Draw an **elevation** of the prism looking in the direction of arrow **A**.

(b) Draw a **plan** of the prism looking in the direction of the arrow **B**, projected from the elevation.

(c) Draw a **surface development** of the prism.

Example
A pictorial view of a **truncated prism**, which is based on the **R-kive** box, is shown over.

(a) Draw a **front elevation** of the truncated prism looking in the direction of arrow **A**.

(b) Draw an **end elevation** looking in the direction of the arrow **B**.

(c) Draw a **development** of the truncated prism.

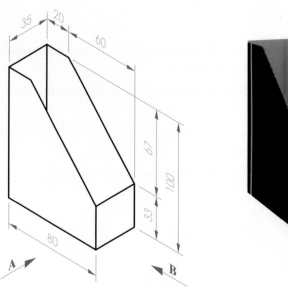

1. The figure below illustrates the faces of the truncated prism unfolding into one plane. The development consists of three rectangles and two trapeziums.

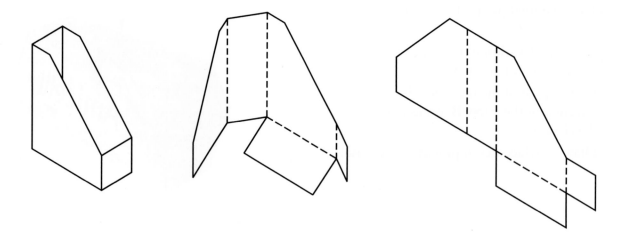

2. The front and end elevations are drawn as shown below.

3. The development can be drawn by transferring the relevant true lengths from the front and end elevations as shown below.

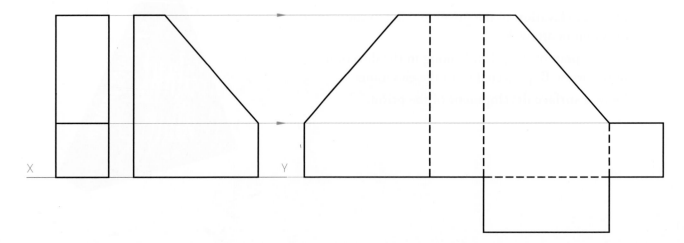

Exercises

1. A pictorial view of a **Disk Box** is shown over.

   (a) Draw a **front elevation** of the box looking in the direction of arrow **A**.

   (b) Draw a **plan** looking in the direction of the arrow **B**, projected from the elevation.

   (c) Draw a **development** of the box.

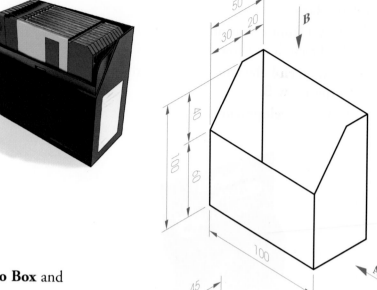

2. A pictorial view of a **Display Box**, a **Biro Box** and a **Litter Box** are shown. In each case:

   (a) Draw a **front elevation** of the box looking in the direction of arrow **A**.

   (b) Draw an **end elevation** looking in the direction of the arrow **B**.

   (c) Draw a **development** of the box.

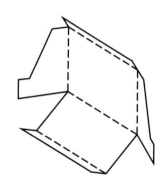

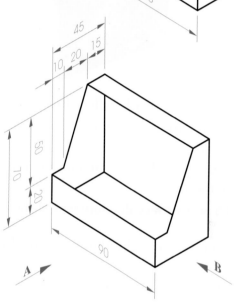

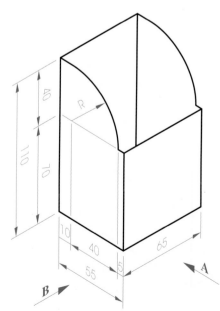

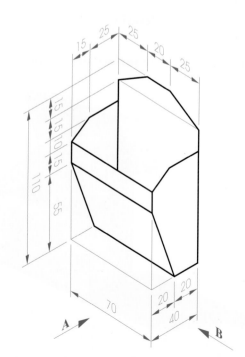

3. The figure over shows a pictorial view of a box for **Gillette Razor Blades**.

    (a) Draw a **front elevation** of the box looking in the direction of arrow **A**.

    (b) Draw an **end elevation** looking in the direction of the arrow **B**.

    (c) Draw a **development** of the box.

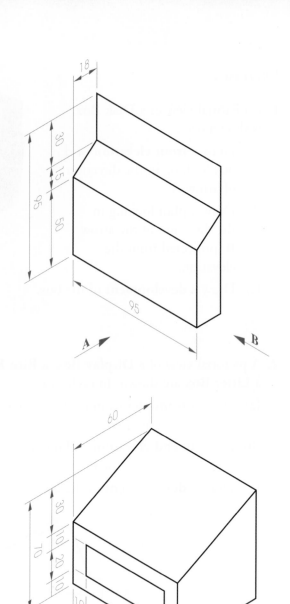

4. A pictorial view of a **Jewellery Box** is shown across.

    (a) Draw a **front elevation** of the box looking in the direction of arrow **A**.

    (b) Draw an **end elevation** looking in the direction of the arrow **B**.

    (c) Draw a **surface development** of the box.

5. The figure below, right, shows a pictorial view of a box.

    (a) Draw a **front elevation** of the box looking in the direction of arrow **A**.

    (b) Draw an **end elevation** looking in the direction of the arrow **B**.

    (c) Draw a complete **surface development** of the box.

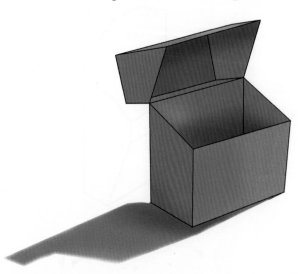

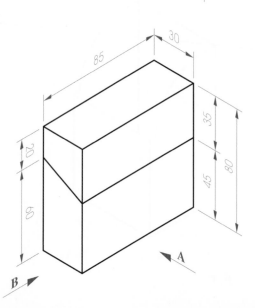

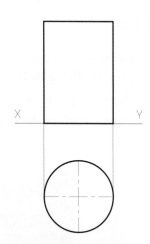

Example
The **Peaches Tin** shown is based on a **cylinder**. The plan and elevation of this cylinder are shown far right. Draw a **complete surface development** of the cylinder.

1. By observing, for example, some kitchen roll it is evident that *the curved surface of a cylinder unrolls into a rectangle.*

   The figure below illustrates the curved surface of a cylinder unrolling into a plane. The development has:
   • a length equal to the circumference of the top or bottom circle.
   • a height equal to the height of the cylinder.

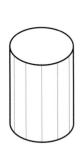
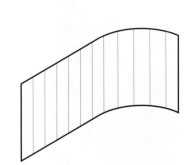
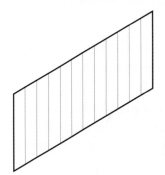

2. The development is constructed as shown below. The circumference of the circle can be approximated by dividing the circle into twelve equal parts and setting out the resulting cord distance twelve times.

3. The true shape of the top and bottom can be transferred directly from the plan.

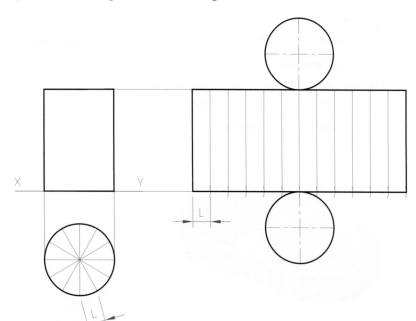

Exercises

1. The elevation and plan of a cylinder, which is based on the **Pringles** box are shown over.

(a) Draw the given views.

(b) Draw a **surface development** of the prism.

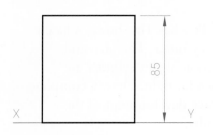

2. The figure over shows a pictorial view of a **bin**.

(a) Draw an **elevation** of the bin looking in the direction of arrow **A**.

(b) Draw a **plan** looking in the direction of the arrow **B**, projected from the elevation.

(c) Draw a **development** of the bin.

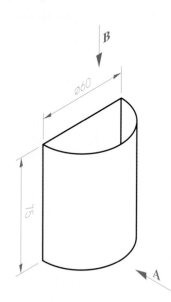

3. A pictorial view of a prism, which is based on the **Herring Fillets** box is shown below, right.

(a) Draw an **elevation** of the prism looking in the direction of arrow **A**.

(b) Draw a **plan** looking in the direction of the arrow **B**, projected from the elevation.

(c) Draw a **surface development** of the prism.

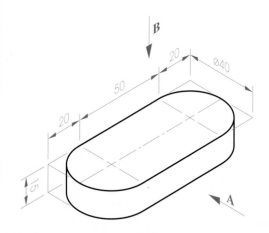

4. The figure over shows a pictorial view of a **container**.

   (a) Draw an **elevation** of the container looking in the direction of arrow **A**.

   (b) Draw an **end elevation** looking in the direction of the arrow **B**.

   (c) Draw a **development** of the container.

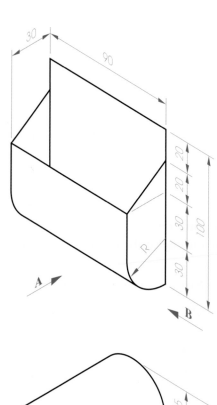

5. A pictorial view of a **Jewellery Box** is shown across.

   (a) Draw an **elevation** of the box looking in the direction of arrow **A**.

   (b) Draw an **end elevation** looking in the direction of the arrow **B**.

   (c) Draw a **surface development** of the box.

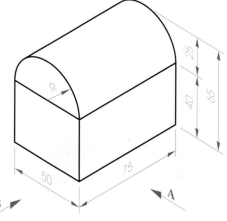

6. The figure over shows a pictorial view of a **box**.

   (a) Draw an **elevation** of the box looking in the direction of arrow **A**.

   (b) Draw an **end elevation** looking in the direction of the arrow **B**.

   (c) Draw a **surface development** of the box.

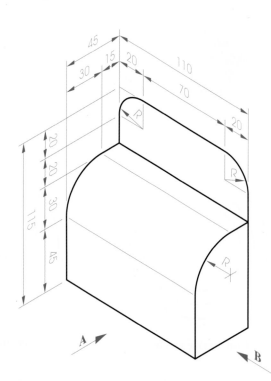

Chapter 11
Circles 1

A **circle** is a plane curve whose points are all the same distance from a fixed point called the **centre**.

Parts of a Circle

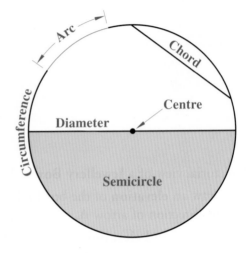

Circumference
The outline of the circle.

Arc
Any part of the circumference.

Chord
A straight line joining two points on the circumference.

Diameter
A chord that passes through the centre. The symbol for diameter is Ø.

Semicircle
Half of a circle.

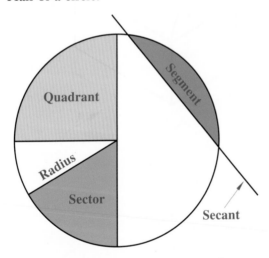

Quadrant
A quarter of a circle.

Segment
The part of a circle enclosed by a chord and its arc.

Radius
A line joining the centre to a point on the circumference. It is often abbreviated to **R**. The plural of radius is **radii**.

Sector
The part enclosed by two radii and an arc.

Secant
A line that intersects a circle at two points.

Concentric and Eccentric Circles

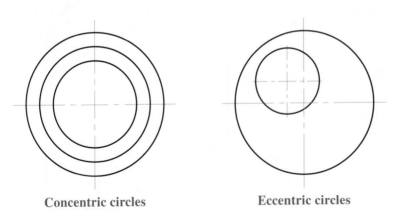

Concentric circles

Eccentric circles

Concentric circles are circles that have the same centre but different radii.
Eccentric circles are circles that have different centres and different radii.

Exercises

1. A drawing of the badge used on **Opel** cars is shown in the figure over.

   (a) Reproduce the drawing to the sizes given.

   (b) You are required to design a sign for use by garages to show that they are Opel agents. Your sign must incorporate the Opel logo.

   Make a drawing of your design. You will find a sketch a great help to start with.

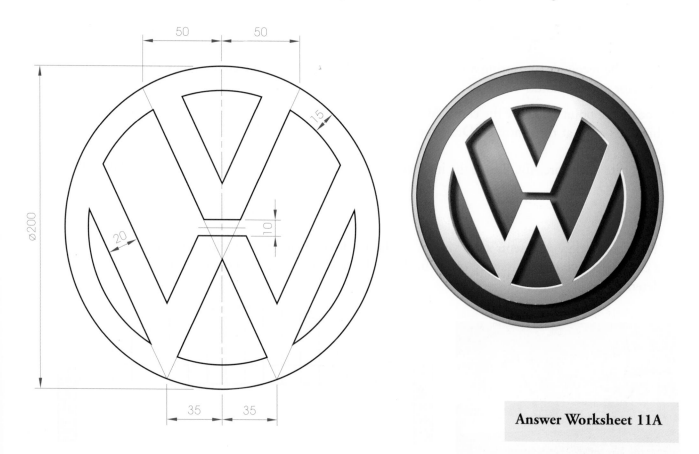

2. The drawing of the **Volkswagen** symbol shown in the figure below includes the letters V and W in a circular logo. Draw the logo full-size. Use shading or colour to enhance your drawing.

Answer Worksheet 11A

Finding the Centre of a Given Circle or Arc

The figure across shows a circle, centre O. Two chords AB and CD are also shown. The chords are bisected to show that the perpendicular bisectors cross at the centre O.

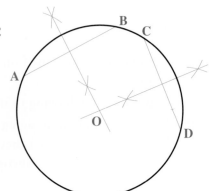

The perpendicular bisector of a chord passes through the centre of the circle.

Example

The figure below shows an elevation of a **globe light fitting**. Reproduce the drawing showing clearly how the centre of the arc is obtained.

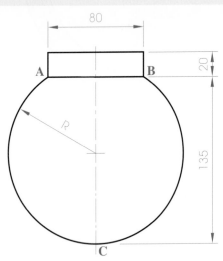

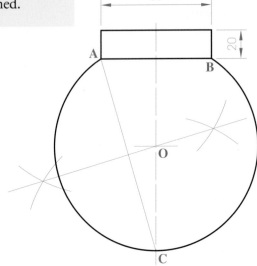

1. Draw the rectangle measuring 80 mm × 20 mm. AB is a chord of the circle. Draw the perpendicular bisector of this chord.

2. Locate the point C. Draw the chord AC and construct its perpendicular bisector. The perpendicular bisectors cross at the centre O. Draw the arc centre O and radius OA.

The centre of the arc ABC lies at the intersection of the perpendicular bisectors of chords AB and AC.

Exercises

1. The figure below represents a drawing of the **James Joyce Bridge** in Dublin. The curve ABC is an arc of a circle. Reproduce the drawing of the bridge full-size showing clearly how the centre for the arc ABC is determined.

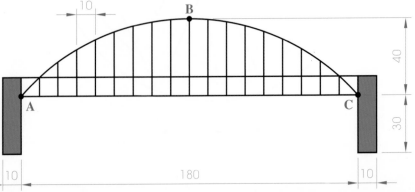

2. A drawing of a logo that was once used by the estate agents **Hamilton, Osborne and King** is shown in the figure below.
Reproduce the given drawing showing all construction lines.

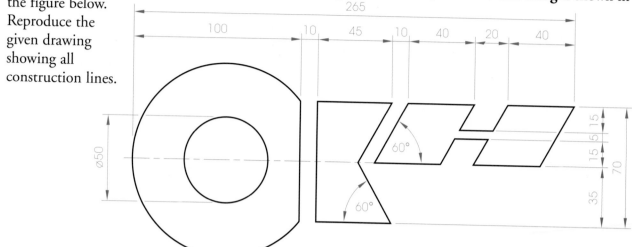

3. Draw the **euro** symbol to the dimensions given.

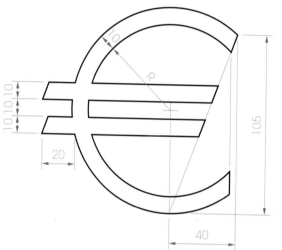

4. The **Shell** logo is a complex one but it can be reproduced accurately by means of a technical drawing. Reproduce the drawing of the **Shell** logo shown below showing all constructions.

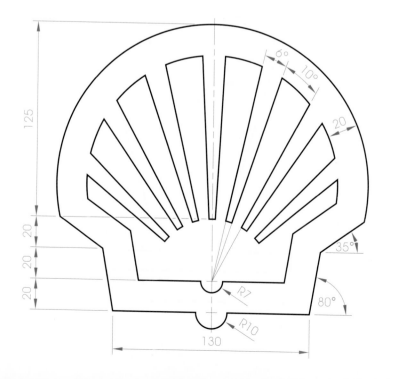

Answer Worksheet 11B

Tangents to a Circle

A **tangent** to a circle is a line that touches the circumference at one point only, called the **point of contact**.

The angle between the radius of a circle and a tangent at the point of contact is 90°.

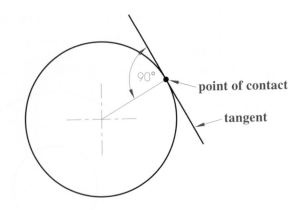

Drawing a Tangent from a Point Outside A Circle

Example
Draw a tangent to the given circle K from the point P.

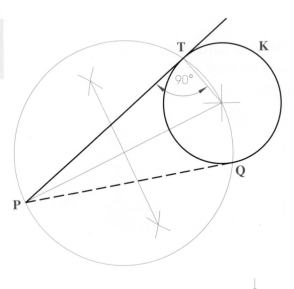

1. Join P to the centre of the circle.

2. Bisect this line and draw the semicircle cutting the circumference of the circle at T. This is the **point of contact**.

3. Join PT. This is a **tangent** from P.

A second tangent PQ can be drawn as shown.

This construction is based on the angle in a semicircle (see page 186).

Exercises

1. Reproduce the given drawing of a **sports trophy** showing clearly how the tangents to the circle are constructed.

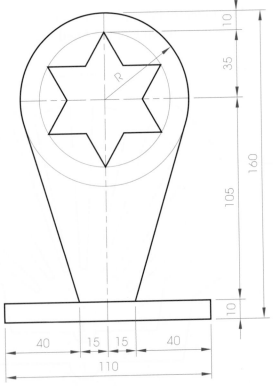

2. The figure across shows a sign for a **golf course**. Reproduce the drawing full-size showing clearly how the **tangent** to the arc is obtained.

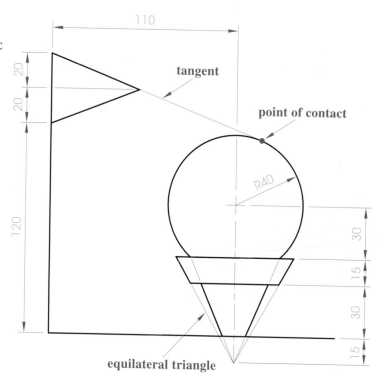

tangent

point of contact

R40

equilateral triangle

3. Reproduce the given drawing of the logo for **Remax Auctioneers** showing clearly how the tangents to the circle are constructed.

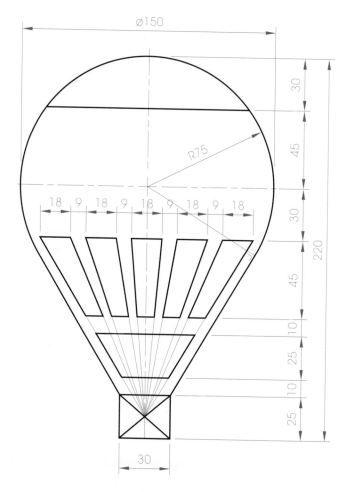

Answer Worksheet 11C

Tangential Circles

Two circles having one point in common are said to **touch** each other. Two circles touch **externally** when one is outside the other – two circles touch **internally** when one is inside the other.

The point at which they touch is called the **point of contact**.

Example 1
Draw an arc of radius 40 mm to touch two circles A and B externally.

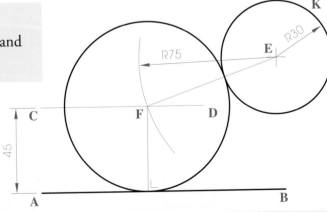

1. With centre A and R60 (20 + 40), draw an arc about circle A as shown in the figure across.
2. With B as centre and R75 (35 + 40), draw a second arc cutting the first at C.
3. Join AC and BC to obtain the points of contact.
4. Draw the arc of radius 40mm from C.

If two circles touch externally, the distance between their centres equals the sum of their radii.

Example 2
Draw an arc of radius 90 mm to touch two circles A and B internally.

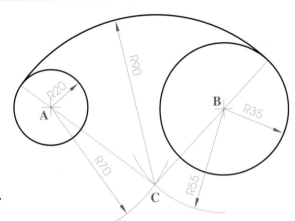

1. With centre A and R70 (90 – 20), draw an arc about circle A as shown in the figure over.
2. With B as centre and R55 (90 – 35), draw a second arc cutting the first at C.
3. Join AC and BC and extend to obtain the points of contact.
4. Draw the arc of radius 90 mm from C.

If two circles touch internally, the distance between their centres equals the difference of their radii.

Example 3
Draw a circle of radius 45 mm to touch a circle K and a straight line AB.

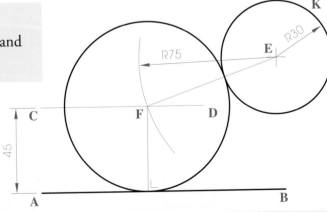

1. Draw a line CD 45 mm above AB.
2. With centre E and a radius equal to the sum of the radii of the two circles (30 + 45), draw an arc to cut CD at F. This is the centre of the required circle.
3. Join FE to obtain the point of contact between the two circles. Draw a line from F perpendicular to AB to obtain the point of contact between the circle and the line. Draw the circle.

Answer Worksheets 11D and 11E

Example

A design for a **hand bell** is shown. Draw the given design, showing clearly all constructions and points of contact.

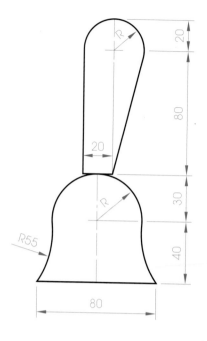

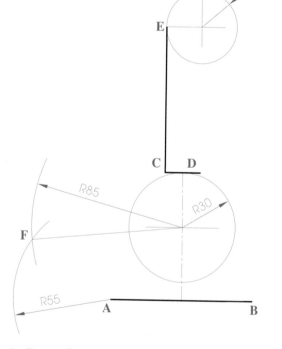

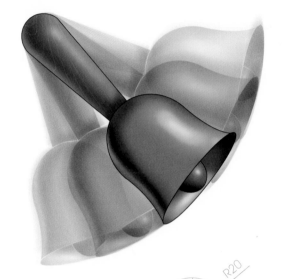

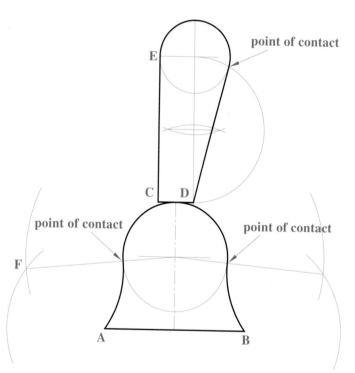

1. Draw the two horizontal lines AB and CD, and the vertical line CE. Locate the centres for the circles of radii 20 mm and 30 mm respectively. Draw these two circles.

2. With centre A and radius 55 mm, draw an arc as shown. Draw another arc of radius 85 mm (55 + 30) about the circle of radius 30 mm cutting the first arc at F.

3. Join F to the centre of the circle to obtain the point of contact. Draw the arc of radius 55 mm from F. Complete the right-hand side using the same procedure.

4. Construct a tangent from D to the circle of radius 20 mm, using the method outlined on page 98.

5. Complete the design by drawing in the outline of the figure.

Exercises

Draw each of the designs shown below showing clearly all constructions and points of contact.

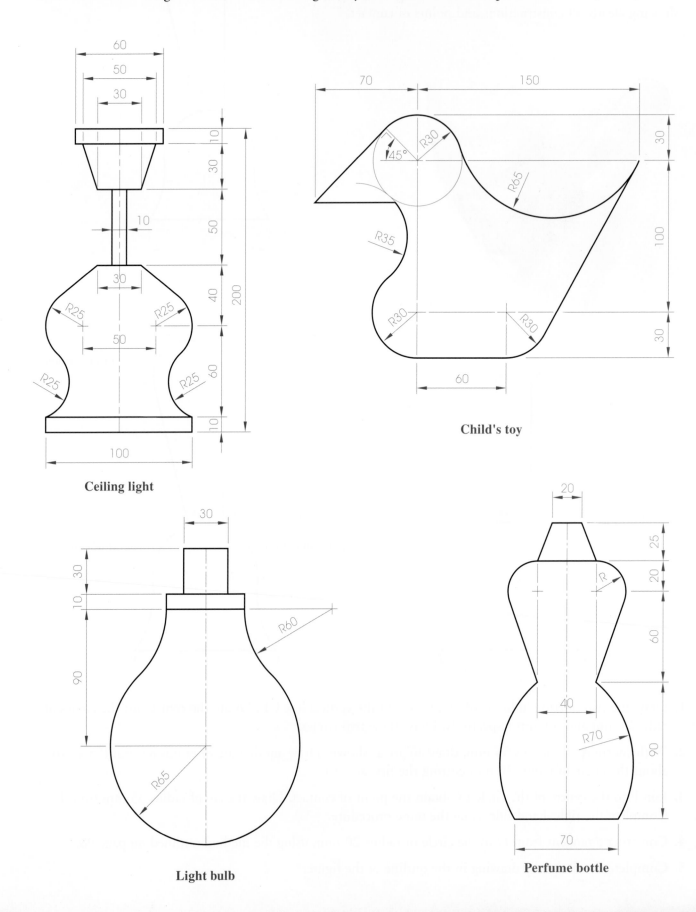

Ceiling light

Child's toy

Light bulb

Perfume bottle

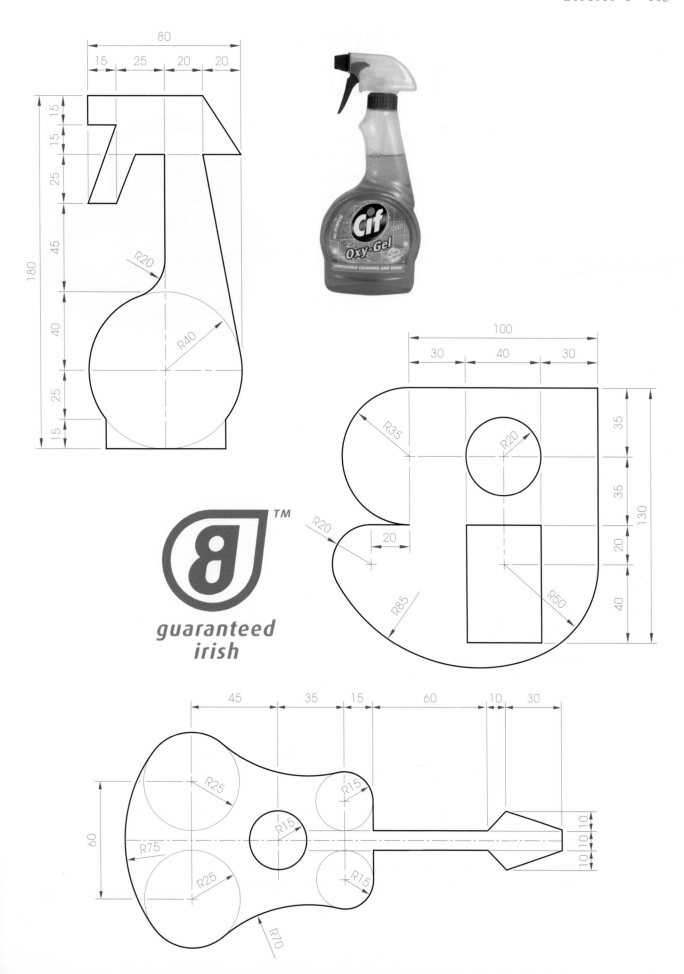

guaranteed
irish

Chapter 12

The Ellipse

The circle is a very common curve in the world around us, but it is not the curve we most often see. This is because a circle seen from an angle appears to be another curve called an **ellipse**. The figure across shows some examples of circles that appear as ellipses in everyday life.

When a cylinder or a cone is cut at an angle to its axis as shown in the figure below, the resulting section is an **ellipse**.

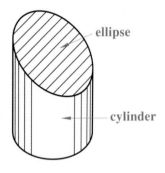

ellipse

cylinder

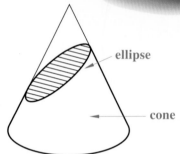

ellipse

cone

Parts of an Ellipse

- The **major axis** is the longest line that can be drawn across the ellipse.

- The **minor axis** is the perpendicular bisector through the midpoint of the major axis.

- The **focal points** are two points that lie on the major axis. They are denoted by F_1 and F_2.

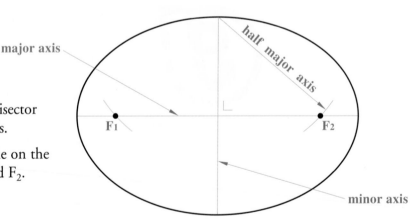

major axis

half major axis

F_1 F_2

minor axis

> The distance from one end of the minor axis to a focal point is always equal to half the length of the major axis.

This information allows us to locate the focal points when we are given the major and minor axes:

1. Set your compass to a length equal to half the length of the major axis.

2. Position the compass point at one end of the minor axis, as shown in the figure above, and swing arcs to cut the major axis at F_1 and F_2 respectively.

Answer Worksheet 12A

Drawing an Ellipse using the Auxiliary Circles Method

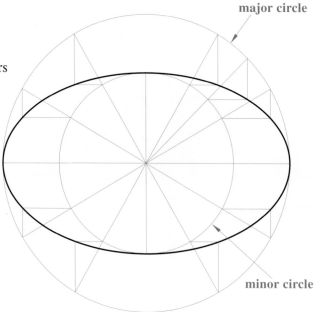

1. Draw the major and minor axes.

2. Draw the major and minor auxiliary circles.

3. For convenience, divide these into twelve equal sectors using the 30°/60° set square. More division lines can be drawn at other angles, e.g. 15°, 45°, 75°, etc.

4. Draw a series of lines parallel to the minor axis from the points where the sector lines cut the major circle.

5. Draw a series of lines parallel to the major axis from the points where the sector lines cross the minor circle. The intersection of the two lines drawn from the same division line gives a point on the ellipse.

6. Draw a smooth curve through these points. Note that an ellipse has rounded ends – not pointed ones.

Use a **flexi curve** to draw the ellipse. This is a length of flexible plastic that can be bent to any curve.

Exercises

1. The figure below shows the logo for **Whiskas** catfood. The design is based on an **ellipse** with a **major axis** of 140 mm and a **minor axis** of 90 mm.

   The ears of the cat are formed by drawing lines from P and Q, respectively, to the **focal points** of the curve.

   Draw the logo showing all construction lines clearly.

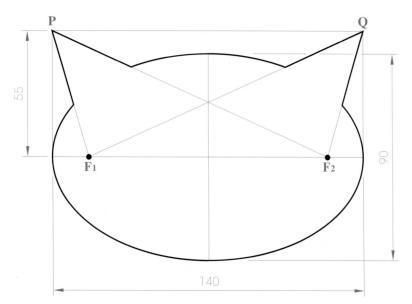

2. A design for an **umbrella** based on a **semi-ellipse** having a **major axis** of 140 mm and a **minor axis** of 80 mm is shown below.

Draw the given design full-size showing clearly how the centres for the four **arcs** are obtained.

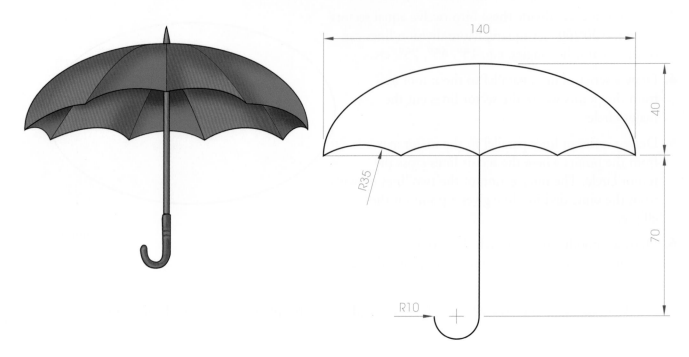

3. The figure below is a drawing of an **entrance gateway**. The curve is in the shape of a **semi-ellipse** having a **major axis** of 120 mm and a **minor axis** of 70 mm. The spacings between the 10 mm vertical members are equal.

Draw this diagram full-size, showing clearly all construction lines.

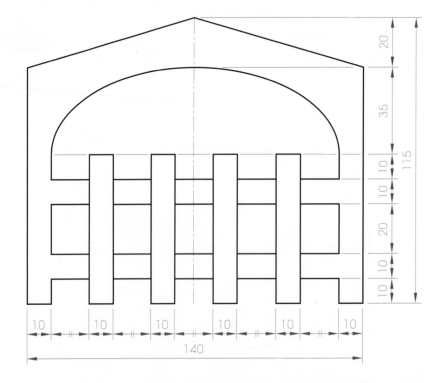

Example

A design for a **bedroom mirror** based on an **ellipse** is shown.

Draw full-size the given design showing clearly how the centre for arc A is obtained.

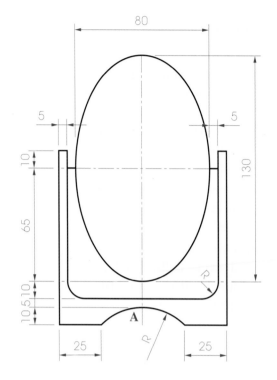

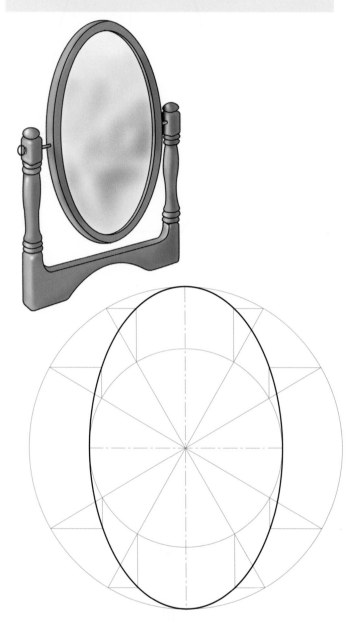

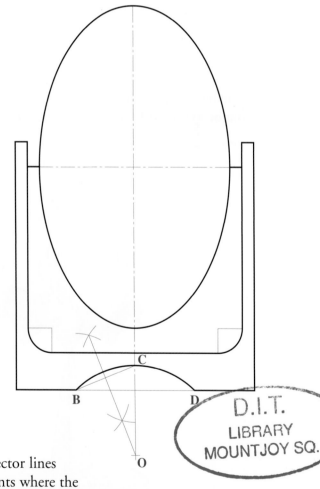

1. Draw the **major axis** of length 130 mm and the **minor axis** of length 80 mm.

2. Draw the major and minor auxiliary circles and divide these into equal sectors as shown.

3. Draw a series of horizontal lines from the points where the sector lines cut the outer circle, and a series of vertical lines from the points where the sector lines cross the inner circle. The intersections give points on the ellipse. Draw the ellipse.

4. Draw the outline of the stand. The centre O of the arc A is obtained by finding the point of intersection of the perpendicular bisectors of the two chords BC and BD.

Exercises

1. The figure across shows a drawing of a **shower gel bottle**. The outline of the bottle is in the shape of a portion of an **ellipse** having a **major axis** of 180 mm and a **minor axis** of 90 mm.

   (a) Draw this figure showing all construction lines clearly.

   (b) Using your freehand drawing skills, sketch a suitable design for a label for the bottle.

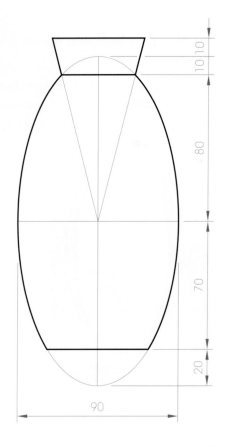

2. The figure below shows a view of a **lamp**. The lampshade is in the form of a **semi-ellipse** having a **major axis** of 140 mm and a **minor axis** of 80 mm. The curve ABC is an **arc** of a circle.

   Reproduce the drawing of the lamp showing clearly all construction lines.

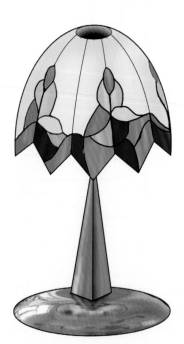

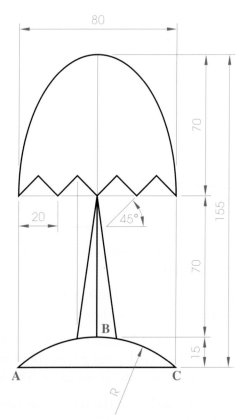

Drawing an Ellipse using the Trammel Method

1. Draw the major and minor axes.

2. Cut a strip of paper with a straight edge to use as a trammel. Mark a point P about 10 mm from the edge of the trammel as shown. From this point mark a point A such that PA is equal to half the minor axis. Locate another point B such that PB is equal to half the major axis.

3. Place the trammel so that A is on the major axis and B is on the minor axis. Then, mark the position of P with a pencil.

4. Move the trammel around, keeping A on the major axis and B on the minor axis as shown. Mark the position of P each time.

5. When enough points have been located, draw a smooth curve through them.

6. Include the trammel with your drawing.

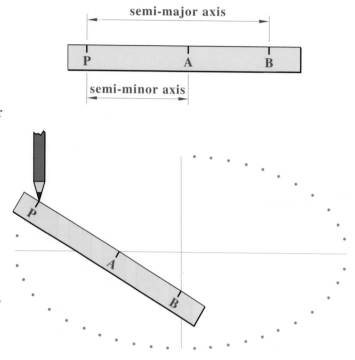

Exercises

1. The figure below shows a design for a **Bed and Breakfast** sign in the shape of an **ellipse**. The **ellipse** has a **major axis** of length 150 mm and a **minor axis** of length 100 mm. F_1 and F_2 are the focal points of the curve.

   Draw the given design full-size, using a **trammel** to construct the ellipse.

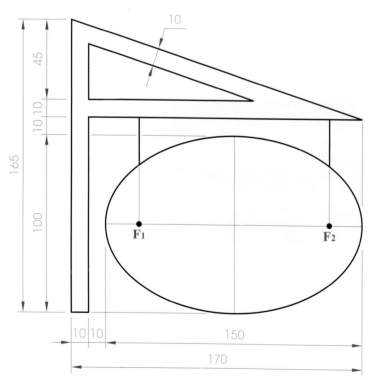

2. The figure below shows a drawing of **entrance gates**. The **semi-ellipse** has a **major axis** of length 140 mm and a **minor axis** of length 80 mm. The boards are 5 mm apart as shown.

Make a drawing of the gates, using a **trammel** to construct the **semi-ellipse**.

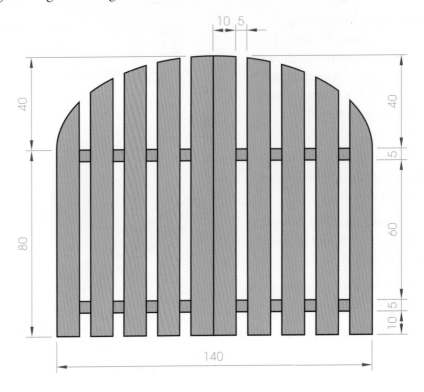

3. A logo for the **Hamburger Inn** based on a **semi-ellipse** having a **major axis** of 130 mm and a **minor axis** of 100 mm is shown in the figure below.

Draw the given logo full-size. Don't forget to include the **trammel** with your drawing.

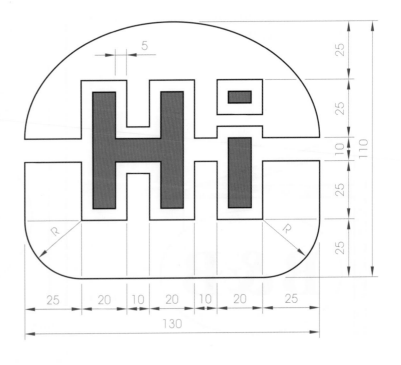

4. The figure across shows the design for a **shampoo bottle**. It has a label in the shape of an **ellipse** attached. The **major axis** is 140 mm and the **minor axis** is 80 mm.

Draw the given design, showing all construction lines. Use a **trammel** to construct the ellipse.

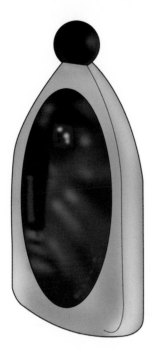

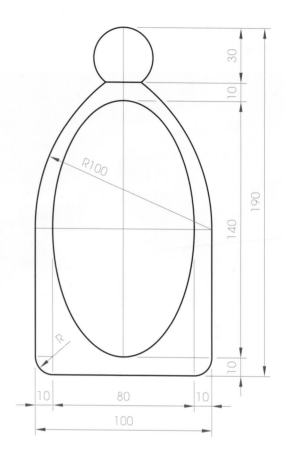

5. A design for a **wine glass** based on a **semi-ellipse** is shown below. The **major axis** of the ellipse is 160 mm long and the **minor axis** is 90 mm long.

Draw the given design full-size using a **trammel** to construct the ellipse.

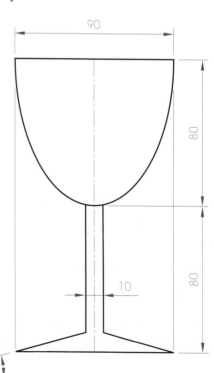

6. Reproduce the drawing of the **rugby ball** shown across, using a **trammel** to draw the **ellipse**.

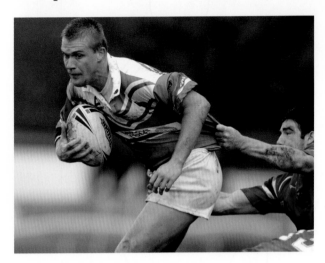

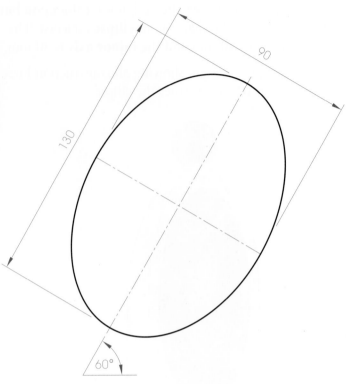

Drawing an Ellipse using the Rectangle Method

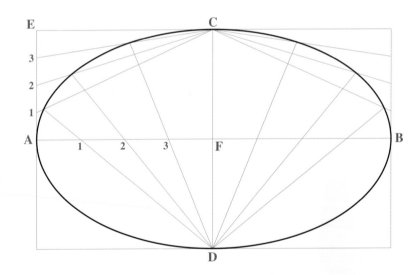

1. Draw the major and minor axes AB and CD, and draw a rectangle about their ends.

2. Divide AE and AF into the same number of equal parts, say four. Number the divisions from A as shown.

3. Join the points on AE to C. Join D to the points on AF and extend as shown.

4. The points where corresponding lines intersect are points on the curve.

5. Repeat in the other quadrants of the rectangle. Join the points of intersection of corresponding lines in a smooth curve.

Answer Worksheet 12B

Drawing a Tangent and a Normal to an Ellipse at a Point P on the Curve

A **tangent** to an ellipse is a line that touches the curve at one point called the **point of contact**.

A **normal** is a line drawn perpendicular to the tangent at the point of contact.

1. Determine the focal points. Join P to F_1 and F_2 respectively.

2. Extend F_2P to E and bisect the angle F_1PE. The bisector of this angle is the required **tangent**.

3. Bisect the angle F_1PF_2. The bisector of this angle is the required **normal**.

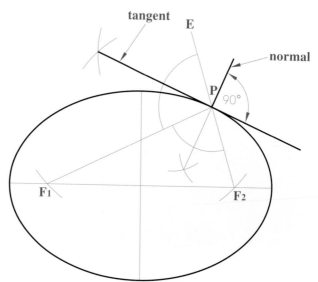

The point of intersection between the ellipse and the tangent is called the **point of contact**.

A **normal** bisects the angle formed by the two lines drawn from the point of contact to the focal points.

Answer Worksheet 12C

Exercises

1. The figure below shows a design based on a **fish**. The curve is based on an **ellipse** with a **major axis** of 140 mm and a **minor axis** of 90 mm.

   F is one of the **focal points** of the curve. The line AB is a **tangent** to the ellipse at the point A.

   Draw the given figure showing all construction lines.

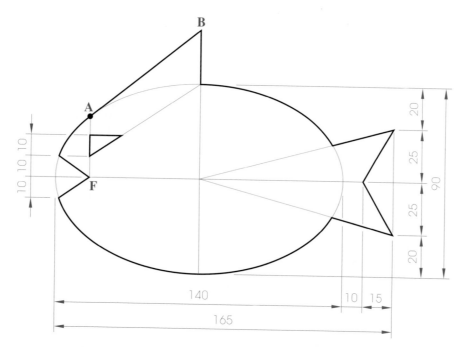

2. The figure below represents a **picture frame** for a photograph that is hanging on a wall. It is based on an **ellipse** having a **major axis** of 120 mm and a **minor axis** of 80 mm.

The lines PT and QT are **tangents** to the ellipse at the points P and Q respectively.

Draw the figure to the dimensions given showing all constructions clearly.

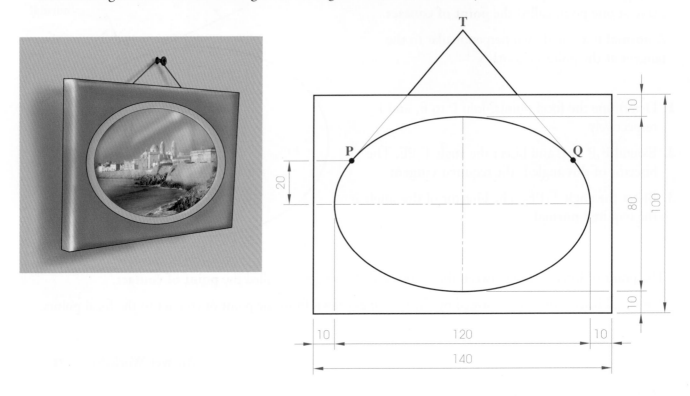

3. The figure below represents a **steering wheel** for a **computer game**. It is based on an **ellipse** having a **major axis** of 120 mm and a **minor axis** of 90 mm.

The line AB is a **normal** to the curve at the point A.

Draw the figure showing all constructions.

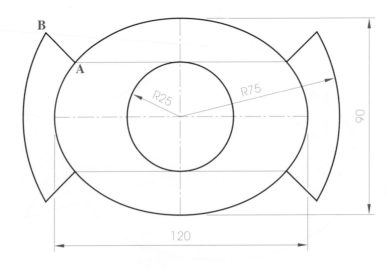

Chapter 13
Orthographic Projection 2

We saw in chapter 7 that orthographic projection is a method of representing a three-dimensional object on a plane surface.

The figure below shows a pictorial view of a cylinder and cone in relation to the **principal planes of projection**. The elevation and plan of the solids are also shown.

Note that the curved surface of the cylinder appears as a rectangle in elevation, while the curved surface of the cone appears as a triangle.

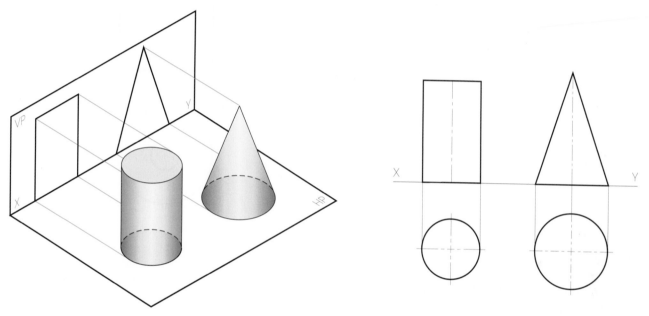

The horizontal plane (HP) and the vertical plane (VP) are known as the principal planes of projection.

Example
A pictorial view of a **Ribena Bottle** is shown over. Draw a plan of the bottle and project an elevation.

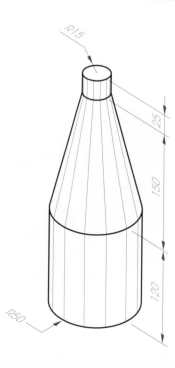

1. The plan will consist of two concentric circles of radii 15 mm and 50 mm as shown across.

2. The elevation can then be projected by marking off the relevant heights of 120, 150 and 25 mm.

3. Note that the truncated cone appears as a trapezium in elevation.

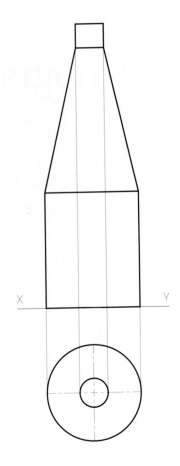

Exercises

1. A pictorial view of a **blocklock** is shown over. The bolt is 100 mm long.

   (a) Draw a **front elevation** looking in the direction of arrow **A**.

   (b) Draw an **end elevation** looking in the direction of arrow **B**.

   (c) Draw a **plan** projected from (a) above.

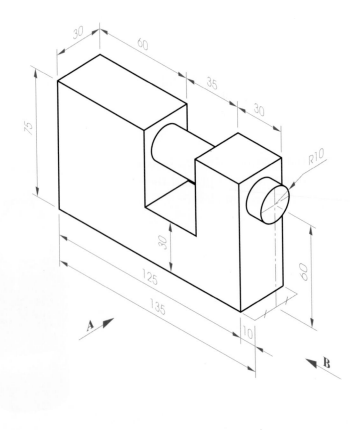

2. The figure over shows a pictorial view of a **school bag**.
A thumb-sketch of the front elevation is shown below.

(a) Draw the **front elevation** looking in the direction of arrow **A**.

(b) Draw an **end elevation** looking in the direction of arrow **B**.

(c) Draw a **plan** projected from (a) above.

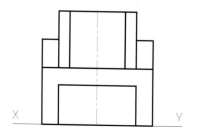

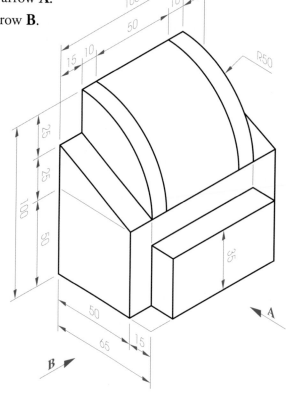

3. The figure over shows a pictorial view of a
lampshade. Using an A3 sheet portrait:

(a) Draw an **elevation** looking in the
direction of arrow **A**.

(b) Draw an **end elevation** looking in the
direction of arrow **B**.

(c) Draw a **plan** projected from (a) above.

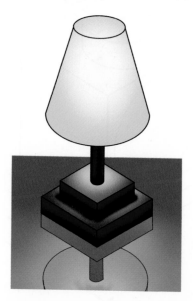

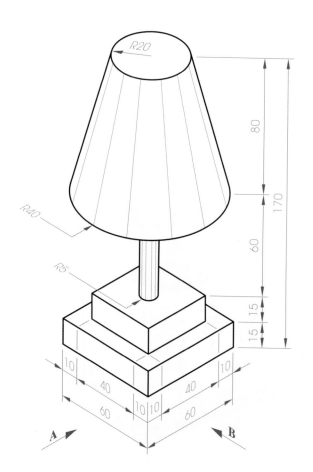

4. The figure below shows a pictorial view of a **food mixer**.
   (a) Draw an **elevation** looking in the direction of arrow **A**.
   (b) Draw an **end view** looking in the direction of arrow **B**.
   (c) Draw a **plan** projected from (a) above.

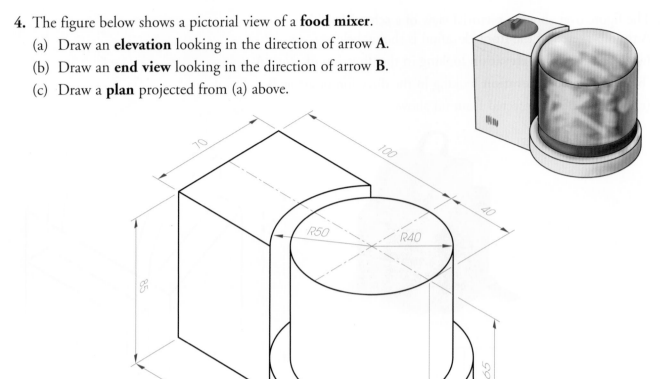

5. A pictorial view of some **kitchen scales** is shown across.
   (a) Draw an **elevation** looking in the direction of arrow **A**.
   (b) Draw an **end view** looking in the direction of arrow **B**.
   (c) Draw a **plan** projected from (a) above.

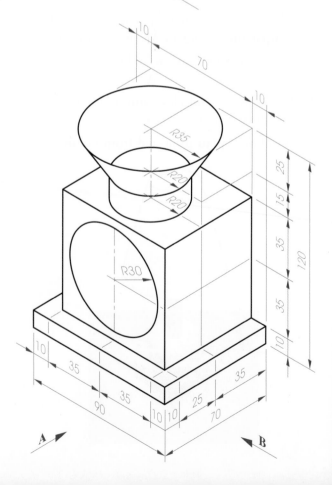

Example

The figure over shows a pictorial view of a
flight of steps.

(a) Draw an **elevation** looking in the
direction of arrow **A**.

(b) Draw an **end view** looking in the
direction of arrow **B**.

(c) Draw a **plan** projected from (a) above.

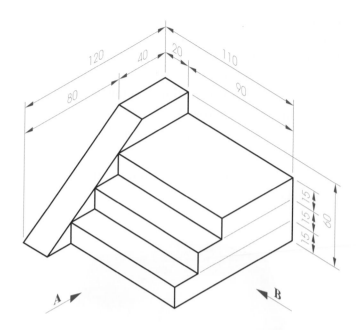

1. The elevation and outline of the end view are
   drawn as shown below.

2. The sloped surface appears as an edge (line) in
   the end view. Therefore the height of each step
   can be projected to intersect this surface (line)
   in the end view.

3. Now that the depth of each step has been determined the plan can be projected in the normal manner.

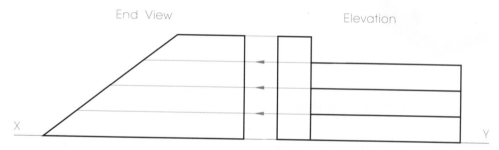

The point of intersection between a line and a plane can be determined in a view in which the plane
appears as an edge.

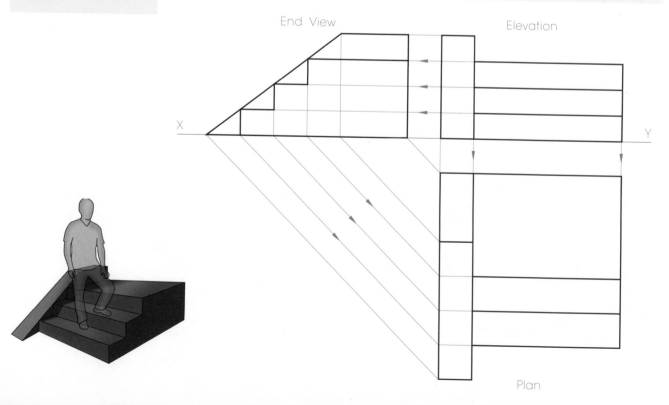

Plan

Exercises

1. A pictorial view of a **toaster** is shown over. The depth of the holes is 65 mm.

   (a) Draw a **front elevation** looking in the direction of arrow **A**.

   (b) Draw an **end view** looking in the direction of arrow **B**.

   (c) Draw a **plan** projected from the front elevation.

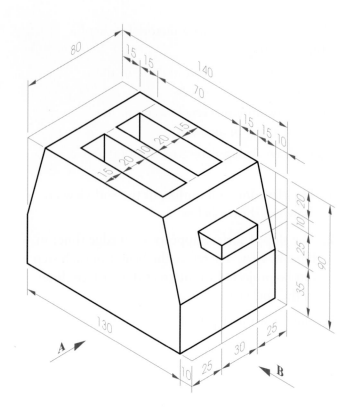

2. Represent each of the solids shown below using **orthographic projection** by drawing the following views:

   (a) A **front elevation** looking in the direction of arrow **A**.

   (b) An **end view** looking in the direction of arrow **B**.

   (c) A **plan** projected from (a) above.

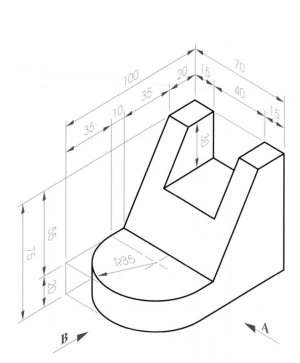

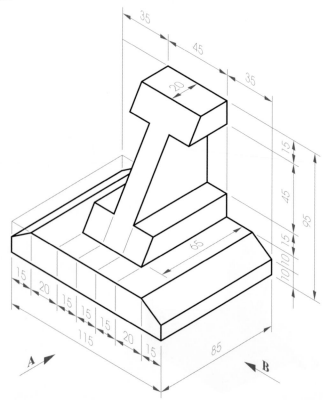

Example

A pictorial view of a **solid** is shown over.

(a) Draw an **elevation** looking in the direction of arrow **A**.

(b) Draw an **end view** looking in the direction of arrow **B**.

(c) Draw a **plan** projected from (a) above.

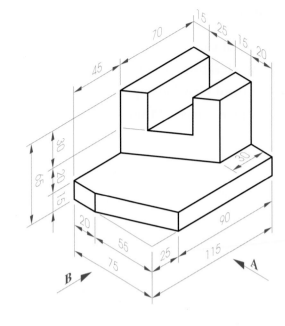

1. The incomplete elevation and the entire end view are drawn as shown below, right.

2. The plan is then projected in the normal manner.

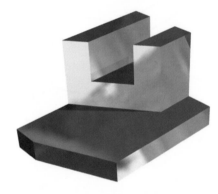

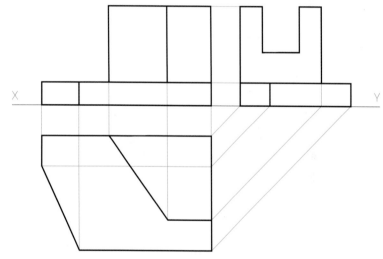

3. The upper inclined surface appears as an edge in the plan. Accordingly, the remaining lines on the object can be projected from the end view to intersect this surface (line) in the plan.

4. Now that the lengths of these lines have been determined, they can be projected to the elevation and the drawing completed as shown below.

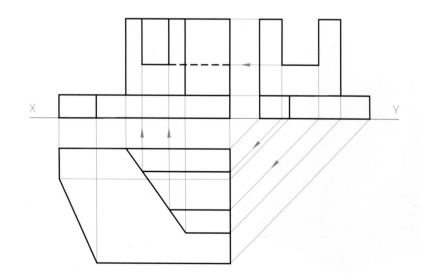

Exercises

1. A pictorial view of each of two components is shown below. In each case draw full-size:

    (a) An **elevation** looking in the direction of arrow **A**.

    (b) An **end view** looking in the direction of arrow **B**.

    (c) A **plan** projected from (a) above.

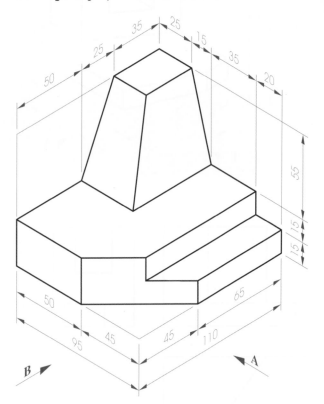

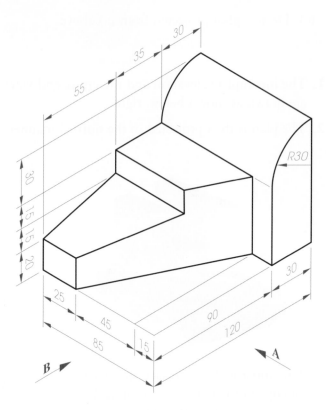

2. The figure below shows a pictorial view of a **platform**. *Each step is of equal height.* Draw full-size:

    (a) An **elevation** looking in the direction of arrow **A**.

    (b) An **end elevation** looking in the direction of arrow **B**.

    (c) A **plan** projected from (a) above.

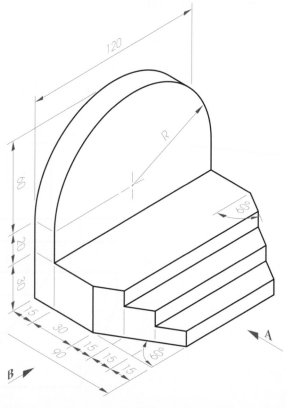

3. A pictorial view of a **knife block** is shown below. Also shown is an elevation of the knife block looking in the direction of arrow A. Using an A2 size sheet draw full-size:

(a) The given **elevation** looking in the direction of arrow **A**.

(b) An **end view** looking in the direction of arrow **B**.

(c) A **plan** projected from (a) above.

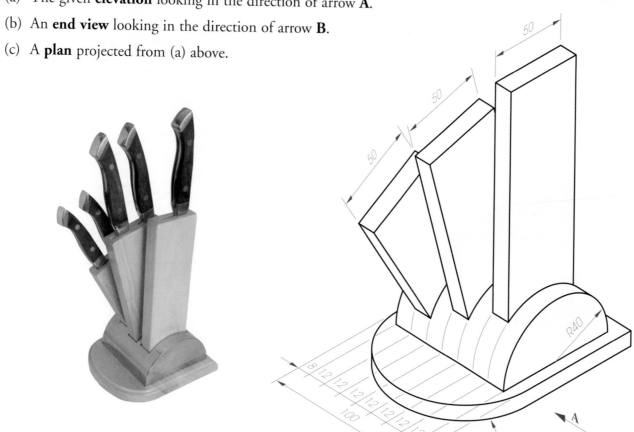

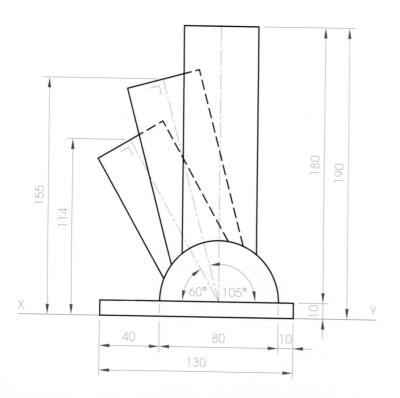

4. The figure over shows a pictorial view of a **component**. A photo-realistic image of the component is also shown. Draw full-size:

(a) An **elevation** looking in the direction of arrow **A**.

(b) An **end view** looking in the direction of arrow **B**.

(c) A **plan** projected from (a) above.

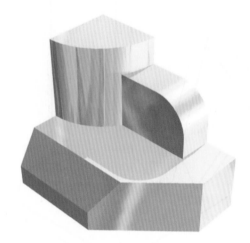

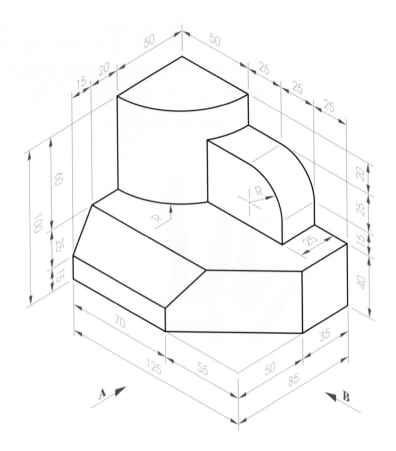

5. A pictorial view of a **component** is shown below. A photo-realistic image of the component is also shown. Draw full-size:

(a) An **elevation** looking in the direction of arrow **A**.

(b) An **end view** looking in the direction of arrow **B**.

(c) A **plan** projected from (a) above.

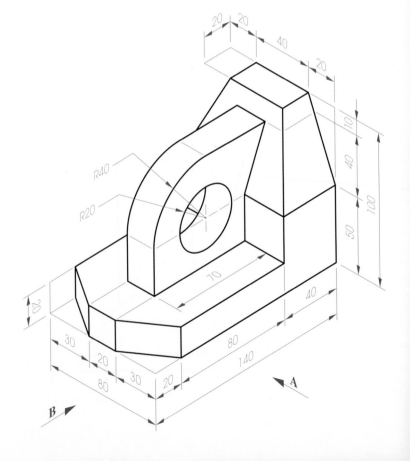

6. The figure over shows a pictorial view of a **camera**. Draw full-size:

(a) An **elevation** looking in the direction of arrow **A**.

(b) An **end view** looking in the direction of arrow **B**.

(c) A **plan** projected from (a) above.

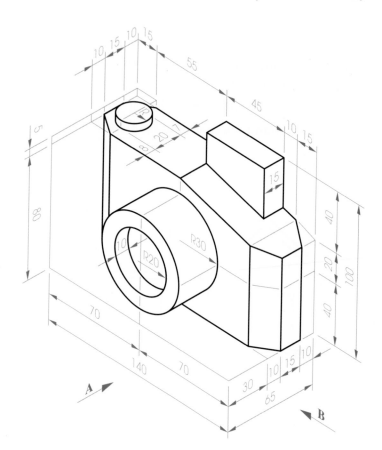

7. A pictorial view of a **component** is shown below. Draw full-size:

(a) An **elevation** looking in the direction of arrow **A**.

(b) An **end view** looking in the direction of arrow **B**.

(c) A **plan** projected from (a) above.

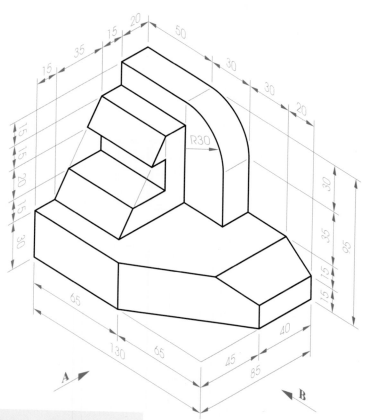

Answer Worksheets 13A and 13B

Example

The figure below shows a pictorial view of a **garage**. Also shown are the front elevation and incomplete end elevation of the garage.

(a) Complete the **end view** of the garage.

(b) Draw a **plan** projected from the front elevation.

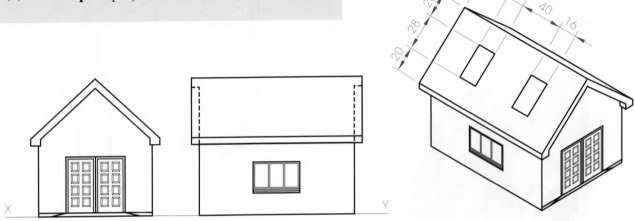

1. The true distances (20 and 28) can be marked-off along the roof surface, which appears as an edge, in elevation as shown below. This establishes the heights for the roof windows.

2. These heights can be projected to the end elevation where the appropriate widths can be marked-off.

3. The plan is then projected in the normal manner.

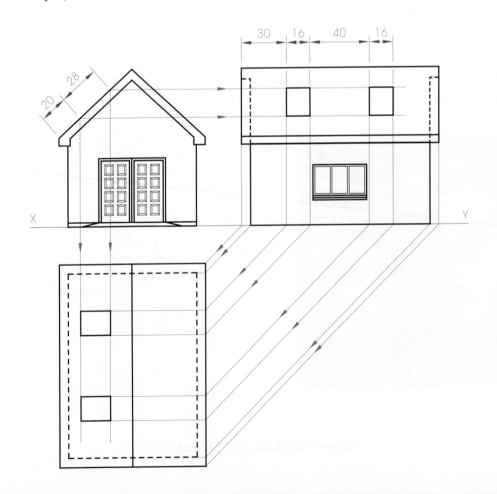

Exercises

1. The figure below, right shows a pictorial view of a **package for sliotars**. It is based on a **regular hexagonal prism**. Draw full-size:

(a) The **front elevation** looking in the direction of arrow **A**.

(b) An **end view** looking in the direction of arrow **B**.

(c) A **plan** projected from the front elevation.

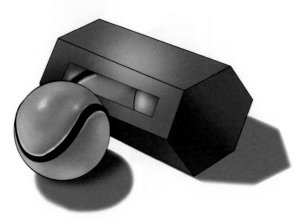

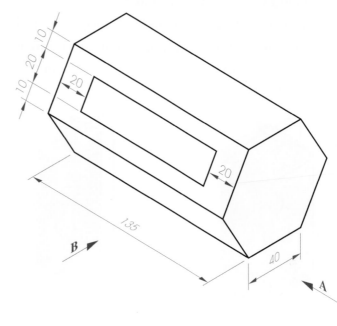

2. A pictorial view of a **drawing table** is shown below. The chamfers on its legs are 5 mm x 5 mm.

(a) Draw the **front elevation** looking in the direction of arrow **A**.

(b) Draw an **end view** looking in the direction of arrow **B**.

(c) Draw a **plan** projected from the front elevation.

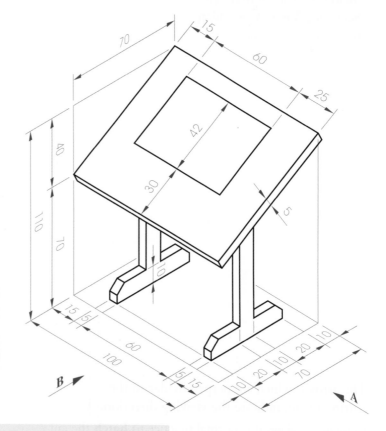

Answer Worksheets 13C and 13D

Sectional Views

An object with internal features can be shown more clearly with a **sectional view**. The pictorials below indicate how a sectional view is created:

(i)   Imagine that the object is cut by an imaginary cutting plane (below, left)

(ii) Imagine the portion of the object nearest you is removed (below, centre).

(iii) The remaining part of the object is projected in the normal manner to yield a sectional view (below, right).

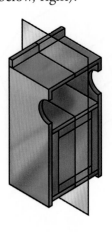 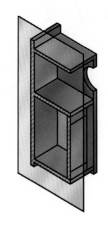 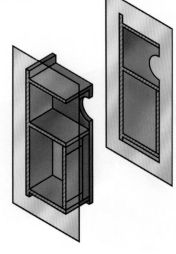

Example
The elevation and plan of a **locker** are shown over. The **Sectional View A–A** which results from the cutting plane AA is also shown.

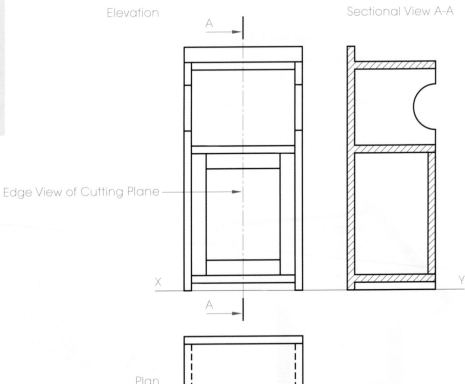

Elevation

Sectional View A-A

Edge View of Cutting Plane

Plan

The arrows, which are perpendicular to the cutting plane, indicate the viewing direction.

In sectional views it is normal practice to **hatch** the cut surface (**section**) with equally spaced light lines at 45 degrees.

Answer Worksheet 13E

Chapter 14
Pictorial Drawing 2

In chapter 8 we were introduced to two types of pictorial drawing, namely oblique drawing and isometric drawing. In this chapter we shall consider:

- Further Isometric Drawing.
- Isometric projection using the Isometric Scale.
- Axonometric Projection.

Lines of Given Slope in Isometric Drawing

In isometric drawing distances must be measured along, or parallel to, the principal axes.
An inclined line can be located in isometric by determining its distances along, or parallel to, two of the isometric axes.

Example
The elevation and plan of a **Mitsubishi logo**, which is based on an equilateral triangle, are shown across.

Construct an **isometric drawing** of the logo.

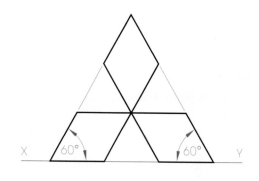

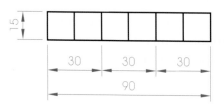

1. Draw the isometric axes and mark off the length and depth of the object.
2. Draw the elevation of the equilateral triangle to determine the overall height of the logo, as shown below, left.
3. Complete the box into which the logo fits by transferring this height as indicated below, middle.
4. Complete the drawing as shown below, right. Recall from chapter 8 that parallel lines on an object appear parallel in an isometric view.

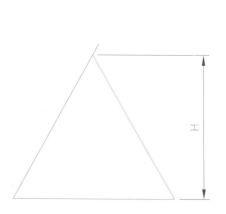

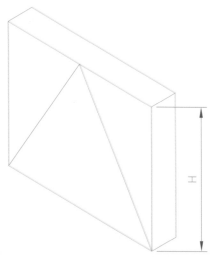

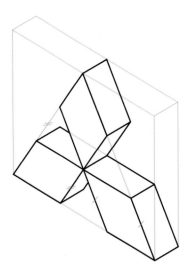

Exercise

The elevation and plan of the box for **Turkish Delight** sweets, which is based on a **regular hexagonal prism**, are shown across.

Construct an **isometric drawing** of the box.

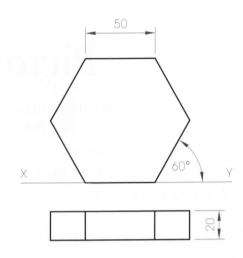

Circles in Isometric Drawing

Circles appear elliptical in isometric drawing.

Example
The elevation and plan of a **shampoo bottle** are shown over.
Make an **isometric drawing** of the bottle.

1. Draw the isometric axes and construct the box into which the bottle fits.

2. Draw the elevation of the semicircle and mark off points (C, 1 and 2) along the base line, say 15 mm apart for convenience, as shown over.

3. Locate these points (C, 1 and 2) on the base line in the isometric drawing.

4. Now locate points on the semi-ellipse by transferring the relevant heights above C, 1 and 2 as shown over, and draw a smooth curve to pass through them.

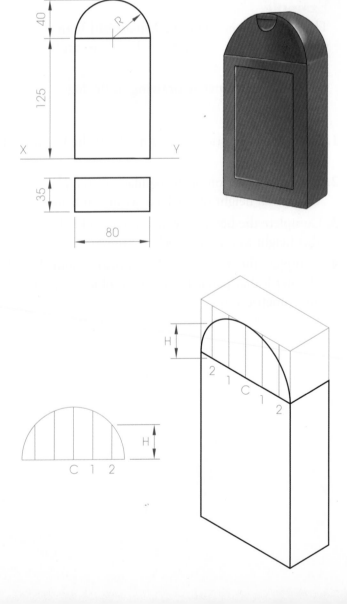

5. The relevant portion of the semi-ellipse on the back surface can be drawn by locating points 35 mm away from the front semi-ellipse, at 30° to the right as shown across.

6. The point of contact for the tangent can be located by drawing the diagonal from the centre as shown.

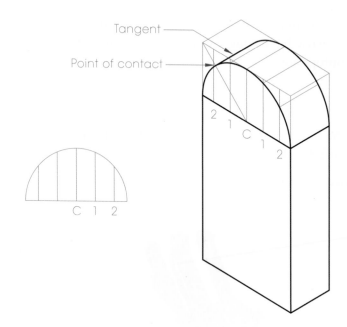

Exercises

1. The figure over shows the elevation and plan of a solid based on the **Milk Tray** box.

Construct an **isometric drawing** of the box.

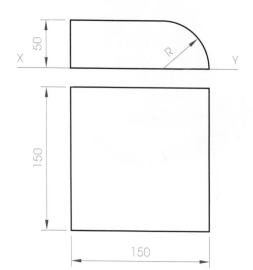

2. The elevation and plan of a **bridge** are shown over. The vertical lines in the railings are 5 mm apart.

Make an **isometric drawing** of the bridge.

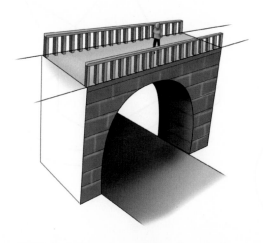

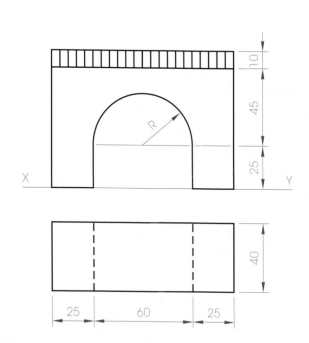

More complicated objects can be drawn in isometric by 'boxing' in their component parts if appropriate.

Example

The figure over shows the elevation and plan of a **knife block**.

Draw an **isometric** view of the block.

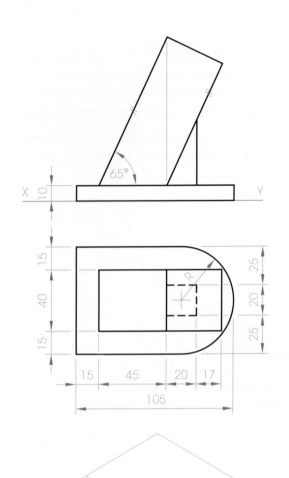

1. Draw the box into which the base fits and construct the base as shown over, top.

2. Draw the partial elevation shown over, bottom, to determine the vertical heights of points **P** and **Q** on the inclined lines.

3. Transfer these heights to the isometric view to determine points **P** and **Q** in the isometric view as shown.

4. Complete the isometric drawing noting that parallel lines on an object will appear parallel in an isometric view.

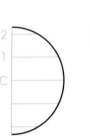

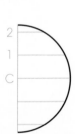

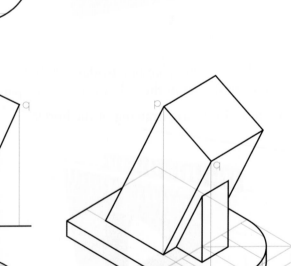

Exercises

1. The elevation and plan of a **solid** are shown over. Also shown is a photo-realistic image of the solid. Draw an **isometric** view of the solid.

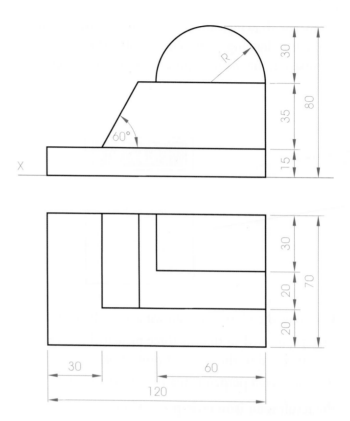

2. The elevation and plan of **plaque** are shown over.

Draw an **isometric** view of the plaque.

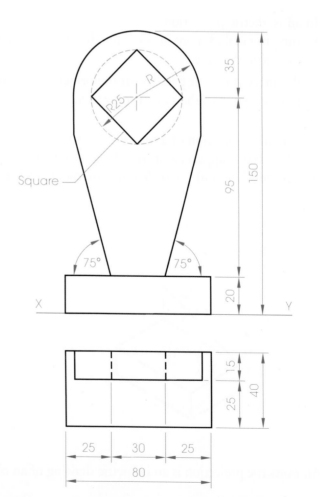

Answer Worksheets 14A, 14B and 14C

Isometric Projection using the Isometric Scale

Isometric drawings are useful to give an overall impression of what an object looks like. However, an isometric drawing of an object makes the object appear larger than it actually is. This can be seen by comparing the orthographic views and the isometric drawing of the box for matches shown below.

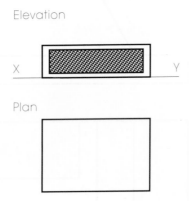

Elevation

Plan

Isometric Drawing

Consider the illustration shown across. If the matchbox is:

(i) positioned so that its three principal faces are equally inclined to the plane of projection,

(ii) projected perpendicularly onto the plane of projection,

the result is an **isometric projection**.

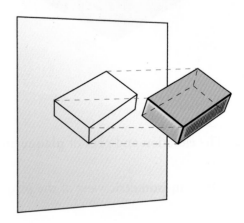

In an isometric projection:
- the principal axes are in the same directions as they are for isometric drawing.
- distances along (or parallel to) the principal axes are foreshortened in the same proportion.

An isometric projection of a matchbox is shown below, left. Imagine that the top surface of the box is rotated so that it appears as a true shape as shown. This allows us to establish the relationship between the actual dimensions and the scaled measurements required for isometric projection, as indicated below right.

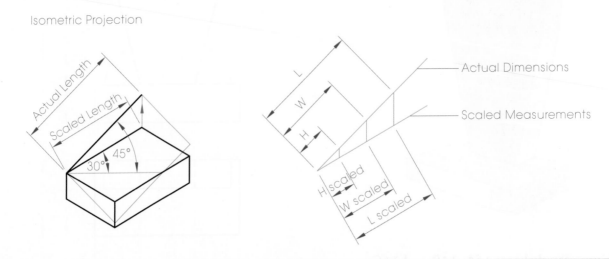

Isometric Projection

Actual Length

Scaled Length

30° 45°

Actual Dimensions

Scaled Measurements

An isometric projection is an isometric drawing of an object which has been scaled to a certain proportion.

Example

The elevation and plan of a **flight of steps** are shown over.
Draw an **isometric projection** of the steps using the **isometric scale**.

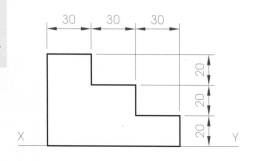

1. Draw a line at 45° and a line at 30° as shown below, left. Then mark off the actual dimensions of 20, 30 and 70 mm along the 45° line as indicated.

2. Transferring these distances vertically downwards to the line at 30° gives the scaled dimensions D1, D2 and D3 which correspond to the actual dimensions.

3. The scaled dimension D1 is marked-off along the vertical axis to represent each length of 20 mm, as shown below, centre.

4. The scaled dimension D2 is marked-off along the axis at 30° to the left to represent each length of 30 mm.

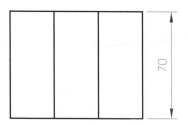

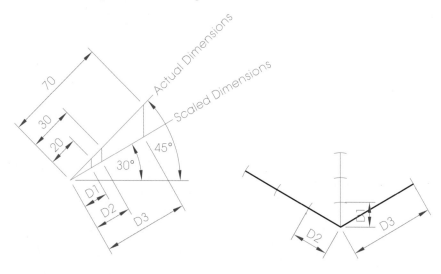

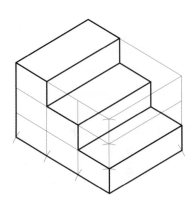

5. The scaled dimension D3 is marked-off along the axis at 30° to the right to represent a length of 70 mm.

6. The isometric projection is completed as shown above, right.

Exercise

The elevation and plan of a **skateboard** ramp and a letter **H** are shown over.
In each case draw an **isometric projection** of the object using the **isometric scale** method.

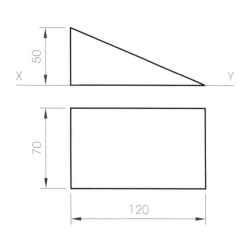

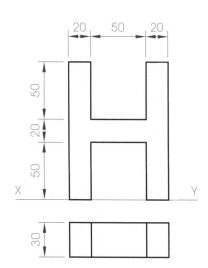

Answer Worksheet 14D

Isometric Projection using the Axonometric Plane

The figure over shows a pictorial view of an **eau de toilette** bottle and its projections on the three principal planes of reference. Also shown is a fourth plane which has been positioned so that it is **equally inclined** to each of the planes of reference. If points on the object are projected perpendicularly onto this plane, the result is an **isometric projection**.

This type of projection is known as **axonometric projection** and the plane of projection is called an **axonometric plane**.

If the principal planes of reference are rotated into the **axonometric** plane, as shown across, then all four planes will appear in true shape.

In this arrangement the plan is orientated at 45° and the elevations are orientated at 15°. This facilitates an efficient method for constructing an axonometric projection of an object as shown overleaf.

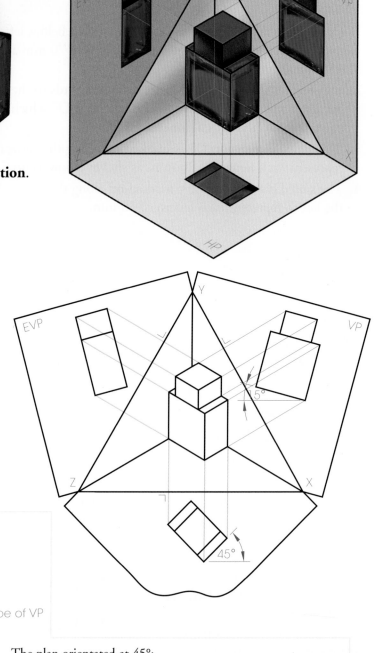

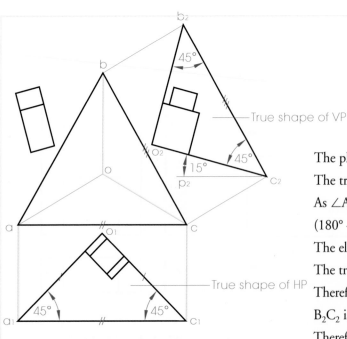

The plan orientated at 45°:

The true shape of $\triangle AOC$ is a right-angled isosceles triangle.

As $\angle A_1 O_1 C_1$ is 90° then $\angle$s $O_1 A_1 C_1$ and $O_1 C_1 A_1$ must be 45°.

(180° − 90° = 90° divided by 2 = 45°).

The elevations orientated at 15°:

The true shape of $\triangle OBC$ is a right-angled isosceles triangle.

Therefore $\angle B_2 C_2 O_2$ is 45° (as above).

$B_2 C_2$ is inclined at 60° (// to side BC of equilateral $\triangle ABC$)

Therefore $\angle P_2 C_2 O_2$ = 60° - 45° = 15°

1. The axonometric plane is equally inclined to the three principal planes of reference. This means that the axonometric axes can be drawn at 30° to the right, vertically and at 30° to the left as shown below, left.

2. Draw the plan orientated at 45° as indicated.

3. Draw the front elevation orientated at 15° as indicated.

4. Project points on the lower part of the bottle vertically from the plan as shown below, left.

5. Project points on the lower part of the bottle at 30° from the front elevation as shown below, left.

6. Join the points, where corresponding lines meet, in order.

7. Complete the axonometric projection by projecting the remaining points from the plan and front elevation as shown below, right.

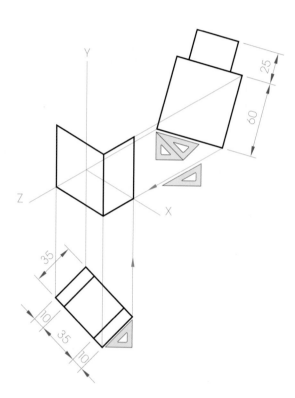

Exercises

1. The figure over shows the incomplete isometric projection of a **flight of steps** using the axonometric axes method.

    (i) Draw the axonometric axes X, Y and Z.

    (ii) Draw the plan orientated at 45° as shown.

    (iii) Draw the front elevation orientated at 15° as shown.

    (iv) Draw the completed axonometric projection of the steps.

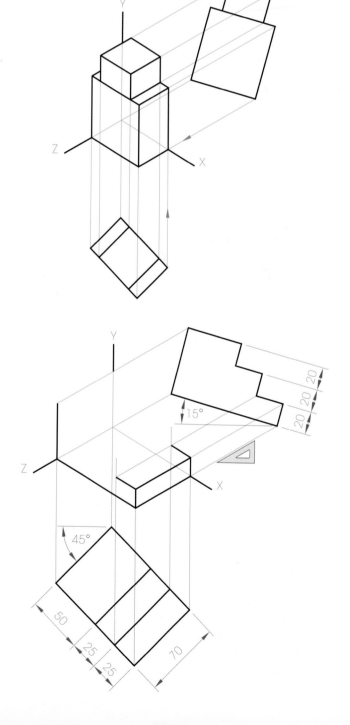

2. The figure below shows the incomplete isometric projection of three objects using the axonometric axes method. In each case, the elevation and plan are also shown in their required positions.

  (i) Draw the axonometric axes X, Y and Z.

 (ii) Draw the plan orientated at 45° as shown.

(iii) Draw the side elevation orientated at 15° as shown.

(iv) Draw the completed axonometric projection.

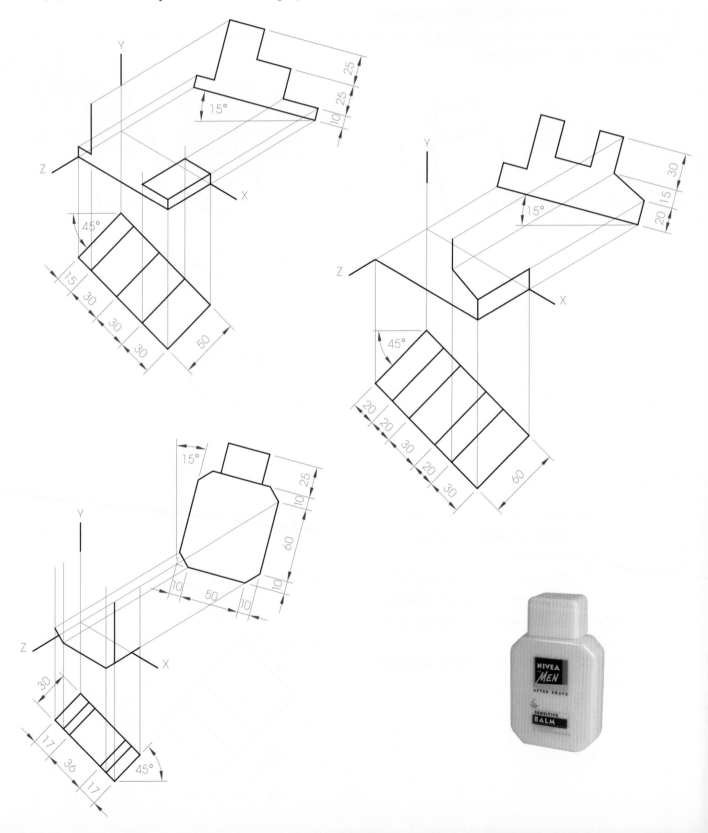

3. The incomplete isometric projections of a **Ferrero Rocher** box and a **square-based lampshade**, using the axonometric axes method are shown over and below, right. In each case the elevation and plan are also shown in their required positions. For each object:

(i) Draw the axonometric axes X, Y and Z.

(ii) Draw the plan orientated at 45° as shown.

(iii) Draw the side elevation orientated at 15° as shown.

(iv) Draw the completed axonometric projection.

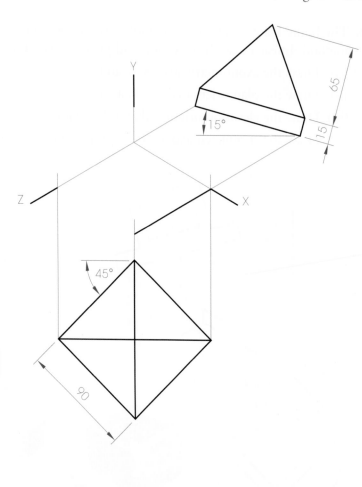

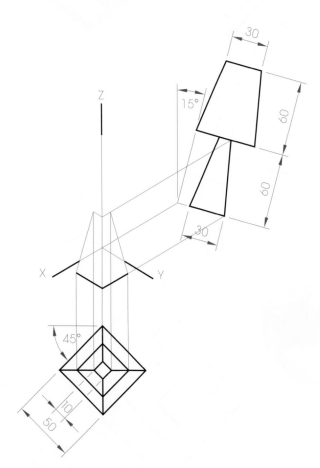

4. The figure below shows the incomplete isometric projection of four objects using the axonometric axes method. In each case the elevation and plan are also shown in their required positions. For each solid:

(i) Draw the axonometric axes X, Y and Z.

(ii) Draw the plan orientated at 45° as shown.

(iii) Draw the elevation orientated at 15° as shown.

(iv) Draw the completed axonometric projection.

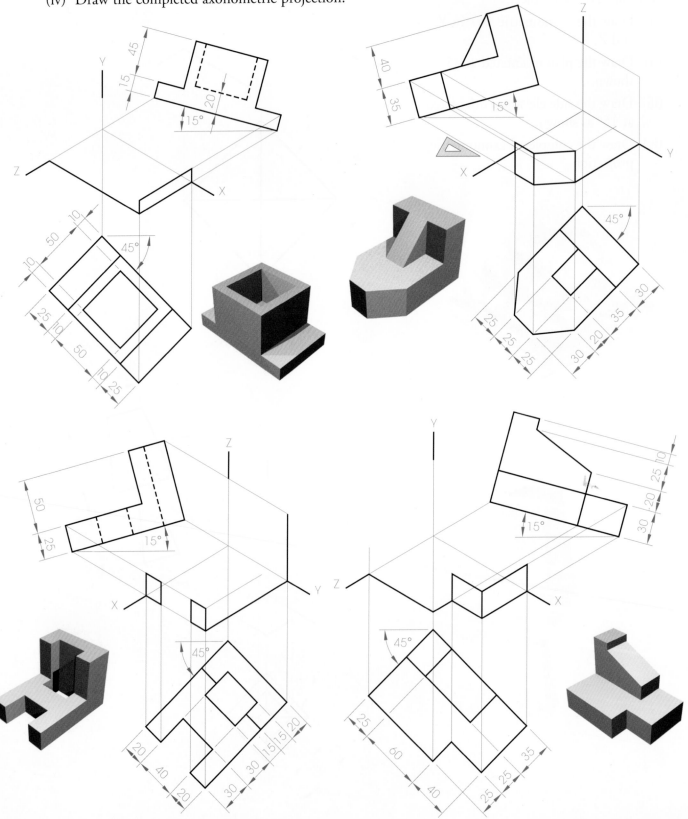

Example

The incomplete isometric projection of the **Amicelli box** using the axonometric axes method is shown below. The box is based on a **regular hexagonal prism**. The front and side elevations are also shown in their required positions.

(i)   Draw the axonometric axes X, Y and Z.

(ii) Draw the elevations orientated at 15° as shown.

(iii) Draw the completed axonometric projection.

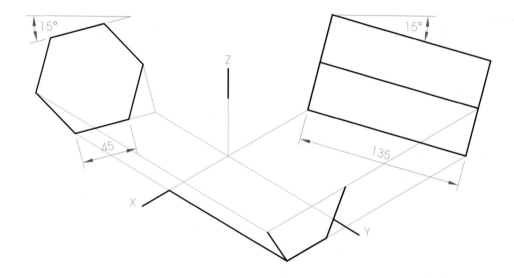

1. Draw the axonometric axes X, Y and Z.

2. Draw the side elevation which is a regular hexagon of side 45 mm as shown below.

3. Draw the front elevation by transferring the heights from the side elevation as indicated below.

4. Project points from the elevations at 30° as shown.

5. Join the points where corresponding lines meet to complete the axonometric projection.

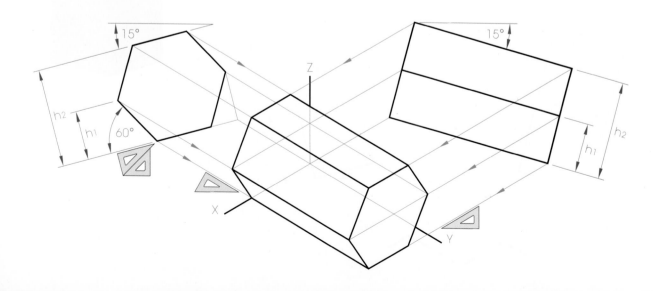

Exercises

1. The figure below shows the incomplete isometric projection of a **container** using the axonometric axes method. The front and side elevations are also shown in their required positions.

  (i) Draw the axonometric axes X, Y and Z.

 (ii) Draw the elevations orientated at 15° as shown.

(iii) Draw the completed axonometric projection.

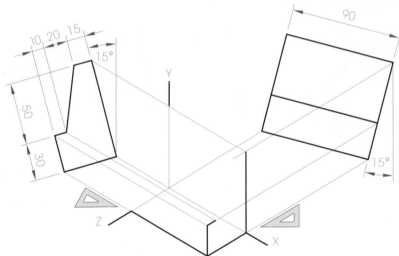

2. The incomplete isometric projection of an **arcade game** using the axonometric axes method is shown below. The front and side elevations are also shown in their required positions.

  (i) Draw the axonometric axes X, Y and Z.

 (ii) Draw the elevations orientated at 15° as shown.

(iii) Draw the completed axonometric projection.

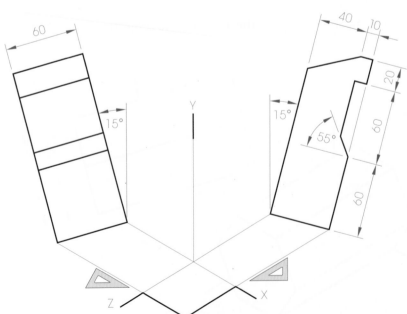

3. The figure below shows the incomplete isometric projection of a
component using the axonometric axes method. The front and side
elevations are also shown in their required positions.

(i)   Draw the axonometric axes X, Y and Z.

(ii) Draw the elevations orientated at 15° as shown.

(iii) Draw the completed axonometric projection.

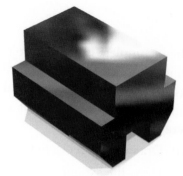

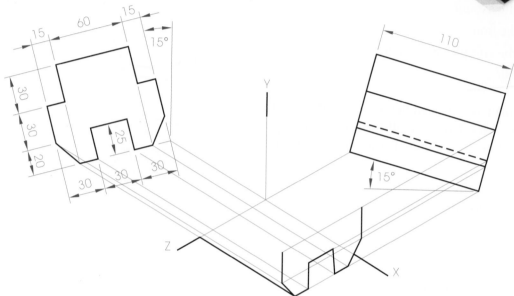

4. The incomplete isometric projection of a **box for tennis
balls** using the axonometric axes method is shown below.
The front and side elevations are also shown in their required
positions.

(i)   Draw the axonometric axes X, Y and Z.

(ii) Draw the elevations orientated at 15° as shown.

(iii) Draw the completed axonometric projection.

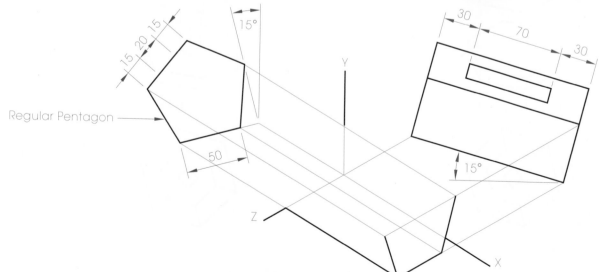

Example

The incomplete isometric projection of a **table lamp** using the axonometric axes method is shown over. The base of the table lamp is a **regular hexagonal prism** and the shade is a frustum of a **regular hexagonal pyramid**.

(i) Draw the plan orientated at 45° as shown.

(ii) Draw the axonometric axes X, Y and Z.

(iii) Draw the front elevation orientated at 15° as shown.

(iv) Draw the completed axonometric projection of the lamp.

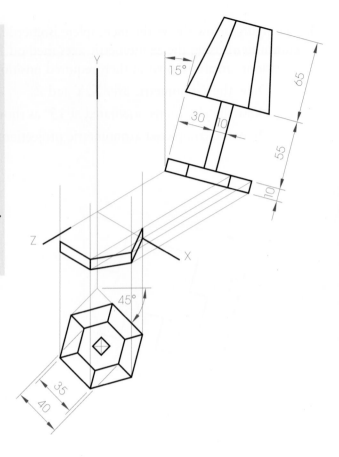

1. Draw the plan as indicated below, left, and insert the axonometric axes. Note that all the sides of the outer hexagon will be 35 mm long because it is a regular hexagon.

2. Transfer the lengths L1, 35 and L1 from the plan to draw the elevation of the base and the base hexagon of the shade.

3. Repeat this process as appropriate for the smaller hexagon and complete the elevation as shown.

4. Complete the axonometric projection in the normal manner.

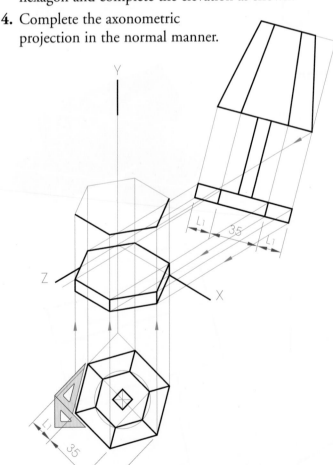

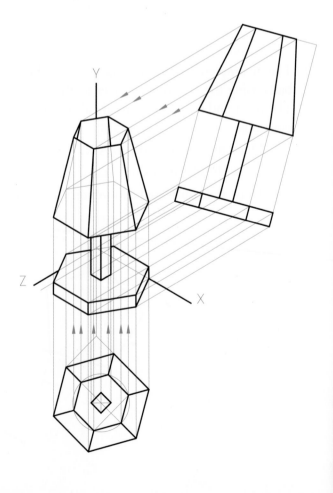

Exercises

1. The figure over shows the incomplete isometric projection of a **podium** using the axonometric axes method. The front elevation and plan are also shown in their required positions.

  (i) Draw the axonometric axes X, Y and Z.

  (ii) Draw the plan orientated at 45° as shown.

  (iii) Draw the elevation orientated at 15° as shown.

  (iv) Draw the completed axonometric projection.

2. The incomplete isometric projection of a **toy aeroplane** using the axonometric axes method is shown across. The front elevation and plan are also shown in their required positions. Use an A2 sheet portrait:

  (i) Draw the axonometric axes X, Y and Z.

  (ii) Draw the plan orientated at 45° as shown.

  (iii) Draw the elevation orientated at 15° as shown.

  (iv) Draw the completed axonometric projection.

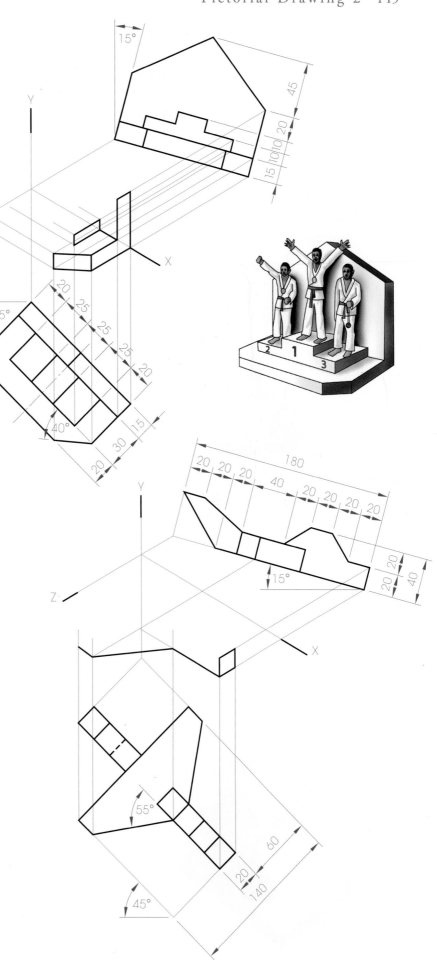

3. The incomplete isometric projection of a **lamp** using the axonometric axes method is shown over. The elevation and plan are also shown in their required positions.

(i) Draw the axonometric axes X, Y and Z.

(ii) Draw the plan orientated at 45° as shown.

(iii) Draw the elevation orientated at 15° as shown.

(iv) Draw the completed axonometric projection.

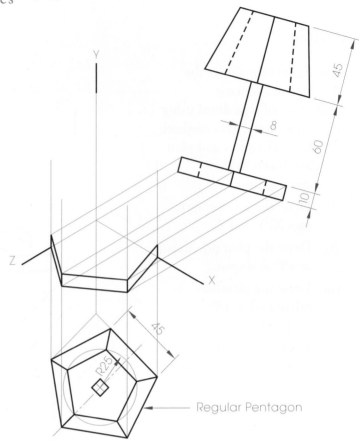

Regular Pentagon

4. The figure over shows the incomplete isometric projection of a **solid** using the axonometric axes method. The front elevation and plan are also shown in their required positions.

(i) Draw the axonometric axes X, Y and Z.

(ii) Draw the elevation orientated at 15° as shown.

(iii) Draw the plan orientated at 45° as shown.

(iv) Draw the completed axonometric projection.

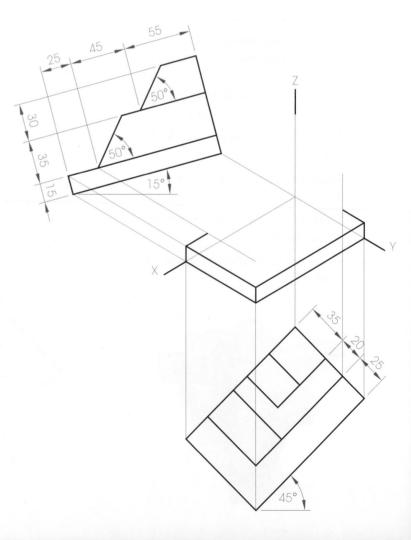

Chapter 15
Transformation Geometry 1

Transformation geometry involves the study of the movement of shapes from one position to another. In our course, we will study the movement of shapes under the following **transformations**:

- **Translations**
- **Rotations**
- **Axial Symmetries**
- **Central Symmetries**
- **Enlargements and Reductions**

We will study the first four transformations in this chapter, and in chapter 26. These are called **isometries**. We will study enlargements and reductions in chapter 28. These are called **similarities**.

> An **isometry** is a transformation that preserves shape and size.
>
> A **similarity** is a transformation that preserves shape but not size.

Translations

> Under a **translation** all points are moved the same distance in the same direction.

In the figure across, every point of the triangle ABC is moved to a new position on the triangle DEF. The triangle ABC is called the **object** and the triangle DEF is called the **image**.

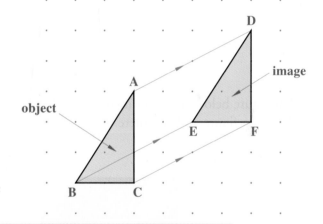

Every translation has a **translation vector**, which tells you the distance and direction of movement. In the figure over, the translation vector is the line joining A to D.

Example
The figure below shows the image of the letter 'E' under a **translation** from point A to A_1.

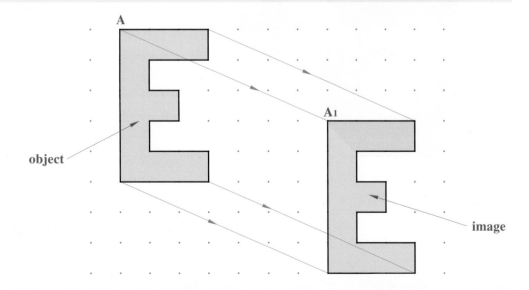

Exercises

1. Each one of the letters of the **AA monogram** is the image of the other under a **translation**. Copy the drawing shown in the figure below and use a **translation** to complete the monogram.

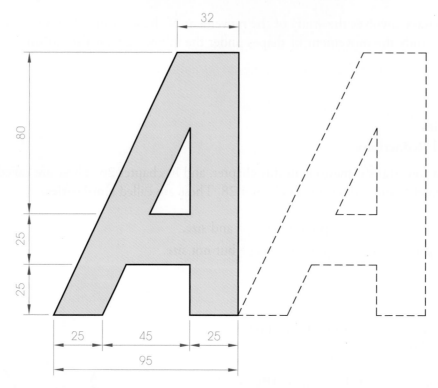

2. The figure below shows an incomplete **Bed and Breakfast** sign drawn on a 10 mm square grid. Copy the given figure and complete the sign by drawing the image of the letter 'B' under a **translation** from point A to A₁.

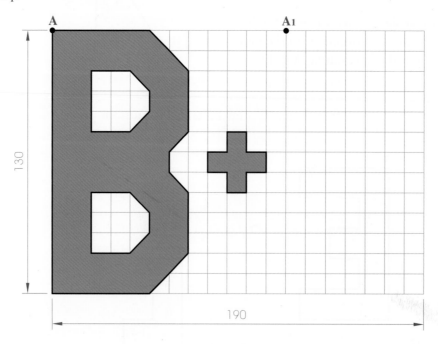

Rotations

Under a **rotation** a figure is turned about a fixed point through a certain angle. The fixed point is called the **centre of rotation** and the angle is called the **angle of rotation**.

The figure across shows a flag that has been rotated clockwise through an angle of 50° about the point R. The point R is fixed and everything else is moved around it. The rotated figure is the same shape and size as the original figure.

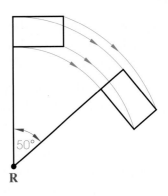

Example 1
Rotate the **flag** ABC anti-clockwise through 70°, about centre O.

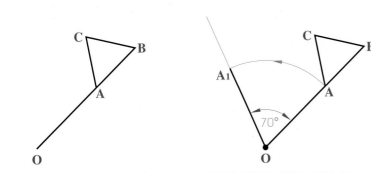

1. With centre O and radius OA, swing an arc in an anti-clockwise direction from A.

2. Draw a line from O at 70° to OA to locate A₁. A₁ is the image of A under the given rotation.

3. Repeat the procedure for the points B and C. Join the points in order to complete the image.

Example 2
Rotate the given parallelogram ABCD **clockwise** through an angle of 65° about the point P.

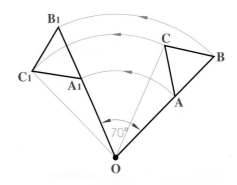

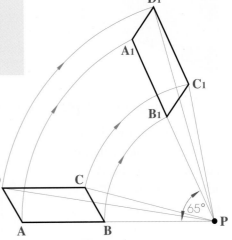

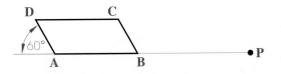

1. With centre P and radii PA and PB respectively, draw arcs in a clockwise direction.

2. Draw a line from P at an angle of 65° to PA to locate points A₁ and B₁ respectively.

3. Join PC. With centre P and radius PC, draw an arc in a clockwise direction. Draw a line from P at an angle of 65° to PC to locate C₁.

4. Repeat the procedure for the remaining point D. Join the image points in order.

Alternative Solution

1. The image of the figure can also be determined by rotating the base AB in a clockwise direction, about P, through an angle of 65°.

2. Extend B_1A_1 beyond A_1. Draw A_1D_1 at an angle of 60° at A_1B_1 and of a length equal to that of AD.

3. Draw a line from B_1 parallel to A_1D_1, and a line from D_1 parallel to A_1B_1, to locate the point C_1. Complete the image by joining the points in order.

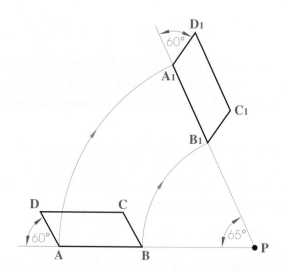

Exercises

Answer Worksheet 15B

1. (a) Copy the view of the **film clipboard** shown in the figure below.

   (b) Draw the image of the shaded portion of the clipboard when it is rotated about the point A through an angle of 40° in an *anti-clockwise* direction.

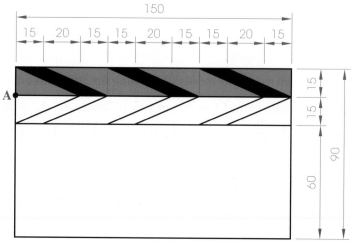

2. (a) Copy the drawing of the **stapler** shown in the figure below.

   (b) Draw the image of the shaded portion of the stapler when it is rotated about the point A through an angle of 120° in a *clockwise* direction.

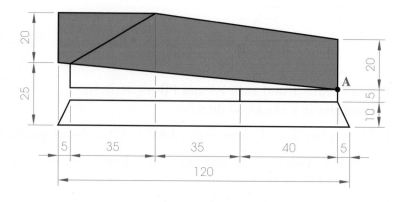

Axial Symmetries (Reflections in Lines)

Under an **axial symmetry**, shapes are flipped over an **axis of reflection** to a new position that is the mirror image. The two shapes in the figure below are **reflections** of each other in a vertical axis of reflection (left) and a horizontal axis of reflection (right).

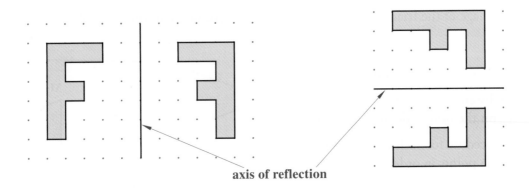

axis of reflection

Under an **axial symmetry**, any point and its image are the same distance from the **axis of reflection**.

Example
Construct the image of the triangle ABC under an **axial symmetry** in the line L.

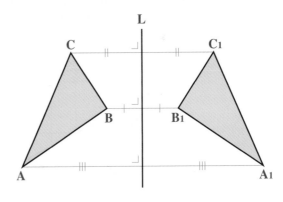

1. Through A, draw a line perpendicular to the line L and extend to the other side.

2. Measure the distance from A to the line L and mark this distance on the other side of L to locate A_1.

3. Repeat the procedure for each of the points B and C. Join the points in order to obtain the image triangle.

Exercise
The *incomplete* designs shown below are made up on a grid of 15 mm squares. Draw the grids and complete each of the designs using an **axial symmetry**.

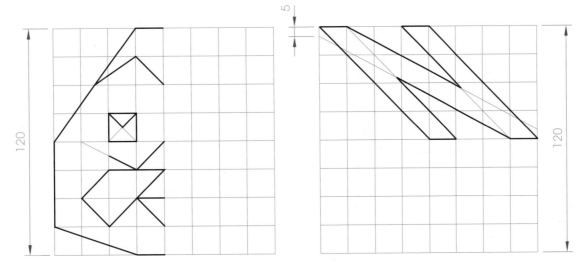

Central Symmetries (Reflections in Points)

Under a **central symmetry** in a point Z, any point and its image are the same distance from Z. The point Z is called the **centre of symmetry**.

> **Example**
> Construct the image of the triangle LMN under a **central symmetry** in the point Z.

1. Join L to Z and extend to the other side.

2. Measure the distance from L to Z and mark this distance on the other side of Z to locate L_1.

3. Repeat the procedure for each of the points M and N. Join the points in order to obtain the image triangle.

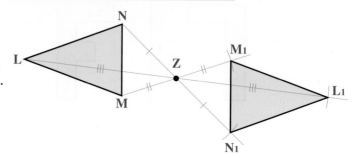

> Under a **central symmetry**, any point and its image are equidistant from the **centre of symmetry**.
>
> A **central symmetry** is equivalent to a **rotation** through 180° about the centre of symmetry.

Exercises

1. The figures shown below are made up on a grid of 15 mm squares. Copy the grids and the associated figures, and draw the image of each figure under a **central symmetry** in the point Z.

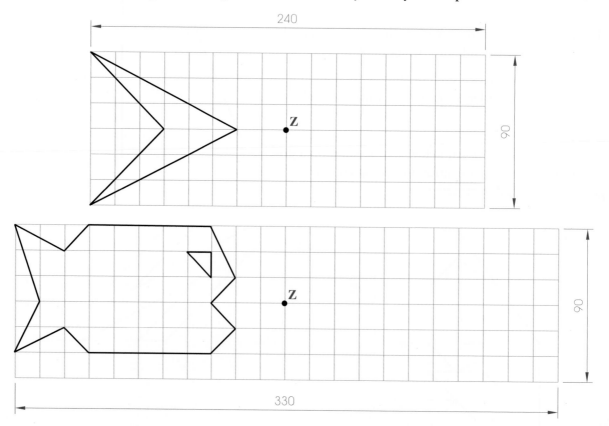

Answer Worksheets 15C and 15D

Example

Draw the figure across and complete the rectangle 150 mm by 120 mm as shown.

Find the image of the given figure under the following transformations:

(a) From point A to A_1 by a **translation**.

(b) From point A_1 to A_2 by an **axial symmetry** in the line XY.

(c) From point A_2 to A_3 by a **central symmetry** in the point Z.

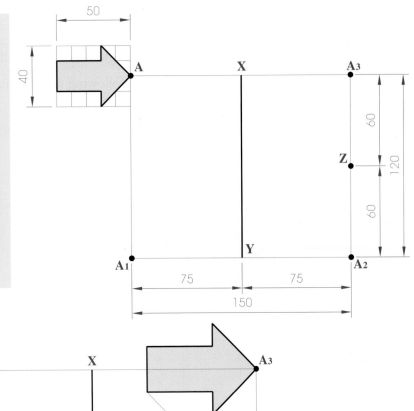

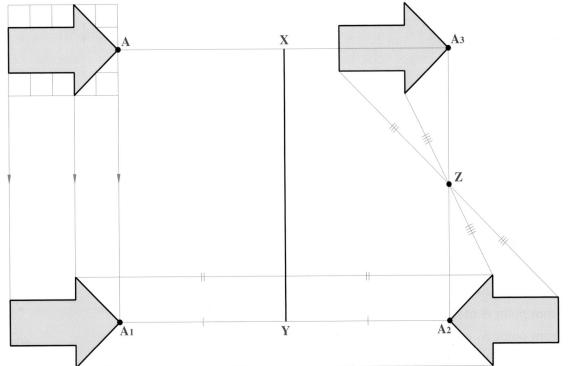

Copy the arrow onto a sheet of tracing paper and use this to help you visualise the solution.

1. Under the **translation**, the point A moves to a new position A_1, which is 120 mm directly below A. *Every point of the arrow is moved the same distance in the same direction.* Slide the tracing paper down the drawing sheet so that the point A lies on the point A_1. This is a **translation**.

2. Under an **axial symmetry** in the line XY, the point A_1 is moved to a new position A_2. *Every point of the arrow and its image are the same distance from the axis of reflection.* Flip the sheet of tracing paper over the axis of reflection XY to a position that is the mirror image. This is equivalent to an **axial symmetry** in the line XY.

3. Under a **central symmetry** in the point Z, the point A_2 is moved to a new position A_3. *Every point moves to Z, and then travels on from Z the same distance in the same direction.* Place the point of your pencil on the tracing paper at the point Z. Rotate the sheet of tracing paper about the pencil point through an angle of 180°. This is equivalent to a **central symmetry** in the point Z.

Exercises

1. Draw the given figure and complete the rectangle 140 mm by 100 mm as shown.

Find the image of the given figure under the following transformations:
(a) From point A to A_1 by a **translation**.
(b) From point A_1 to A_2 by an **axial symmetry** in the line PQ.
(c) From point A_2 to A_3 by a **central symmetry** in the point Z.

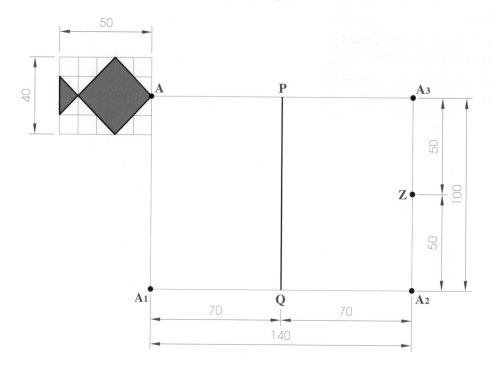

2. Draw the given figure and complete the rectangle 100 mm by 120 mm as shown.

Find the image of the given figure under the following transformations:
(a) From point A to A_1 by a **translation**.
(b) From point A_1 to A_2 by an **axial symmetry** in the line PQ.
(c) From point A_2 to A_3 by a **central symmetry** in the point Z.

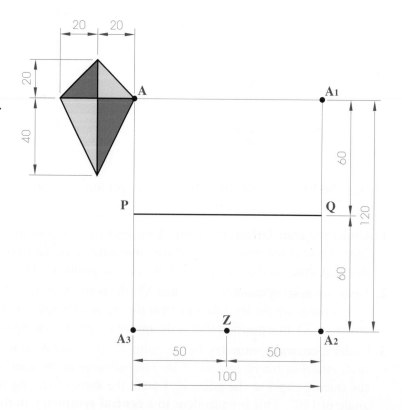

3. Draw the given figure and complete the rectangle 120 mm by 100 mm as shown.

Find the image of the given figure
under the following
transformations:

(a) From point A to A_1 by a
translation.

(b) From point A_1 to A_2 by an
axial symmetry in the line XY.

(c) From point A_2 to A_3 by a
central symmetry in the
point Z.

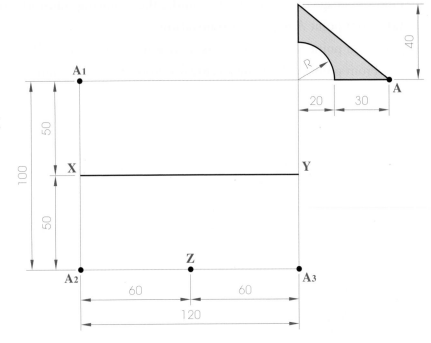

4. Draw the given figure and locate the image points A_1, A_2 and A_3.

Find the image of the given figure under the following transformations:

(a) From point A to A_1 by a **translation**.

(b) From point A_1 to A_2 by an **axial symmetry** in the line PQ.

(c) From point A_2 to A_3 by a **central symmetry** in the point Z.

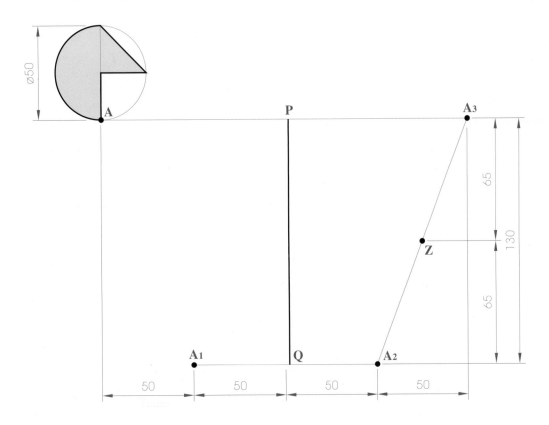

5. Draw the given figure and complete the rectangle as shown.

Find the image of the given figure under the following transformations:

(a) From point A to A₁ by a **translation**.

(b) From point A₁ to A₂ by an **axial symmetry** in the line XY.

(c) From point A₂ to A₃ by a **central symmetry** in the point Z.

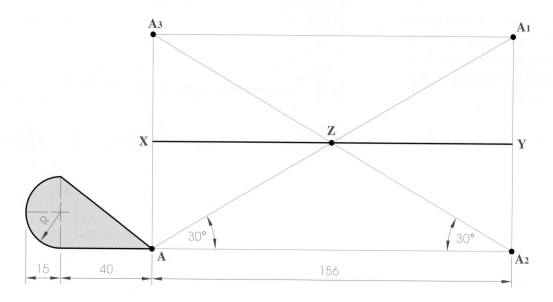

6. Draw the given figure and locate the image points A_1, A_2 and A_3.

Find the image of the given figure under the following transformations:

(a) From point A to A₁ by a **translation**.

(b) From point A₁ to A₂ by an **axial symmetry** in the line joining A to A₃.

(c) From point A₂ to A₃ by a **central symmetry** in the point Z.

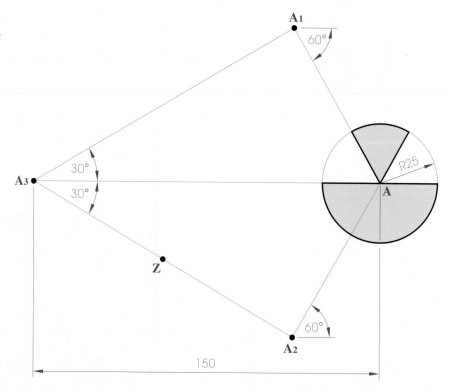

Chapter 16

Scales

When a drawing is made the same size as an object on a standard-size sheet of drawing paper, we get what is called a **full scale** drawing. In this case the scale is written as 1:1. However, there are many times when an object cannot be drawn full scale, e.g. a multistorey building. In these cases, the drawing is made much smaller than the object and is called a **reduced scale** drawing. Other objects like a watch are so small that they need to be drawn much larger than full-size. These drawings are called **enlarged scale** drawings. The scale is usually written as a ratio of the size of the drawing to the size of the object.

A ratio of 1:2 is a **reducing ratio** and means that every measurement on the scaled drawing will be half the corresponding measurement of the object.

A ratio of 2:1 is an **enlarging ratio** and means that every measurement on the scaled drawing will be twice the corresponding measurement of the object.

Constructing Plain Scales

It would be time-consuming if every measurement of the object had to be multiplied or divided proportionally to obtain their scaled measurement on a drawing. Using a **plain scale** avoids this.

Example

Construct a **plain scale** of 1:20 to measure up to 4 metres and to show tenths of a metre.

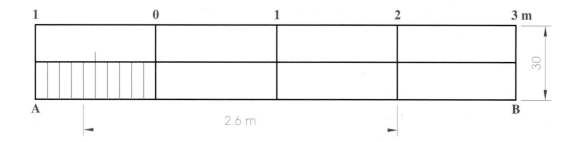

1. The scale must read up to 4 metres which is 4000 mm. The reducing ratio is 1:20. Thus 4000 mm will be represented by 200 mm (4000 ÷ 20).

2. Draw a line AB 200 mm long representing 4 m. Make a block of any width, say 30 mm, on this line. Draw a horizontal line across the middle of the scale as shown.

3. Divide the block into four equal parts by drawing vertical lines as shown. Each of these represents one metre.

4. Divide the first of the equal spaces into ten equal parts. Each part represents one tenth of a metre.

5. The finished scale can then be numbered as shown. A length of 2.6 m is shown.

The zero is always placed at the first major graduation line.

To read off 2.6 m, place the point of the compass on the 2 m mark and open the compass out to the point on the sixth graduation to the left of the zero mark. Now the compass is opened to a distance of two large spaces plus six small spaces, totalling 2.6 metres.

Exercises

1. Construct a **plain scale** of 1:20 to measure up to 3 metres and to show tenths of a metre.

   Using this scale, make a drawing of the **window** shown in the figure below

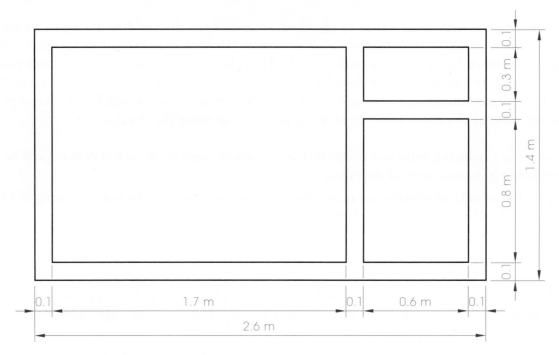

2. Construct a **plain scale** of 1:200 to measure up to 50 metres and to show metres.

   Use this scale to draw the plan of the **car park** shown in the figure below.

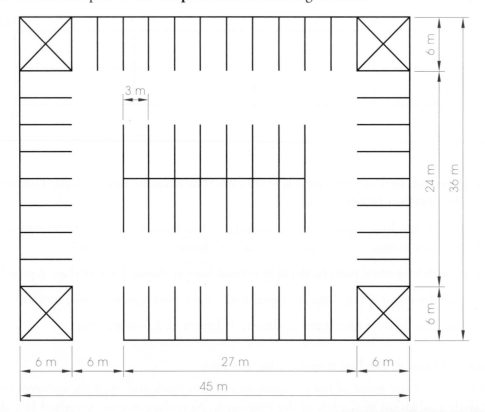

Answer Worksheets 16A and 16B

Constructing Diagonal Scales

Sometimes we need to show very small divisions on a drawing. In such cases, we use **diagonal scales**.

Example

Construct a **diagonal scale** of 1:20 to measure up to 4 metres and to show hundredths of a metre. Show lengths of 1.25 m and 2.68 m on the scale.

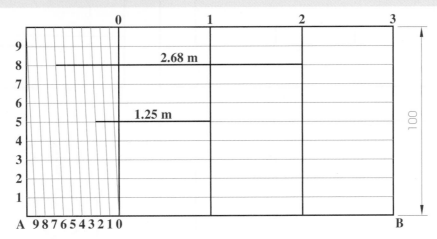

1. The scale must read up to 4 metres which is 4000 mm. The reducing ratio is 1:20. Thus 4000 mm will be represented by 200 mm (4000 ÷ 20). Draw a line AB 200 mm long representing 4 metres.

2. Make a block of any width, say 100 mm, on this line. Divide the block into four equal parts by drawing vertical lines as shown. Each of these represents 1 metre.

3. Divide the first vertical line into ten equal parts numbering them as shown, and draw horizontal lines from these across the scale.

4. Divide the top and base lines of the first *box* into ten equal spaces. Join these graduations by inclined lines. Number all graduations as shown. Each inclined line travels one hundredth of a metre as it crosses each horizontal division when rising from the base line. The required lengths of 1.25 m and 2.68 m are drawn on the scale.

Exercises

1. Construct a **diagonal scale** of 1:200 to measure up to 40 metres and to show tenths of a metre. Using this scale, draw the **cabin cruiser** shown in the figure below.

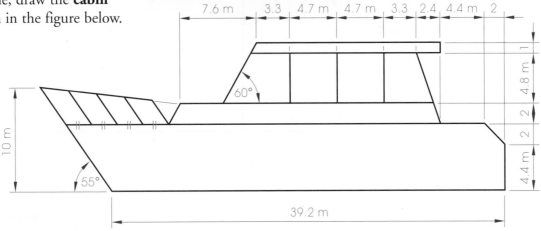

2. Construct a **diagonal scale** of 1:10 to measure up to 2 metres and to show hundredths of a metre. Use this scale to draw the elevation, plan and end view of the **couch** shown below.

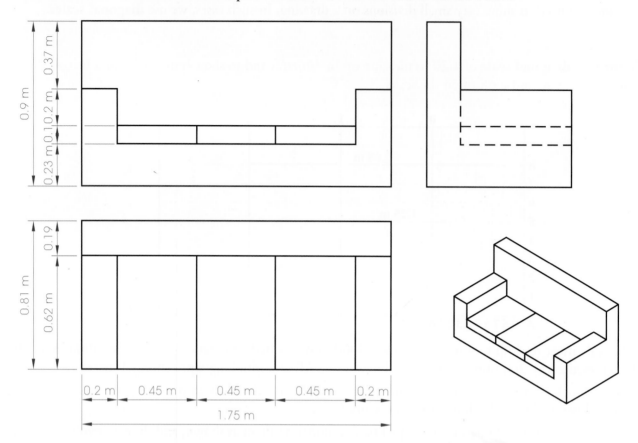

3. Construct a **diagonal scale** of 1:200 to measure up to 30 metres and to show tenths of a metre. Use this scale to draw the view of the **basketball court** shown in the figure below.

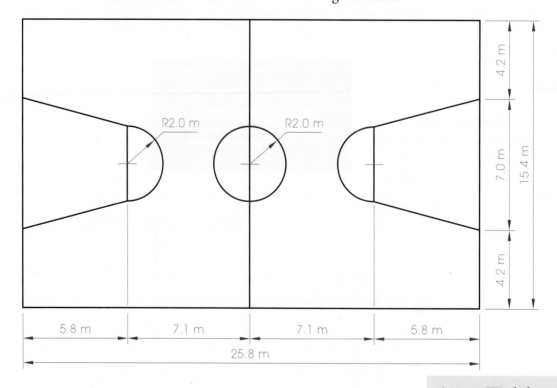

Answer Worksheet 16C

Example

A line 177 mm long represents 2.5 metres. Construct a **diagonal scale** to read up to 3 metres and to read metres and hundredths of a metre. Show lengths of 2.57 m and 1.34 m on the scale.

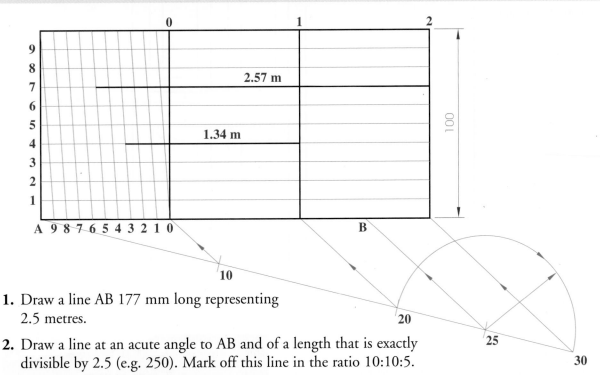

1. Draw a line AB 177 mm long representing 2.5 metres.

2. Draw a line at an acute angle to AB and of a length that is exactly divisible by 2.5 (e.g. 250). Mark off this line in the ratio 10:10:5.

3. Join the end of the line to B, and draw lines parallel to this line through points 10 and 20. The scale is now divided into metre divisions.

4. Extend the line AB as shown so that it is 3 metres long.

5. Complete the scale as in the previous example to show tenths of a metre and hundredths of a metre. The lengths of 2.57 m and 1.34 m are shown on the scale.

Exercises

1. Construct a **diagonal scale** in which 280 mm represents 70 metres. Use this scale to draw the plan of the **soccer pitch** shown across.

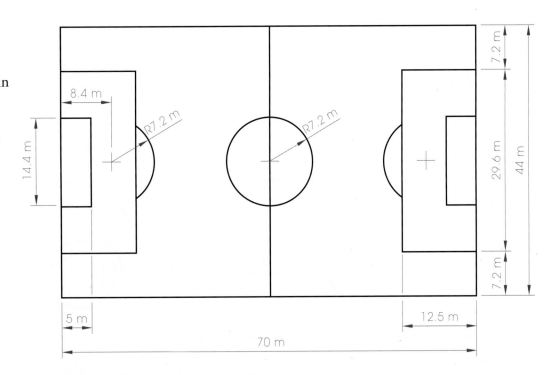

2. A line 117 mm long represents 1.5 metres. Construct a **diagonal scale** to read up to 2 metres and to show metres and hundredths of a metre.

Use this scale to draw the elevation of the **door** shown in the figure across.

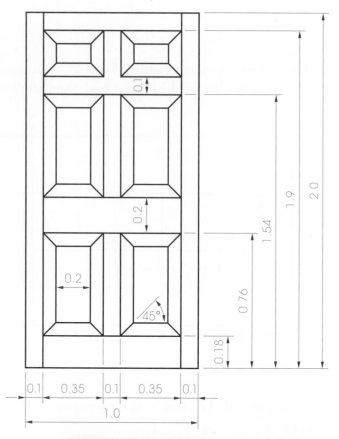

3. A line 195 mm long represents 10 metres. Construct a **diagonal scale** to read up to 13 metres and to show metres and hundredths of a metre.

Use this scale to draw the **Bus Éireann bus** shown below.

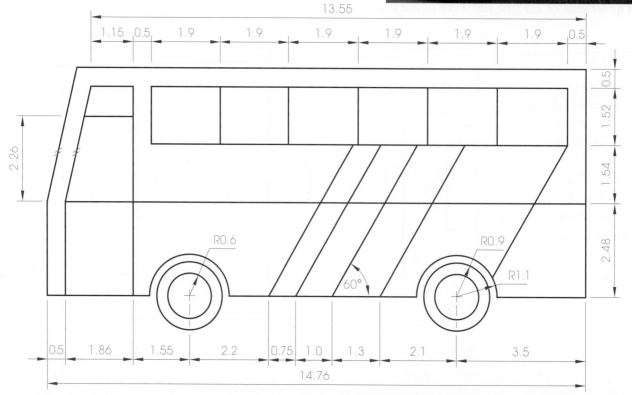

Chapter 17

The Parabola

Whenever a ball is thrown into the air, it travels along a path in the shape of a curve called a **parabola**.

> A **parabola** is the path traced out by a point which moves in a plane so that its distance from a fixed line is always equal to its distance from a fixed point.

Parts of a Parabola

1. The fixed line is called the **directrix**.

2. The fixed point **F** is called the **focal point**.

3. The **vertex V** lies midway between the directrix and the focal point.

4. The **axis** is a line drawn perpendicular to the directrix through the focal point.

Drawing a Parabola by the Locus Method

1. Position the directrix and the focal point F. Bisect AF to locate the vertex V.

2. Draw lines parallel to the directrix. With centre F and radius AB, swing arcs to intersect the line through B at P_1 and P_2. These are two points on the parabola.

3. With centre F and radius AC, swing arcs to intersect the line through C at P_3 and P_4. These are two more points on the parabola.

4. Other points on the curve can be located in the same way.

5. Draw a smooth curve through the points.

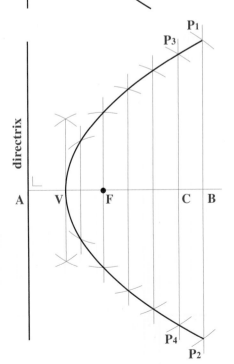

Answer Worksheet 17A

Exercises

1. The figure represents a **bow and arrow**. The curve AVC is based on a **parabola** with the **vertex** at V and the **focal point** at F. The line DD is the **directrix** for the curve.

   Draw the figure full-size.

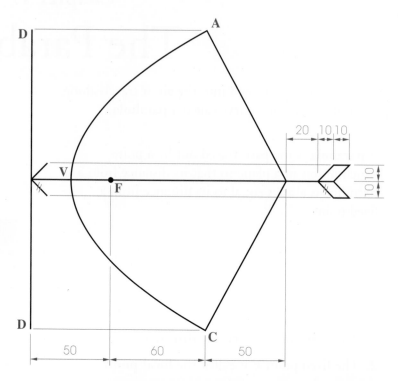

2. The figure below shows a drawing of a portion of the **Golden Gate Bridge** in San Francisco. The curve ABC is based on a parabola with the **vertex** at B and the **focal point** at F. The line DD is the **directrix** of the curve. *The vertical cables are equally spaced.*

   Reproduce the figure to the given measurements, showing clearly how to obtain the vertex B and the points A and C.

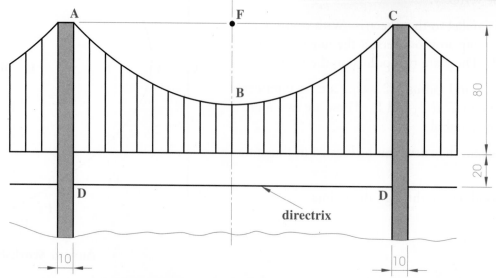

directrix

Inscribing a Parabola in a Given Rectangle PQRS

1. Bisect SR to get V, the vertex of the parabola.

2. Draw the axis VU of the parabola.

3. Divide PS and PU into the same number of equal parts, say four.

4. Draw lines from each of the points on PS to V.

5. Draw lines through the points on PU parallel to the axis to intersect the lines through V at P_1, P_2 and P_3. These points of intersection lie on the parabola.

6. Repeat steps 3, 4 and 5 for the other half of the curve. Draw a smooth curve through the intersections as shown.

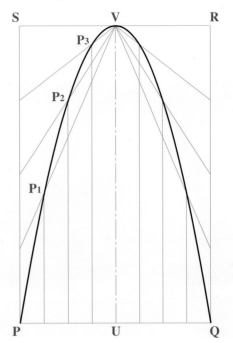

Answer Worksheet 17B

Exercises

1. The figure across shows a **candle holder**. Also shown is a drawing of the holder. Both curves are **parabolas**.

   Reproduce the drawing to the given dimensions showing all construction lines.

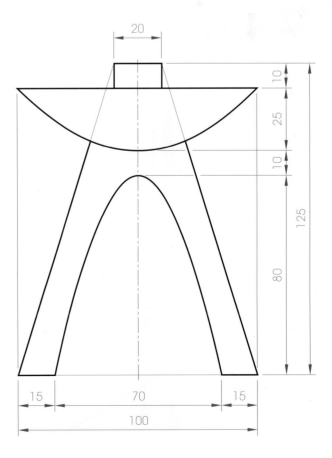

2. The figure across shows a drawing of the famous **Gateway Arch** at St Louis, Missouri, in the United States of America. The arch contains two **parabolic** curves.

Reproduce the drawing of the arch showing all constructions.

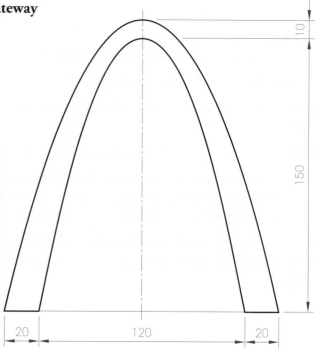

3. The figure across shows a drawing of a **lava lamp**, which is composed of two **parabolic** curves ABC and ADC, with vertices at B and D, respectively.

Make a copy of the drawing showing all construction lines clearly.

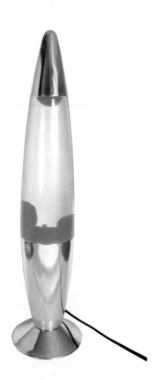

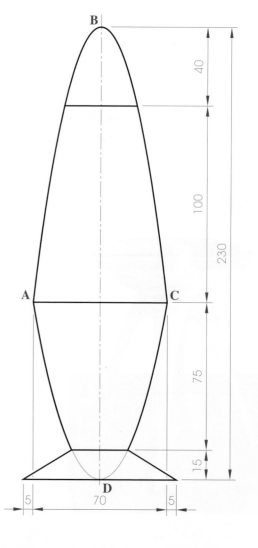

4. The figure below shows the **McDonald's** logo. A drawing of the logo, consisting of two **parabolas**, is also shown in the figure.

Draw the logo to the dimensions given.

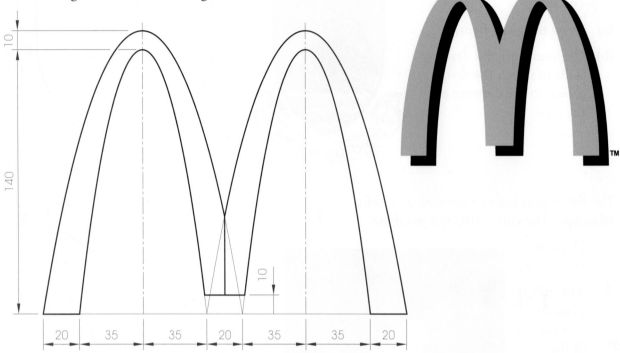

5. The figure across shows a drawing of the **Motorola** sign. It contains two **parabolas** with vertices at A and B respectively.

Reproduce the given drawing of the sign showing all construction lines clearly.

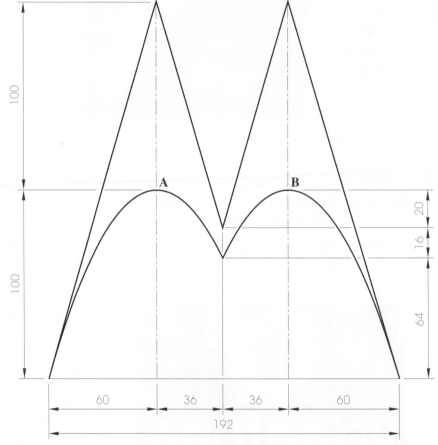

6. The figure across represents the outline of a **crest** for a county jersey. The curves AC and BC are **semi-parabolas** with vertices at A and B respectively.

(a) Draw the given figure.

(b) Use your freehand drawing skills to sketch the design shown in the drawing of the crest.

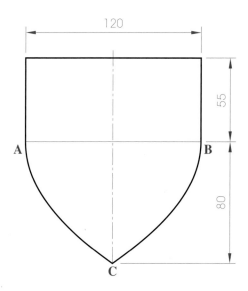

7. The figure over shows a drawing of a **radio telescope**. The curve ABC is a **parabola**.

(a) Draw the given view.

(b) The dish is tilted so that the axis of the **parabola** is at an angle of 45° to the ground. On a separate diagram, draw a view of the telescope in this position.

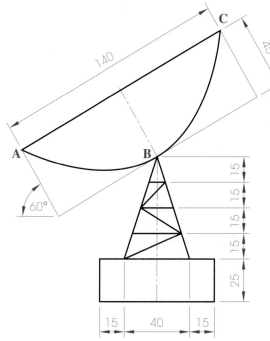

8. A drawing of the **Vodafone** symbol is shown over. The curves AD and ABC are based on **parabolas** with vertices at A and B respectively.

Reproduce the given drawing full-size showing all construction lines.

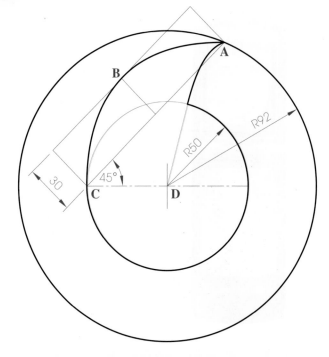

Chapter 18
Auxiliary Elevations and Plans

Auxiliary Elevations

The pictorial view of the thatched cottage shown below indicates how the **front elevation** is:

(i) Obtained from a viewing direction looking in the direction of arrow A.

(ii) Projected onto the vertical plane, which is positioned at right angles to the viewing direction.

Auxiliary elevations can be obtained by changing the viewing direction. Consider, for example, the new viewing direction also shown below:

(i) An auxiliary vertical plane (AVP) can be located in any convenient position *at right angles to the viewing direction.*

(ii) Points on the object are projected perpendicularly onto the AVP and joined in order.

(iii) The planes are rotated into one plane allowing the views to be transferred to a sheet of paper as shown below.

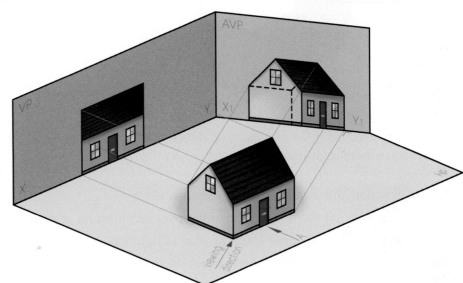

The line of intersection between the auxiliary vertical plane and the horizontal plane is called the X_1Y_1 line and is the new ground line.

Note that changing the viewing direction relative to the plan will not affect the heights of an object. Accordingly, heights can be transferred from the front elevation to an auxiliary elevation as indicated over.

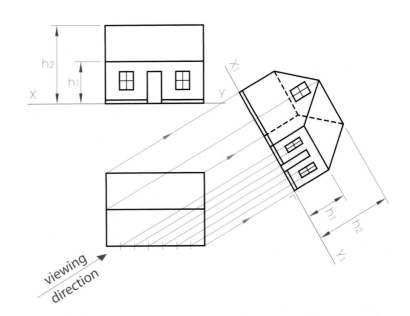

Example

Represent the object shown over by drawing the following views:

(a) An **elevation** looking in the direction of arrow **A**.

(b) A **plan** looking in the direction of the arrow **B**, projected from the elevation.

(c) An **auxiliary elevation** with the viewing direction at 30° from the right-hand side.

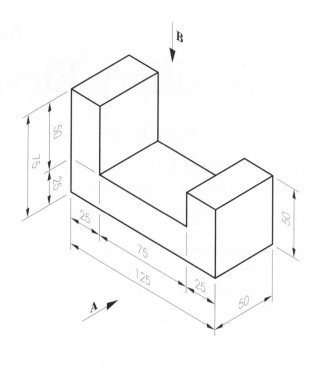

Build the object from 25 mm cubes as shown above. View the model from the viewing direction to help you visualise the solution.

1. The elevation and plan are drawn as shown below.

2. Draw the new ground line X₁Y₁ in any convenient position at right angles to the viewing direction.

3. Project points on the object from the plan at right angles to the new ground line.

4. Transfer the heights from the front elevation to the auxiliary elevation.

5. Line in the auxiliary elevation as appropriate.

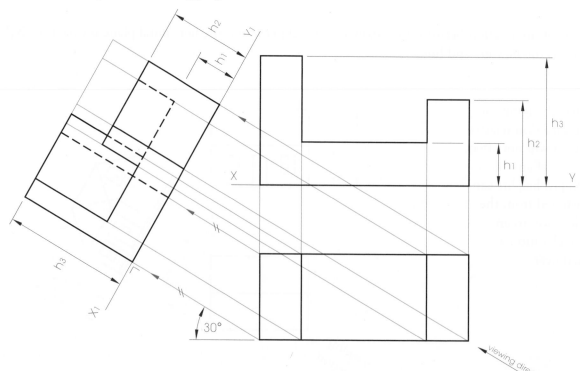

Exercises

1. Represent each of the objects shown below by drawing the following views:
  (a) An **elevation** looking in the direction of arrow **A**.
  (b) A **plan** looking in the direction of the arrow **B**, projected from the elevation.
  (c) An **auxiliary elevation** with the viewing direction at 30° from the right-hand side.

Build each of the objects from 25 mm cubes and use the models to help you visualise the solutions.

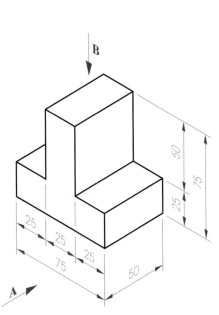
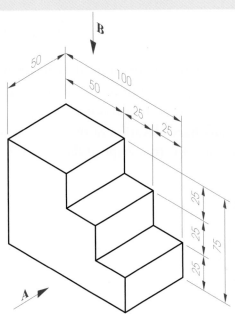

2. Represent each of the objects shown below by drawing the following views:
  (a) An **elevation** looking in the direction of arrow **A**.
  (b) A **plan** looking in the direction of the arrow **B**, projected from the elevation.
  (c) An **auxiliary elevation** with the viewing direction at 45° (first object from the left-hand side and second object from the right-hand side).

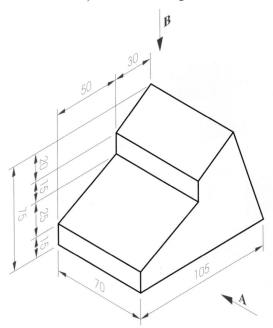
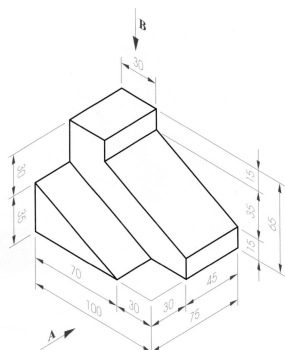

Answer Worksheets 18A and 18B

Determining True Shape using Auxiliary Elevations

A surface will appear in true shape in an auxiliary elevation in which the viewing direction is at right angles to that surface.

Example

Represent the object shown over by drawing the following views:

(a) An **elevation** looking in the direction of arrow **A**.

(b) A **plan** looking in the direction of the arrow **B**, projected from the elevation.

(c) An **auxiliary elevation** of the object, which will show the true shape of the surface S.

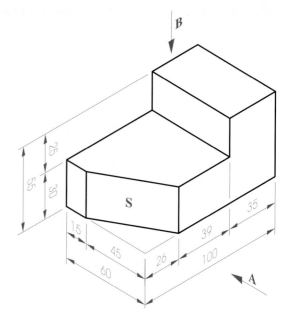

1. Consider the pictorial shown below. The true shape of surface S will appear in an auxiliary elevation in which the viewing direction is at right angles to the surface S, as indicated.

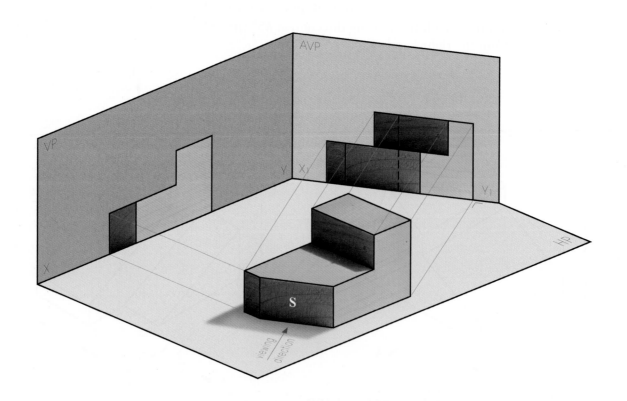

2. The elevation and plan are drawn as shown below.

3. The viewing direction will be ⊥ to the plan of surface S. Draw the new ground line X_1Y_1 in any convenient position at right angles to the viewing direction (parallel to the plan of surface S).

4. Project points on the object from the plan at right angles to the new ground line.

5. Transfer the heights from the front elevation to the auxiliary elevation.

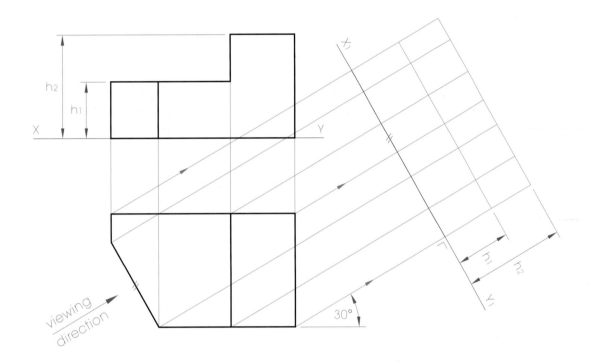

6. Line in the auxiliary elevation as shown below.

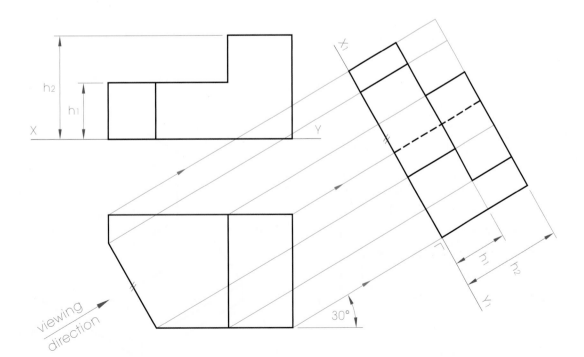

Exercises

The figure below shows pictorial views of some solids. In each case:

(a)   Draw an **elevation** looking in the direction of arrow **A**.

(b)   Draw a **plan** looking in the direction of arrow **B**, projected from the elevation.

(c)   Draw an **auxiliary elevation** of the *entire object,* which will show the true shape of the surface S.

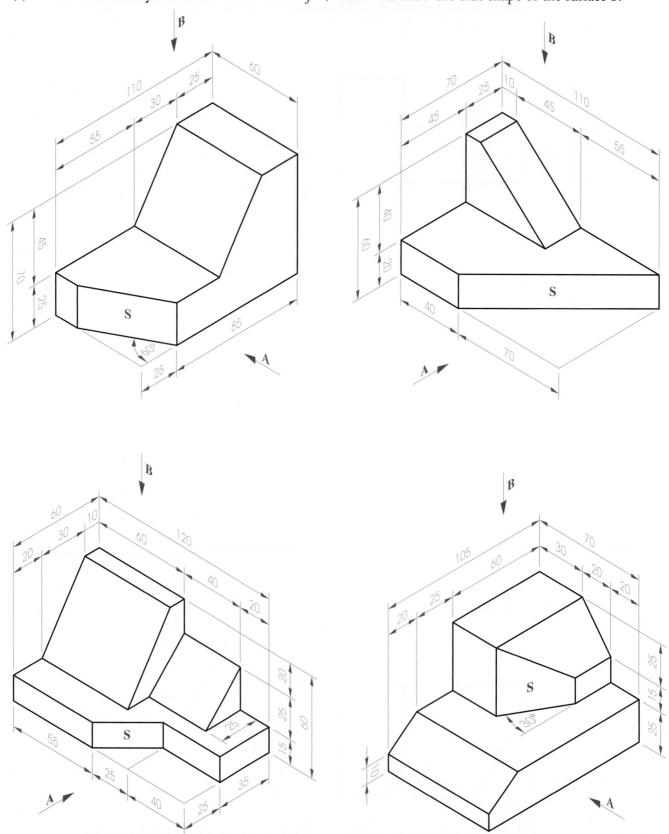

Circles in Auxiliary Elevations

> Circles appear elliptical in auxiliary elevations.

Example
The elevation and plan of an archway based on the **Arc de Triomphe** are shown over.

(a) Draw the given views.

(b) Draw an **auxiliary elevation** of the *entire archway* on the given ground line X_1Y_1.

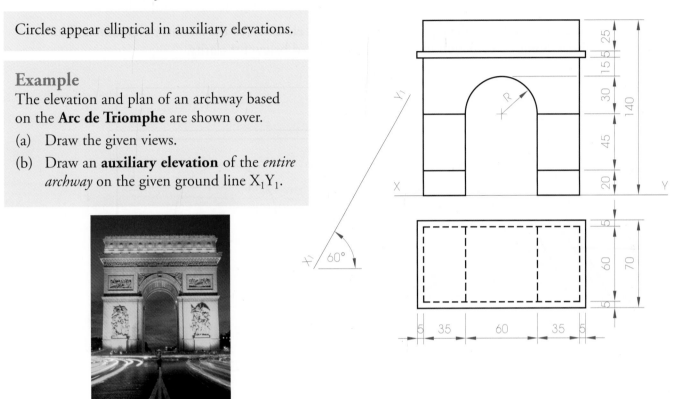

1. The elevation and plan are drawn as shown below.

2. Set up the auxiliary elevation of the archway in the normal manner, omitting the curved surface.

3. Locate points on the elevation of the semicircles (use 30° divisions for convenience) and project them to the plan.

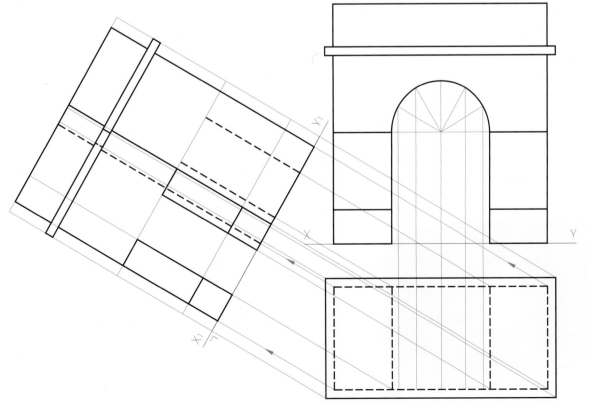

4. The semicircles will appear as semi-ellipses in the auxiliary view. These curves can be drawn by first projecting the points on the plan of the semicircles to the auxiliary view as shown below.

5. Then transfer the heights of these points from the front elevation to the auxiliary elevation and join them in order. Some construction lines have been omitted below for clarity.

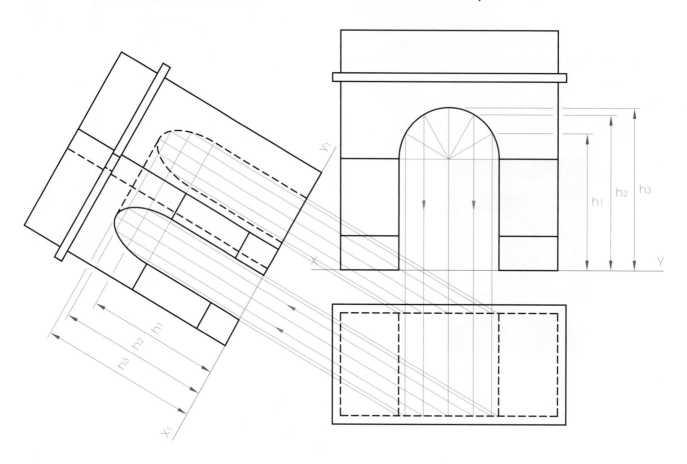

Exercises

1. The elevation and plan of an **archway** are shown across.

   (a) Draw the given elevation and plan.

   (b) Draw an **auxiliary elevation** of the *entire archway* on the given ground line X_1Y_1.

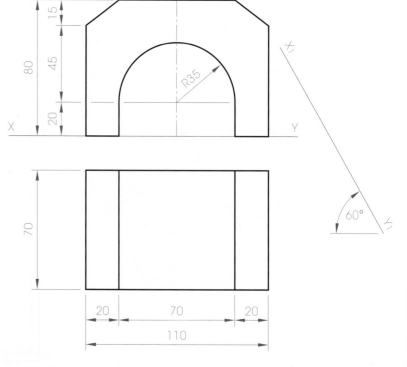

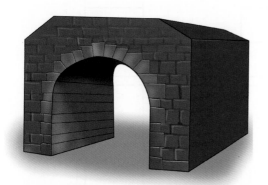

2. The elevation and plan of a **flight of steps** are shown below.

   (a)   Draw the given views.

   (b)   Draw an **auxiliary elevation** of the *entire structure* on the given ground line X_1Y_1.

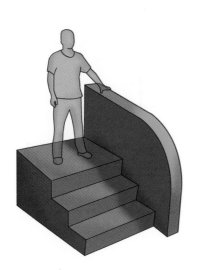

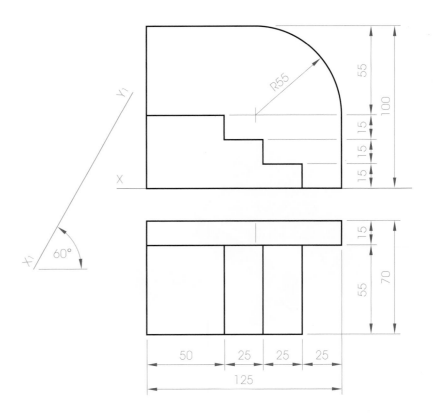

3. The figure below shows the elevation and plan of a **solid**.

   (a)   Draw the elevation and plan.

   (b)   Draw an **auxiliary elevation** of the solid on the given ground line X_1Y_1.

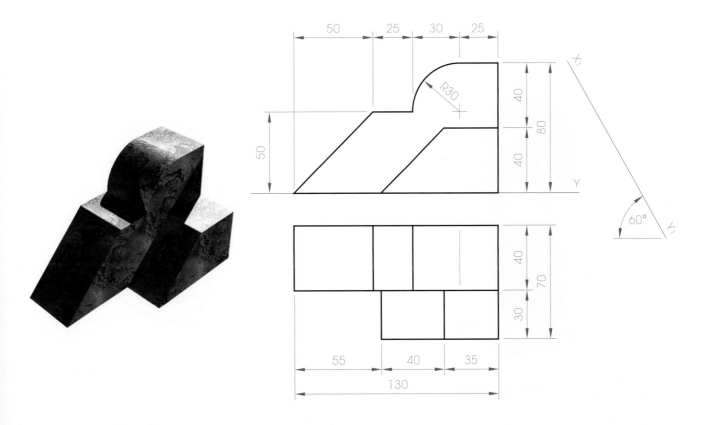

4. The elevation and plan of a **component** are shown across.

(a) Draw the given views.

(b) Draw an **auxiliary elevation** of the *entire component* which will show the true shape of the surface S.

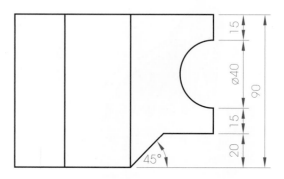

5. The figure over shows a pictorial view of a **trophy**, which contains a **regular hexagon**.

(a) Draw an **elevation** of the trophy looking in the direction of arrow **A**.

(b) Draw a **plan** looking in the direction of arrow **B**, projected from the elevation.

(c) Draw an **auxiliary elevation** of the trophy, which will show the true shape of the surface S.

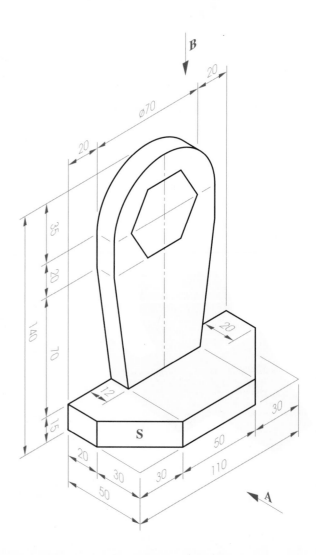

Answer Worksheets 18C and 18D

True Length using Auxiliary Elevations

A line will appear in true length in an auxiliary elevation in which the viewing direction is at right angles to the plan of the line.

Example

The elevation and plan of a **solid** are shown over. Draw an **auxiliary elevation** of the *entire solid* which will show the true length of the line AB.

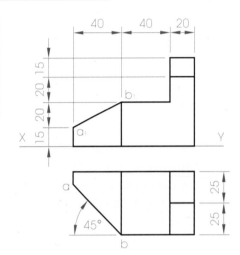

1. The true length of the line AB will appear in an auxiliary elevation in which the viewing direction is at right angles to the plan of the line AB, as illustrated below, right. Accordingly, draw the X_1Y_1 line parallel to the plan of the line AB and project the auxiliary elevation as shown below, left.

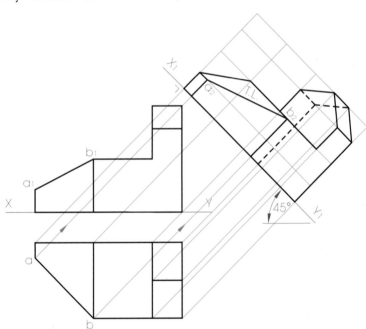

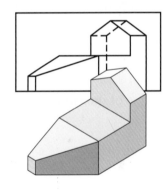

Exercise

The elevation and plan of a **birdhouse** are shown over.

(a) Draw the given views.

(b) Draw an **auxiliary elevation** of the birdhouse which will show the true length of the line AB.

Answer Worksheet 18E

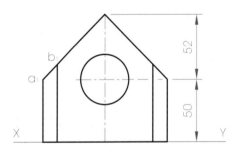

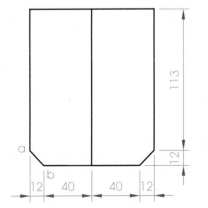

Auxiliary Plans

Auxiliary plans can be obtained by changing the viewing direction also. Take for example the pictorial view of the corner unit shown over. It shows:

(i) A viewing direction inclined to the HP.

(ii) An auxiliary plane (AP) positioned *at right angles to the inclined viewing direction.*

(iii) The auxiliary plan of the unit obtained by projecting points on the object perpendicularly onto the AP and joining them in order.

The planes are rotated into one plane allowing the views to be transferred to a sheet of paper as shown below.

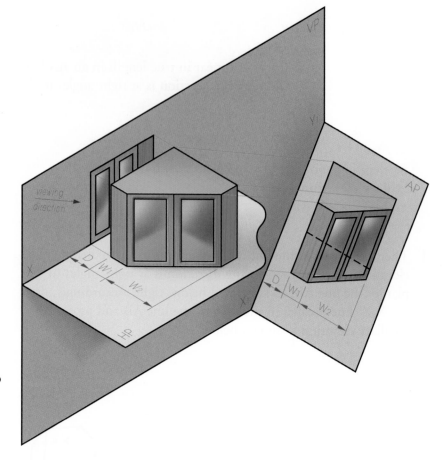

The line of intersection between the auxiliary plane and the vertical plane is called the X_1Y_1 line.

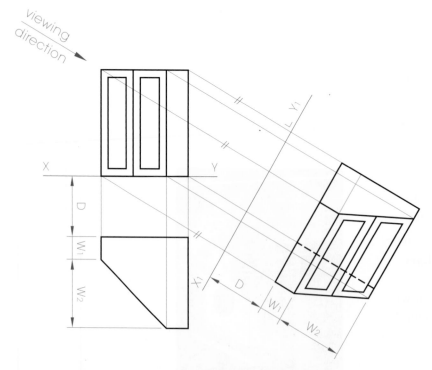

Note that the widths in the auxiliary plan are the same as those in the plan. This facilitates an efficient method of constructing auxiliary plans as shown in the following example.

Example

The elevation and plan of a solid which forms the basis for a **corner unit** is shown over.

(a) Draw the given views.

(b) Draw an **auxiliary plan** of the solid with the viewing direction as indicated by the arrow.

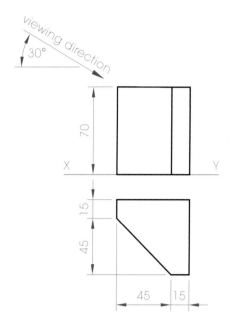

1. The elevation and plan are drawn in the normal manner.

2. Draw the X_1Y_1 line in any convenient position at right angles to the viewing direction for the auxiliary plan.

3. Project all points on the object from the elevation at right angles to the X_1Y_1 line.

4. Transfer the widths from the plan to the auxiliary plan as indicated below, left.

5. Line in the auxiliary plan as shown below, right.

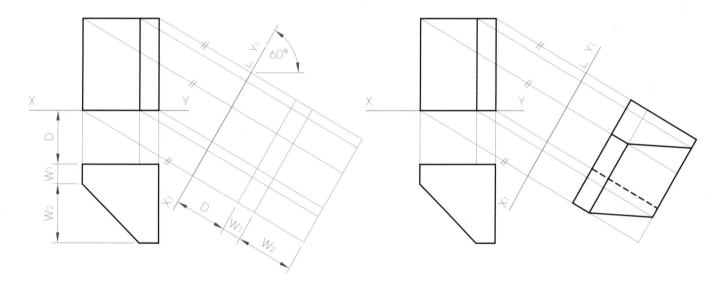

Exercises

1. The figure over shows the elevation and plan of the **Toblerone box** which is based on an equilateral triangular prism.

   (a) Draw the given views.

   (b) Draw an **auxiliary plan** of the box using the viewing direction indicated by the arrow.

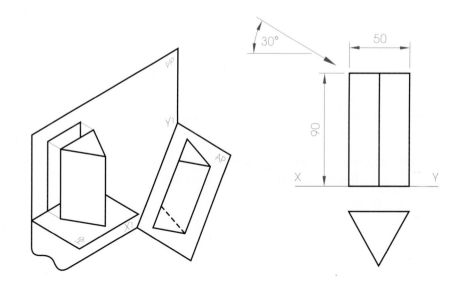

2. The elevation and plan of a **tea box** are shown over.

    (a) Draw the given views.

    (b) Draw an **auxiliary plan** of the box using the viewing direction indicated by the arrow.

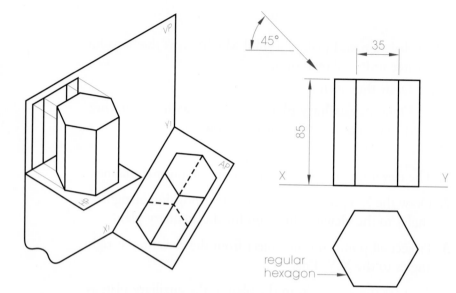

3. The elevation and plan of **two solids** are shown below. In each case:

    (a) Draw the elevation and plan as given.

    (b) Draw an **auxiliary plan** of the solid on the X_1Y_1 line shown.

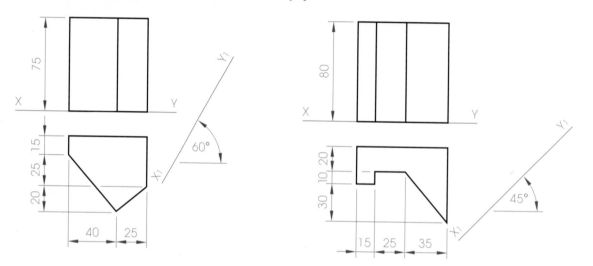

Determining True Shape using Auxiliary Plans

Earlier we determined the true shape of surfaces using auxiliary elevations having noted that:

> A surface will appear in true shape in a view in which the viewing direction is at right angles to that surface.

The same principles can be applied to auxiliary plans.

Example

The elevation and plan of a **solid** are shown over.

    (a) Draw the given views.

    (b) Draw an **auxiliary plan** of the *entire solid*, which will show the true shape of the surface S.

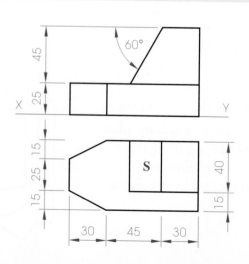

1. The elevation and plan are drawn as shown below.

2. The true shape of surface S will appear in an auxiliary plan in which the viewing direction is at right angles to that surface as illustrated over. Accordingly, the viewing direction will be ⊥ to surface S in elevation.

3. Draw the X_1Y_1 line in any convenient position ⊥ to the viewing direction (parallel to the elevation of surface) and project points on the object from the elevation at right angles to the X_1Y_1 line.

4. Transfer the widths from the plan to the auxiliary plan and complete the new view as shown below.

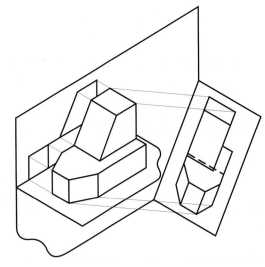

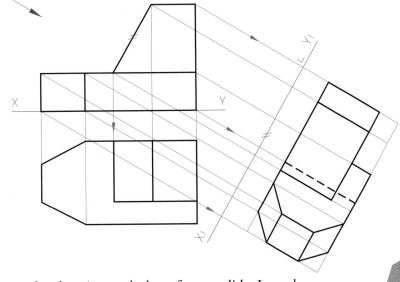

Exercises

The figure below shows the elevation and plan of two solids. In each case:

(a) Draw the given elevation and plan.

(b) Draw an **auxiliary plan** of the *entire solid*, which will show the true shape of the surface S.

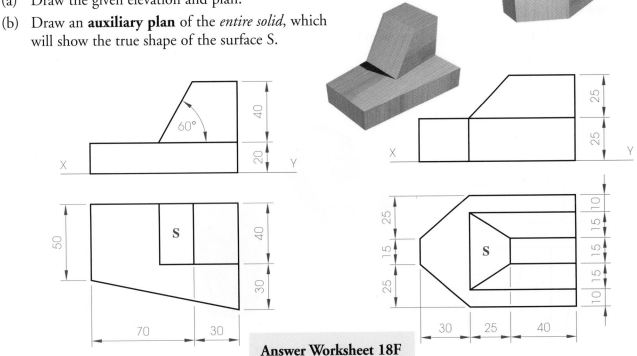

Answer Worksheet 18F

Circles in Auxiliary Plans

Circles appear elliptical in auxiliary plans.

Example
The elevation and plan of a **bin** are shown over.

(a) Draw the given views.

(b) Draw an **auxiliary plan** of the *entire bin* which will show the true shape of the surface S.

1. The elevation and plan are drawn as shown over.

2. The viewing direction for the auxiliary plan will be ⊥ to the elevation of surface S. Draw the X_1Y_1 line ⊥ to the viewing direction (parallel to the elevation of surface S).

3. Complete the auxiliary plan of the object, excluding the curves, in the normal manner.

4. Locate additional points on the plan of the curves (use 30° divisions for convenience) and project them to the elevation.

5. Then locate these points in the auxiliary plan by transferring the appropriate widths and draw smooth curves to pass through them as shown over.

Exercises

The elevation and plan of two objects are shown below. In each case:

(a) Draw the given elevation and plan.

(b) Draw an **auxiliary plan** of the *entire object* which will show the true shape of the surface S.

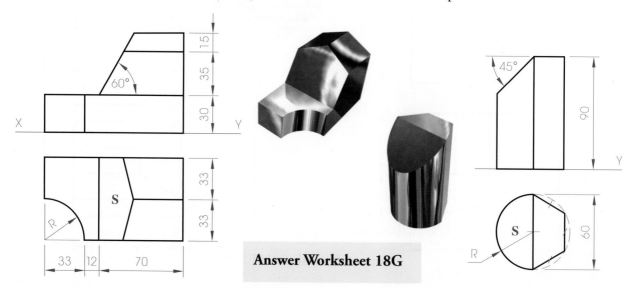

Answer Worksheet 18G

Chapter 19

Circles 2

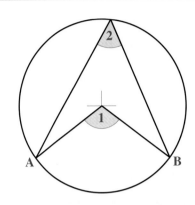

The Circle Theorems

> The measure of the angle at the centre of a circle is twice the measure of the angle at the circumference, standing on the same arc.

The figure across shows a circle with two angles standing on the same arc AB. ∠1 is the angle at the centre of the circle and ∠2 is the angle at the circumference. The measure of ∠1 is twice the measure of ∠2.

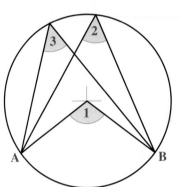

> Two angles standing on the same arc are equal in measure.

In the figure across, ∠2 and ∠3 are standing on the same arc AB and are equal in measure. This is because the measure of each angle is equal to half that of ∠1 at the centre of the circle.

Example
Construct a triangle ABC equal in area to the rectangle shown in the figure (below, left) given that the angle ACB is to be 60°.

1. Draw a line L parallel to AB and a distance equal to twice the width of the rectangle away from AB. The apex C of the triangle will lie on L.

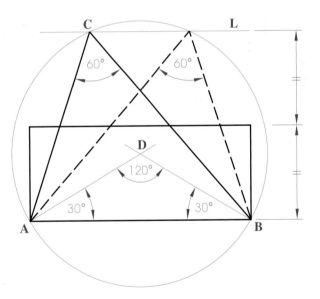

2. Draw a circle, centre D, such that the angle ADB at the centre of the circle is 120°.

> ΔABD is isosceles. ∠ADB is 120°. Thus, ∠DAB = ∠ABD = 30° (180° - 120° = 60° ÷ 2 = 30°).

The measure of the angle at the centre of the circle is twice the measure of the angle at the circumference, standing on the same arc. Thus, vertex C will lie on the circle, centre D.

3. The points of intersection of the line L and the circle give two possible positions for C. Draw the triangle ABC.

The Angle in a Semicircle

Every angle drawn in a semicircle is a right angle.
You may verify this by drawing a series of angles in
a semicircle and measuring them with a protractor.
You will find that each angle measures 90°.

> The angle in a semicircle is a right angle.

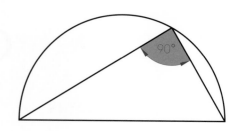

This important fact is used in many constructions.
Here are some examples:

Example 1
Construct the **right-angled triangle** ABC
shown in the figure across.

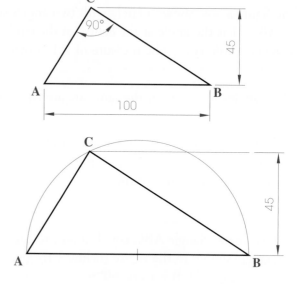

1. Draw the base AB and on it draw a semicircle.
   Every triangle inscribed in this semicircle will be
   right-angled. Thus vertex C will lie on the arc of
   the semicircle.

2. Draw a line parallel to AB and 45 mm from it.
   The vertex C will lie on the intersection of this
   line and the semicircle as shown across.

3. Draw the required triangle ABC.

Example 2
Construct the rectangle ABCD shown in the
figure over.

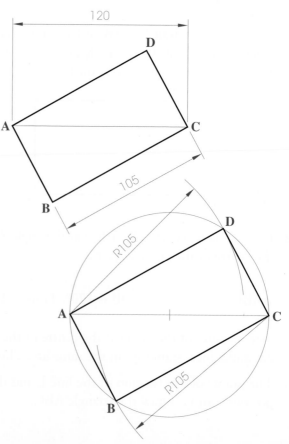

1. Draw the diagonal AC 120 mm long and on it draw a
   circle. Every triangle inscribed in each semicircle will
   be right-angled.

2. Vertex B is readily located with a compass as it is 105
   mm from vertex C.

3. Vertex D may be located by drawing an arc of radius
   105 mm from A as shown.

4. Draw the rectangle by joining the points in order.

Exercises

1. Reproduce the drawing of the logo for the auctioneering firm **Going, Going, Gone** shown in the figure over.

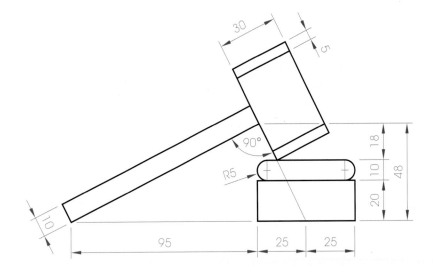

2. Reproduce the drawing of the **CCTV camera** shown in the figure across.

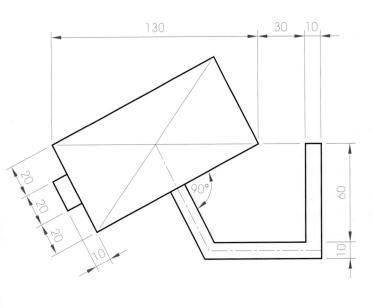

3. Make a full-size drawing of the **sellotape holder** shown across showing all construction lines.

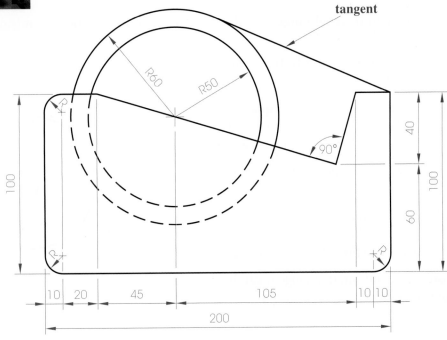

Common Tangents

A tangent can be drawn to two circles as shown across. The tangent is called a **common external tangent** when the circles are located on the same side of it, and a **common internal tangent** when the circles are located on opposite sides of it.

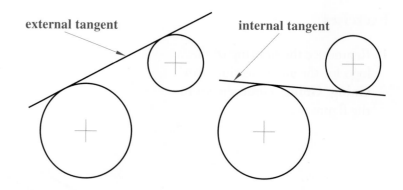

Drawing External and Internal Tangents

Example 1

Construct an **external tangent** to the two circles. Show how both points of contact are determined.

1. Join the centres A and B. Bisect AB and draw a semicircle.

2. With centre A, and radius equal to the difference between the radii of the given circles $(R_A - R_B)$, draw a circle to intersect the semicircle at C.

3. Join AC, and produce the line to intersect the larger circle at D, the point of contact.

4. Draw BE parallel to AD and on the same side of AB as D, to obtain the second point of contact at E. The line DE is the required tangent.

Note: A second external tangent can be drawn on the other side of AB.

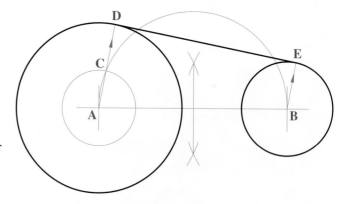

Example 2

Construct an **internal tangent** to the two circles. Show how both points of contact are determined.

1. Join the centres A and B. Bisect AB and draw a semicircle.

2. With centre A, and radius equal to the sum of the radii of the given circles $(R_A + R_B)$, draw a circle to intersect the semicircle at C.

3. Join AC. D, the point of intersection of AC and the larger circle, is one point of contact.

4. Draw BE parallel to AC but on the opposite side of AB as D. Then E is the second point of contact. The line DE is the required tangent.

Note: A second internal tangent can be drawn to the two circles.

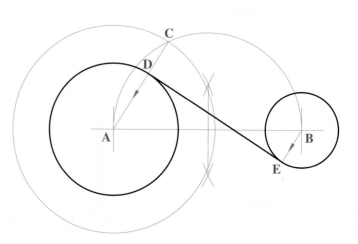

Answer Worksheet 19B

Exercises

1. The elevations of an **Anne French** container and an **Irish Breeze** bottle are shown in the figure below. Draw the given elevations, showing clearly all constructions and points of contact.

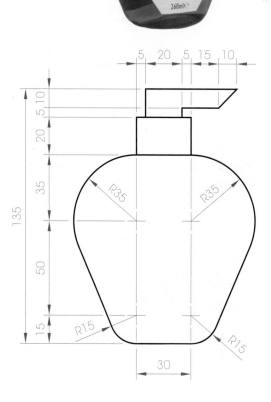

2. The figure below shows a design for a **candle holder**. Reproduce the given figure, showing clearly all constructions and points of contact.

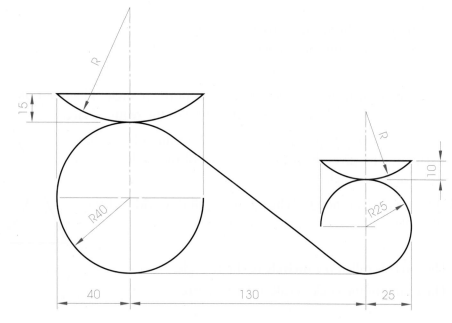

3. Draw the given view of an **electric guitar**, showing clearly all constructions and points of contact.

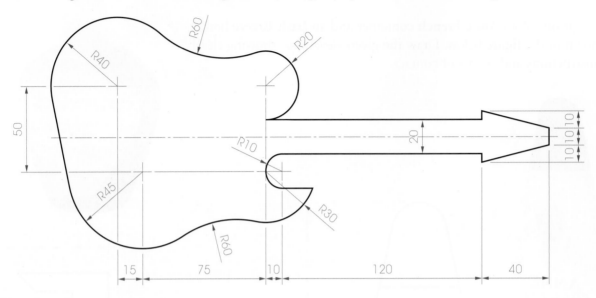

Circle Constructions

Example 1
Describe a circle about the given triangle PQR.

1. Construct the perpendicular bisectors of any two sides of the triangle. The point of intersection C of the perpendicular bisectors is the centre of the required circle.

2. Draw the circle, centre C, passing through the three vertices P, Q and R.

The circle is called the **circumcircle** of the triangle.
The centre of the circle is called the **circumcentre**.

Example 2
Inscribe a circle in the given triangle LMN.
Determine the points of contact.

1. Construct the bisectors of any two angles of the triangle. The point of intersection C of the bisectors is the centre of the required circle.

2. Draw lines from C perpendicular to each of the sides of the triangle. This gives the points of contact of the circle with the sides of the triangle.

3. Draw a circle, centre C, which touches all three sides of the triangle.

The circle is called the **incircle** of the triangle.
The centre of the circle is called the **incentre**.

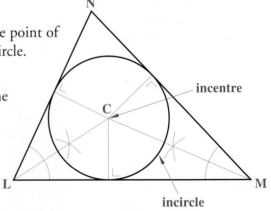

Answer Worksheet 19C

Chapter 20
Areas of Figures

The **area** of a plane figure is the amount of space that is enclosed by its sides. **One square unit** is the area enclosed by a square of side one unit. The area of this square is 1 unit × 1 unit = 1 square unit.

The **area** of a figure is given by the number of squares or fractions of a square that cover it exactly.

Approximate Determination of Areas of Irregular Figures

Example 1
Determine the **area** of the irregular figure (below, left) in square units.

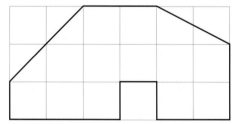

1 square = 1 unit × 1 unit

1. Count all the squares that are completely contained inside the figure – i.e. 12 (above, right).
2. Triangles A and B together make a full square. Triangles C and D also make a full square.
3. The area of the figure is 12 + 1 + 1 = 14 square units.

Example 2
Determine approximately the **area** of the irregular figure (below, left) in square units.

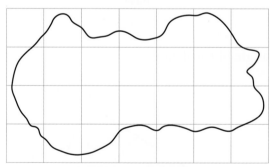 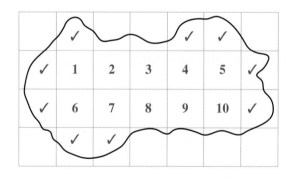

1 square = 1 units × 1 unit

1. Count all the squares that are completely contained within the area – i.e. 10 (above, right).

2. The areas of the squares that are partially contained within the figure can only be approximated.

If more than half the area of a square is occupied, count it as a whole square.
If less than half the area of a square is occupied, do not count it at all.

Thus, only 9 more squares are counted.

3. The area of the figure is approximately 19 square units.

Answer Worksheets 20A and 20B

Area of a Rectangle

The figure over shows a rectangle 4 cm long and 3 cm wide. This rectangle can be divided into 12 square centimetres. Thus, its area is 12 cm². The area may be calculated by multiplying the length and the width.

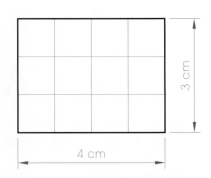

Area of a Rectangle = length × width

Area of a Parallelogram

Shown over is a parallelogram having a base of length 4 cm and a height of 2 cm. The area is calculated by multiplying the base and the height: 4 cm × 2 cm = 8 cm².

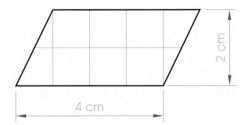

Area of a Parallelogram = base × height

Cutting out the triangle ADE and laying it on the space BCF, shows how to convert the area of the parallelogram ABCD to a rectangle CDEF of equal area.

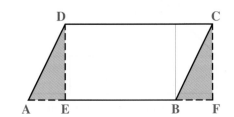

Area of a Triangle

A diagonal of a parallelogram divides it into two equally sized triangles. The triangle has half the area of the parallelogram.

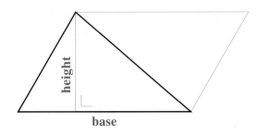

Area of a Triangle = half base × perpendicular height

The **perpendicular height** is the line drawn from the apex perpendicular to the base of the triangle.

Example 1

Convert the area of the **triangle** ABC (below, left), to a **rectangle** of equal area.

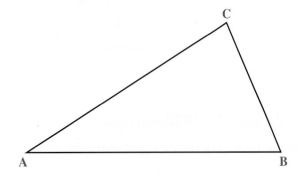
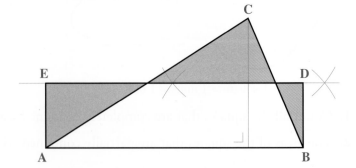

1. Draw the perpendicular height from the apex C to the base AB of the triangle.
2. Construct the perpendicular bisector of the height of the triangle.
3. Erect perpendiculars from A and B to meet the perpendicular bisector at E and D respectively. ABDE is the required rectangle.

Example 2
Convert the area of the given **rectangle** ABCD to an **isosceles triangle** of equal area.

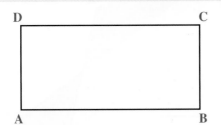

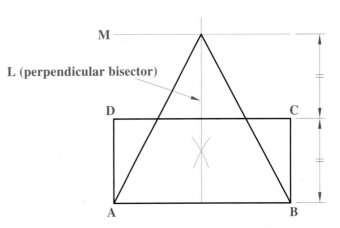

L (perpendicular bisector)

1. Construct the perpendicular bisector L of AB. The apex of the isosceles triangle will lie on L.

2. Draw a line M parallel to AB and a distance equal to twice the width of the rectangle from AB. The apex of the triangle will lie on M.

3. The point of intersection of L and M is the apex of the required triangle. Draw the triangle.

Answer Worksheets 20C and 20D

Triangles

Triangles on the same base and between the same parallels are equal in area.

Area ΔABC = ¹/₂ base × height
Area ΔABD = ¹/₂ base × height
⇒ Area ΔABC = Area ΔABD

Example 1
Construct a **triangle** equal in area to a given ΔABC, and having one side of length 100 mm.

1. Through C, draw a line L parallel to AB. Any triangle having AB as its base and having its third vertex on L is equal in area to ΔABC.

2. With centre A, swing an arc of radius 100 mm to intersect L at D. ΔABD is one solution as it is equal in area to ΔABC and AD is of length 100 mm.

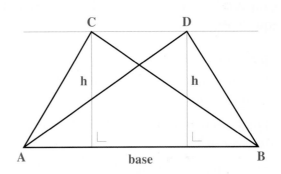

Example 2
Construct a **right-angled triangle** equal in area to ΔABC.

1. Through C, draw a line L parallel to AB. Any triangle having AB as its base and having its third vertex on L is equal in area to ΔABC.

2. Draw a line from B perpendicular to the base to locate D on the line L. ΔABD is one solution.

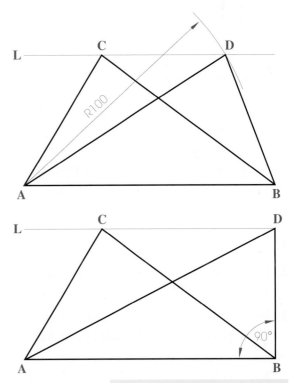

Answer Worksheet 20E

Reducing Polygons to Triangles of Equal Area

Example 1

Convert the **quadrilateral** PQRS into a **triangle** of equal area.

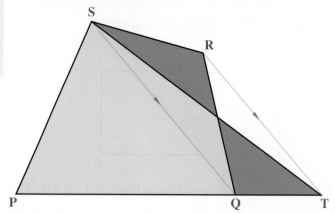

1. Join SQ, thus dividing the quadrilateral into two triangles.

2. Extend the base PQ to the right.

3. Draw a line from R parallel to SQ and cutting the base at T.

4. Join TS to give the required ∆PTS, which is equal in area to the quadrilateral PQRS.

Example 2

Convert the **pentagon** ABCDE into a **triangle** of equal area.

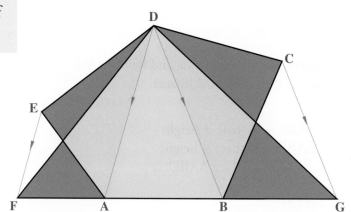

1. Join AD and BD, thus dividing the pentagon into three triangles. Extend the base AB in both directions.

2. Draw a line from E parallel to AD and cutting the base at F.

3. Draw a line from C parallel to BD and cutting the base at G.

4. Join FD and GD. The ∆FGD is the required triangle, which is equal in area to the pentagon ABCDE.

Example 3

Convert the **quadrilateral** ABCD (which contains a re-entrant angle ADC) into a **triangle** of equal area.

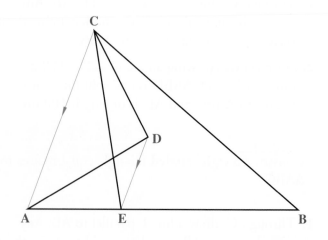

1. Join AC.

2. Draw a line from D parallel to AC cutting the base at E.

3. Join EC to obtain the required triangle EBC, which is equal in area to the quadrilateral ABCD.

Answer Worksheet 20F

Example 1
Convert the **rectangle** ABCD into a **square** of equal area.

Figures of Equal Area

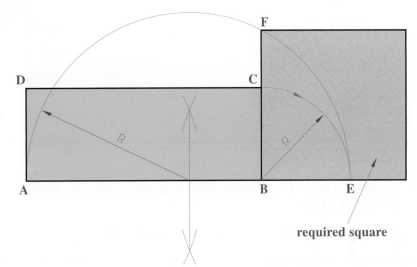

1. Extend the side AB to the right. With B as centre and BC as radius, swing an arc to intersect the side AB produced at E.

2. Bisect AE and draw a semicircle on the line AE.

3. Extend side BC to intersect the semicircle at F. BF is one side of the required square. Draw the square.

The line BF is called the **mean proportional** between AB and BC.

Example 2
Convert the **quadrilateral** ABCD into a **square** of equal area.

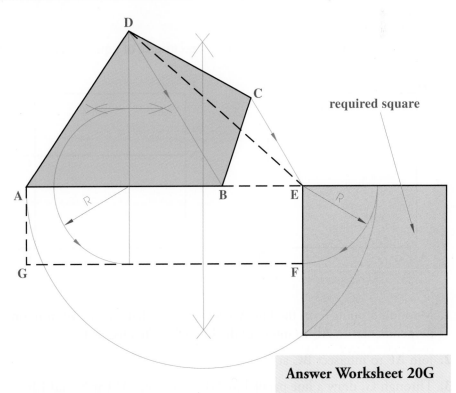

1. Reduce the quadrilateral ABCD to a triangle AED of equal area.

2. Reduce the triangle AED to a rectangle AEFG of equal area.

3. Reduce the rectangle to a square of equal area using the method outlined in Example 1 above.

Answer Worksheet 20G

Example 3

Convert the **rectangle** ABCD into a **rectangle** of equal area and having a length of 140 mm.

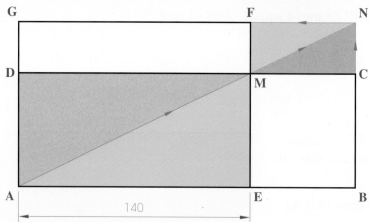

1. Mark off a point E so that the length of AE is 140 mm. Draw a line from E perpendicular to AB to intersect CD at M.

2. Join AM and extend to intersect BC extended at N.

3. Through N, draw a line parallel to AB to intersect AD extended at G. Extend EM to intersect NG at F. AEFG is the required rectangle.

	area ΔABN	=	area ΔANG				
But	area ΔAEM	=	area ΔAMD	and	area ΔMCN	=	area ΔMNF
∴	area ▱BCME	=	area ▱DMFG				
⇒	area ▱ABCD	=	area ▱AEFG				

Example 4

Convert a **square** of side 90 mm into a **rectangle** of equal area and having a length of 150 mm.

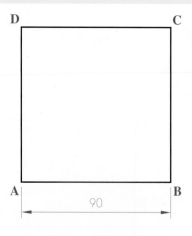 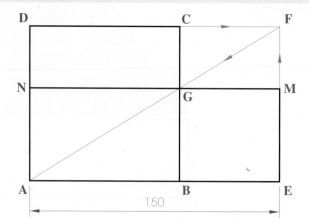

1. Mark off a point E on the line AB extended so that AE is 150 mm long. Draw a line from E perpendicular to AB to intersect the line DC extended at F.

2. Join AF to intersect BC at G.

3. Through G, draw a line parallel to AB to intersect AD at N and EF at M. AEMN is the required rectangle.

Answer Worksheet 20H

Division of Area

Example 1

Draw a line from A which will divide the area of the triangle ABC (below, left) into two equal parts.

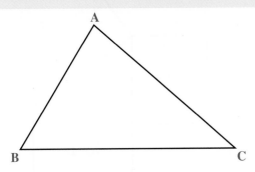

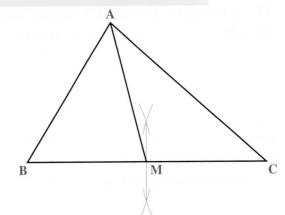

1. Bisect the side opposite A at M.

2. Join AM. AM is the required line.

Example 2

Draw a line from P which will divide the area of the triangle PQR (below, left) into two parts whose areas are in the ratio 2:3.

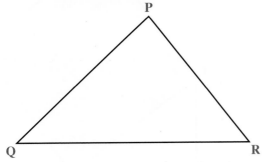

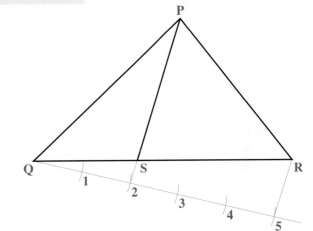

1. Divide the side opposite P in the ratio 2:3.

2. Join PS. PS is the required line.

Example 3

Draw a line from D that will bisect the area of the quadrilateral ABCD.

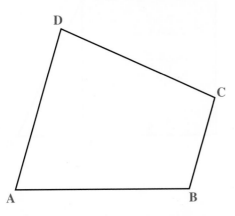

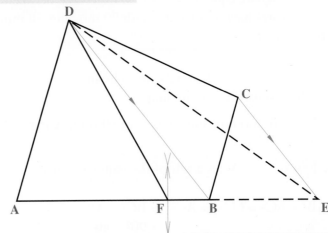

1. Reduce ABCD to a triangle AED of equal area.

2. Bisect AE at F. Join DF. DF is the required line.

Answer Worksheet 20I

Pythagoras's Theorem

The theorem of Pythagoras states:

> The square on the hypotenuse of a **right-angled triangle** is equal to the sum of the squares on the other two sides.

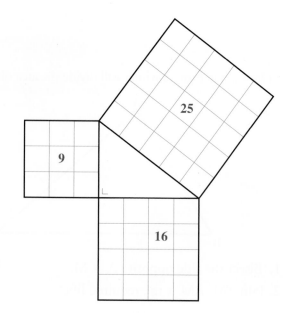

The figure over shows a right-angled triangle having sides of 3 cm, 4 cm and 5 cm, respectively. Squares are drawn on each of the three sides. Counting the small squares verifies that $3^2 + 4^2 = 5^2$.

Pythagoras's Theorem holds true for all right-angled triangles.

Addition and Subtraction of Squares

Example 1
Draw a square equal in area to the sum of the areas of two squares having sides of length 75 mm and 55 mm respectively.

1. Draw two lines AB and AC at right angles to each other. Make AB 75 mm long and AC 55 mm long.

2. Join B to C. BC is a side of the required square. The square on BC is equal in area to the sum of the areas of the other two squares.

$$AB^2 + AC^2 = BC^2 \Rightarrow 75^2 + 55^2 = BC^2$$

Example 2
Draw a square equal in area to the difference between two squares having sides of length 90 mm and 40 mm respectively.

1. Draw two lines AB and AC at right angles to each other. Make AB 40 mm long.

2. Using B as centre and a radius of 90 mm, swing an arc to cut AC at C.

3. Join B to C. AC is a side of the required square.

$$AB^2 + AC^2 = BC^2 \Rightarrow AC^2 = BC^2 - AB^2$$
$$= 90^2 - 40^2$$

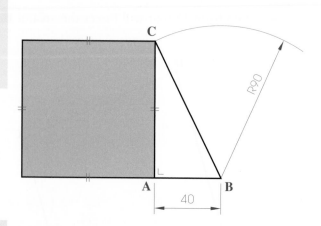

Chapter 21

The Ellipse and Parabola

The **ellipse** and **parabola** may be combined in the drawing of many designs. In this chapter, we will look at some typical examples. The first example is the **Sydney Harbour Bridge**.

Example

Shown below is a drawing of the **Sydney Harbour Bridge**. The main arch of the bridge is in the form of a portion ABC of an **ellipse** having a **semi-major axis** of length 150 mm and a **focal point** F.
The second arch is a **parabola** DEF having its vertex at E. The vertical cables are equally spaced.
Draw the given figure showing all constructions.

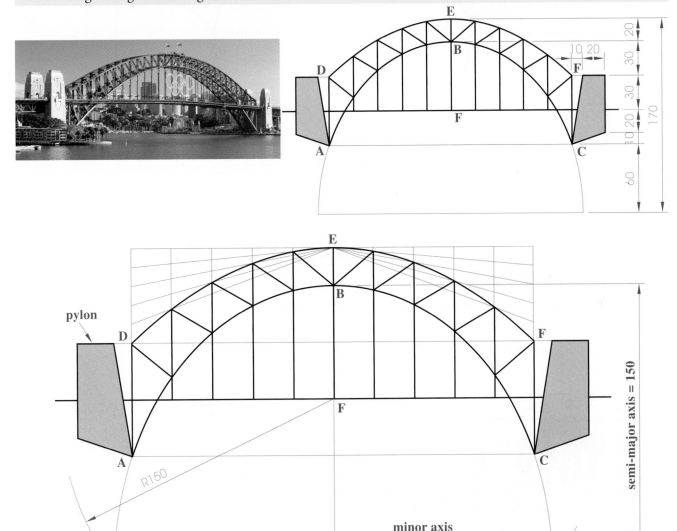

1. Draw the semi-major axis of length 150 mm and locate the focal point F. Draw the direction of the minor axis. With centre F and radius 150 mm (half the major axis), swing arcs to locate the points M and N. MN is the minor axis. Draw the portion ABC of the ellipse.

2. Draw the two pylons to the given sizes.

3. Locate the points D, E and F and draw the rectangle to enclose the parabola DEF. Draw the parabola using the construction outlined on page 165. Complete the outline of the design.

Exercises

1. The figure shows a design based on a **fish**. The curve ABCDE is based on an **ellipse** with **major axis** 130 mm and a **focal point** F. The line BP is **tangential** to the ellipse at point B.

The curve QDR is based on a **parabola** with vertex D.

Draw the given figure showing all construction lines.

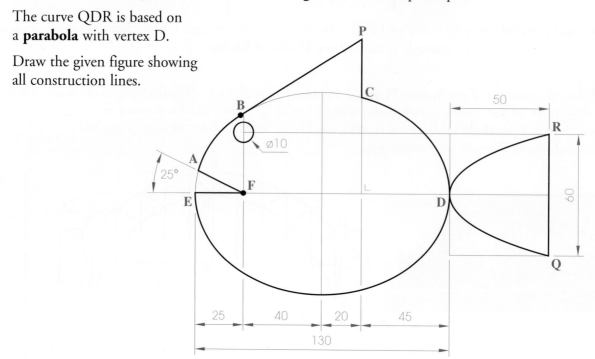

2. Shown below (left) is a photograph of the logo for the **Credit Union of Ireland**. A drawing of part of this logo is shown in the figure (right). The curve ABCD is based on an **ellipse** with **major axis** 180 mm and **focal points** F_1 and F_2.

The curves BV_1D and BV_2D are based on the same parabola with the vertices located at V_1 and V_2 respectively.

Reproduce the given drawing full-size showing all construction lines.

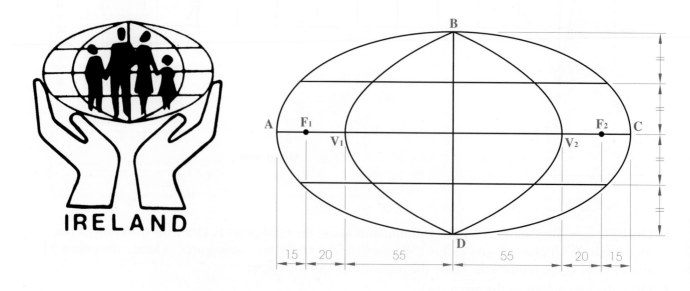

3. The figure across represents a **wine glass**. The curve
ABC is based on an **ellipse** with **major axis** 130 mm
long and a **focal point** F.

The curve JKL is based on a **parabola** with vertex K.

Draw the given figure
full-size showing all
constructions
clearly.

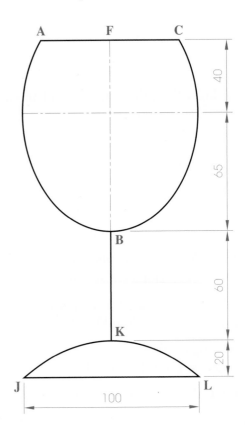

4. The figure shows a design based on the elevation
of a **lamp**. The curve ABCD is based on an
ellipse with **major axis** 150 mm and **minor axis**
80 mm. The **focal points** E and F are indicated.

The line AT is a **tangent** to the ellipse at A. The
curve GAH is based on a **parabola** with vertex A.

Draw the design showing all construction lines.

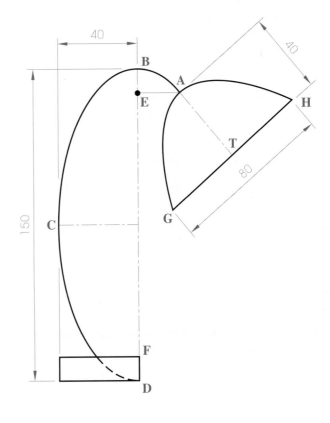

More Problems on the Ellipse

Example
The line MN is the **major axis** of an **ellipse** and P is a point on the curve. Construct the ellipse.

M ——————————————— N

1. Bisect MN to get C, the centre of the ellipse. Draw the major auxiliary circle.

2. Through P, draw a line perpendicular to the major axis to locate D. Join D to C.

3. Through P, draw a line parallel to the major axis to locate E on the line CD.

4. CE is the radius of the minor auxiliary circle.

5. Construct the ellipse using the auxiliary circles method.

The solution involves a reversal of the auxiliary circles method.

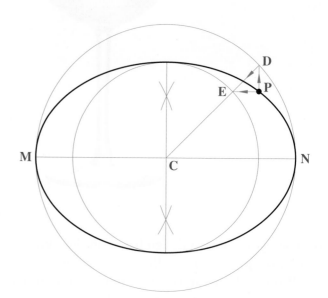

Alternative Solution

1. Bisect MN to get C, the centre of the ellipse. Draw the position of the minor axis.

2. Make a trammel and mark points P and B where PB equals half the length of the major axis.

3. Place the trammel so that P is at the point P and B is on the minor axis.

4. Point A may be marked where the trammel crosses the major axis. Then PA equals half the minor axis.

5. Mark the minor axis and draw the ellipse.

The solution involves a reversal of the trammel method.

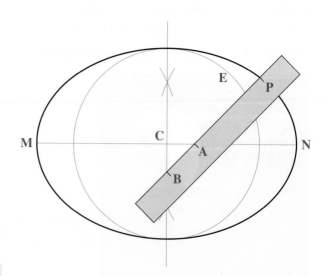

Answer Worksheet 21A

Example

The figure represents a two-button **computer mouse** and **cable**.

The curve ABCD is an **ellipse** with **major axis** 120 mm long.

The curves QA and QR are based on the same **semi-parabola** with the vertex at Q for each parabola.

Draw the figure to the dimensions given showing all constructions clearly.

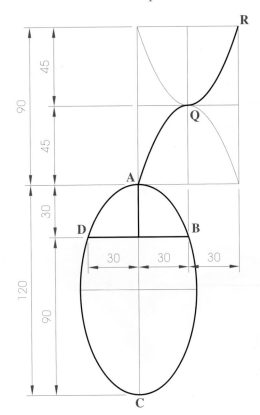

1. Draw the rectangles measuring 45 mm × 30 mm as shown to enclose the semi-parabolas QA and QR. Use the method outlined on page 165 to draw the two curves.

2. Draw the major axis AC of length 120 mm and locate the line DB. Locate E, the centre of the ellipse, and draw the major auxiliary circle of radius 60 mm.

3. D is a point on the curve. Through D, draw a line perpendicular to the major axis to locate F. Join F to E.

4. Through D, draw a line parallel to the major axis to locate G on the line FE. With centre E and radius equal to the length of EG, draw the minor auxiliary circle

5. Construct the ellipse using the auxiliary circles method.

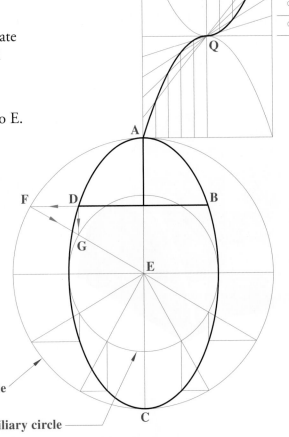

major auxiliary circle

minor auxiliary circle

Exercises

1. The figure across shows a drawing of the **Star Trek** emblem. The curve ABCDE is based on an **ellipse** with **major axis** 150 mm.

   The curves PQR and PSR are **parabolas** with vertices at Q and S respectively.

   Draw the figure to the given dimensions showing all construction lines.

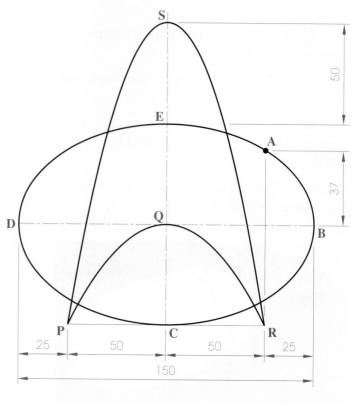

2. The figure below represents the outline elevation of a **stadium**. The curve ABC is a **semi-ellipse** with **minor axis** 120 mm.

   The curves DEF and D_1E_1F are based on the same parabola with vertices located at E and E_1 respectively.

   Draw the outline of the building showing all constructions clearly.

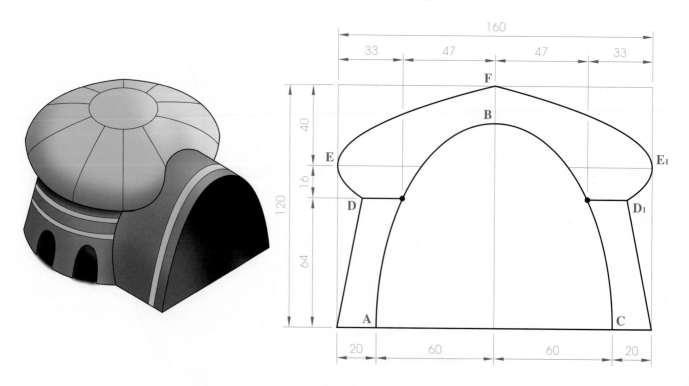

3. A drawing of the **Kawasaki** logo is shown in the figure below. The curves DEF and GHI are based on the same **ellipse** with **minor axis** 50 mm.

The curves AB and AC are **semi-parabolas** with vertices located at B and C respectively.

Reproduce the drawing of the logo showing all construction lines clearly.

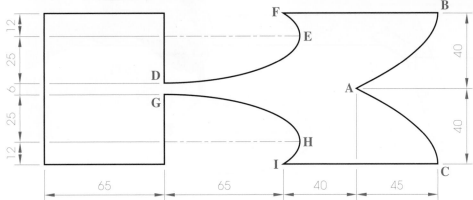

4. A drawing of the **Atlantic Homecare** trademark is shown below. A portion of an **ellipse** and a **parabola** have been linked together in the formation of the letter A.

The curve ABC is based on an **ellipse** with **minor axis** 80 mm and the curve AC is a **parabola** with vertex A.

Reproduce the drawing of this trademark.

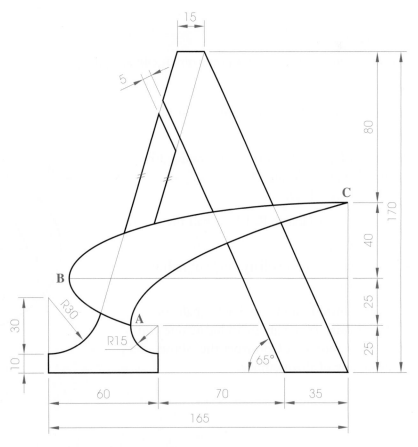

Focal Points of an Ellipse

The simplest way to draw an ellipse is to use two thumbtacks and a piece of string. Stick the thumbtacks in a sheet of paper and hook a piece of string around them. Keep the string stretched with the point of a pencil as shown in the figure below, and move the pencil around the tacks to trace an ellipse.

The thumbtacks are positioned at the **focal points** of the ellipse. The sum of the distances from the pencil point to the focal points is always the same and is equal to the length of the major axis.

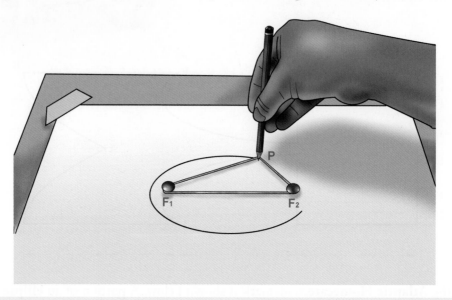

$PF_1 + PF_2$ = major axis.   This property holds for every point on the ellipse.

Example

In the triangle PF_1F_2, P is a point on an ellipse and F_1 and F_2 are the focal points. Construct the ellipse.

1. Bisect F_1F_2 to locate the centre C of the ellipse.

2. Extend F_2P. With centre P and radius PF_1, draw an arc to locate Q. $PF_1 + PF_2$ = major axis = F_2Q.

3. Bisect F_2Q to locate R. RF_2 = half the major axis.

4. Draw the major auxiliary circle of radius RF_2 about C.

5. With centre F_1 and radius RF_2 (half the major axis), swing an arc to locate one end of the minor axis. Construct the ellipse using any of the methods.

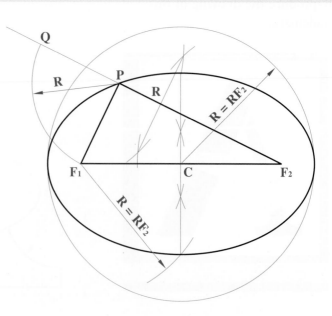

Example

The figure shows a design based on the elevation of a **sports stadium**. The curve ABCDE is based on a **semi-ellipse** with **major axis** 100 mm and **minor axis** 60 mm. The **focal points** F and G are indicated.

The lines BR and DR are tangential to the ellipse at points B and D respectively. *The curve QRS is based on the same ellipse.*

The curves AP and ET are **semi-parabolas** with vertices at A and E respectively.

Draw the design showing all construction lines.

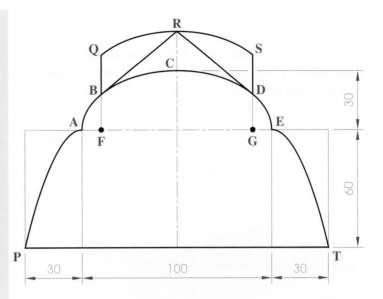

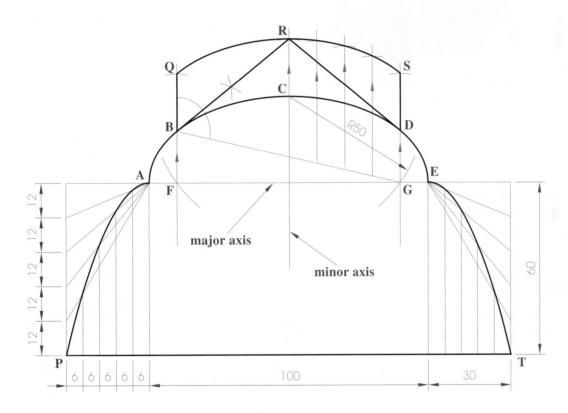

1. Draw the line PT and the two rectangles measuring 60 mm × 30 mm. Construct a semi-parabola in each of the rectangles using the method outlined on page 165.

2. Draw the major and minor axes of the ellipse. Any suitable method for drawing the semi-ellipse may be used.

3. Locate the focal points F and G of the ellipse. Locate the points B and D on the semi-ellipse directly above F and G respectively. Construct the tangent BR, using the method outlined on page 113. Join D to R to obtain the second tangent.

4. The curve QRS is obtained by **translating** the portion BCD of the semi-ellipse upwards a distance equal to CR.

Exercises

1. The figure represents a two-button **computer mouse** and **cable**. The curve ABCDE is based on an **ellipse** with **major axis** 130 mm long. The curve AE is based on the same ellipse.

   The curves VB and VF are based on the same **semi-parabola** with the vertex at V for each parabola.

   Draw the figure to the dimensions given showing all construction lines.

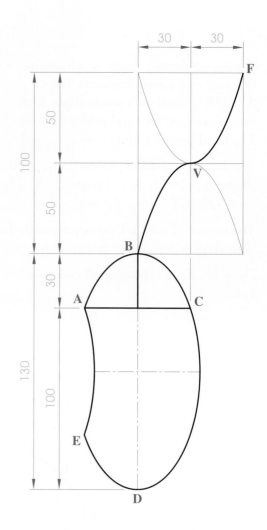

2. The figure represents a design for a **mask**. The curve ABCDE is based on an **ellipse** having a **minor axis** of 60 mm and the curve JKL is based on the same ellipse. The curve AFE is **parabolic**.

   Draw the figure to the dimensions given showing all constructions clearly.

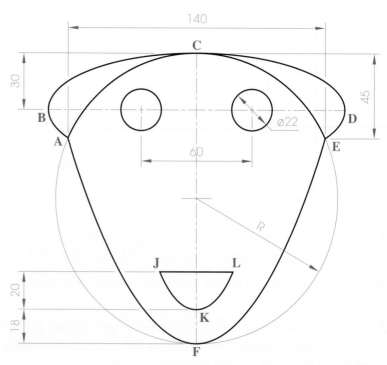

Tangents to an Ellipse from a Point Outside

Example 1
Construct a **tangent** to an ellipse from a point P outside the curve.

1. Determine the focal points. With P as centre and radius PF$_1$, draw an arc as shown.

2. With F$_2$ as centre and the length of the major axis as radius, draw an arc to intersect the first arc at M and N.

3. Join M to F$_2$ to intersect the ellipse at Q. PQ is the required tangent and Q is the point of contact.

4. Join N to F$_2$ to intersect the ellipse at R. PR is a second tangent that can be drawn to the curve from P and R is the point of contact.

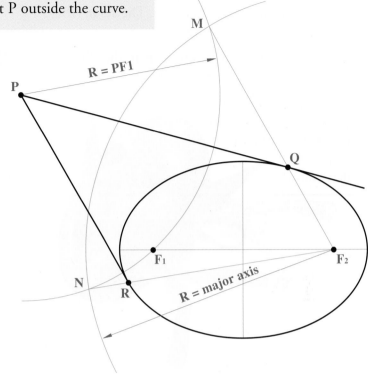

Example 2
Construct a **tangent** to an ellipse that makes an angle of 30° with the major axis.

1. Determine the focal points.

2. Draw the major auxiliary circle.

3. Draw line L at 30° to the major axis.

4. Draw lines from F$_1$ and F$_2$ perpendicular to the line L to locate points A and B on the major auxiliary circle. AB is the required tangent.

5. With A as centre and radius AF$_1$ draw a semicircle to locate C. Join CF$_2$ to locate P on the tangent. This is the required point of contact.

Perpendiculars from the focal points to a tangent meet the tangent on the major auxiliary circle.

The **point of contact** must be located each time a tangent is drawn to an ellipse.

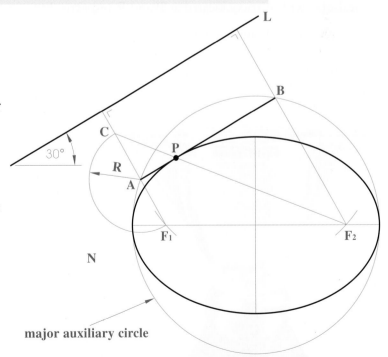

Answer Worksheet 21C

Exercises

1. The figure represents a design for a **mask**. It is based on an **ellipse** having a **major axis** of 120 mm and a **minor axis** of 70 mm. The curve ABC is **parabolic**, with a B as vertex.

The lines PQ and RS are **tangents** to the ellipse drawn from Q and S respectively.

Draw the given figure showing clearly how the **points of contact** P and R are determined.

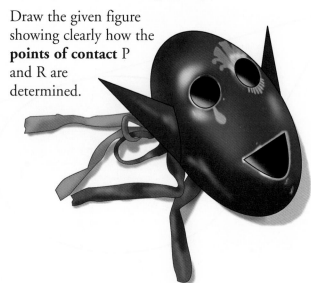

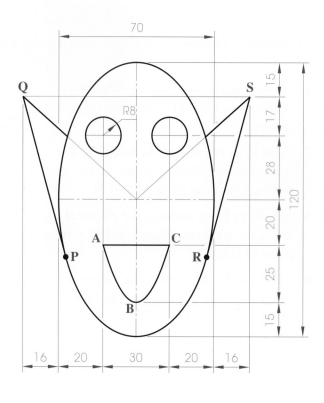

2. The figure shows a design for a **sports cup**. It consists of a **semi-ellipse** with **major axis** 190 mm and **minor axis** 86 mm. The lines AB and CD are tangents to the ellipse. The curves PQ and RQ are **semi-parabolas** with vertices located at P and R respectively.

Draw the given design showing clearly the construction required to determine the **points of contact** A and C between the ellipse and the tangents.

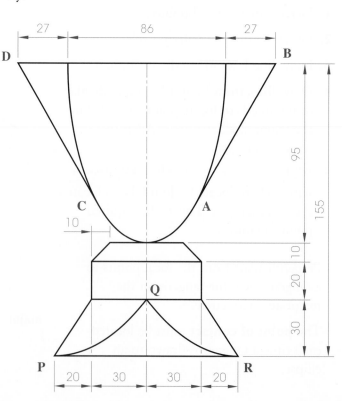

3. The figure across represents the outline of a **radar station**. The curve ABC is based on a **semi-ellipse** having a **major axis** of 140 mm and **minor axis** of 80 mm.

The curve DEF is a **parabola**. The two curves are tangential at the point E.

Draw the outline of the building showing clearly how the point of contact E is established.

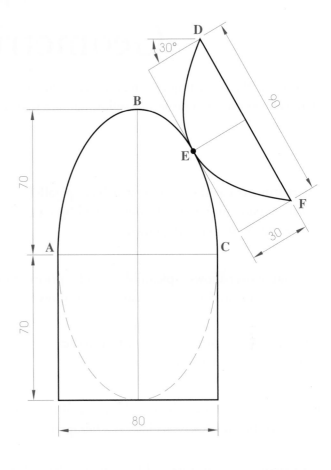

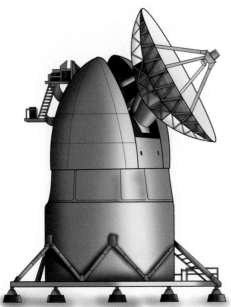

4. The figure below represents the logo for the **King Chess Club**. It is based on an **ellipse** having a **major axis** of 120 mm and a **minor axis** of 70 mm. The lines AF and EG are tangents to the ellipse at the points F and G respectively.

The curves ABC and CDE are **parabolas** with vertices at B and D respectively.

Draw the outline of the logo showing clearly how the points of contact F and G are obtained.

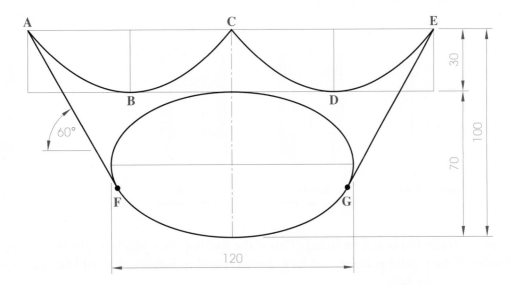

Chapter 22
Geometrical Solids

In some of the preceding chapters we have already encountered many geometrical solids. In this chapter we shall concentrate on two sets of solids, namely **prisms** and **pyramids**.

Prisms

A **prism** has equal end faces, which are parallel and similarly oriented polygons, joined by side faces which are parallelograms.

The figure over shows a pictorial view of a prism. Note its faces, edges and vertices. Its axis is also shown.

The **axis** is an imaginary line which passes through the centre of a prism.

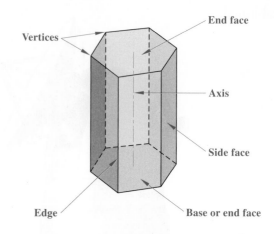

Prisms are named according to the shape of their end faces. Accordingly, the solid shown above is a hexagonal prism because its base is a hexagon.

A **prism** is regular if its end faces are regular polygons.

A **right prism** is a prism whose axis is perpendicular to its end faces. The side faces of right prisms are rectangles.

The figure below shows some right regular prisms. In each case the prism is:

- right because its axis is perpendicular to its end faces.
- regular because its end faces are regular polygons.

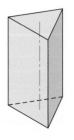

Equilateral triangular prism

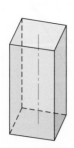

Square prism

Regular pentagonal prism

Regular hexagonal prism

Cylinder – circular prism

A right circular prism (cylinder) is also included. This is the limiting case which results if we imagine that the number of sides of the regular polygon end faces are increased to infinity. The end faces are now circular and the side faces are straight lines.

All prisms referred to in this text are **right** unless otherwise stated.

Example

The figure below, left shows a pictorial view of a **regular hexagonal prism** whose base is resting on the horizontal plane.

(a) Draw the plan of the solid and project an elevation.

(b) Draw an end elevation of the solid.

(c) Index all vertices on the upper end face of the solid in each view.

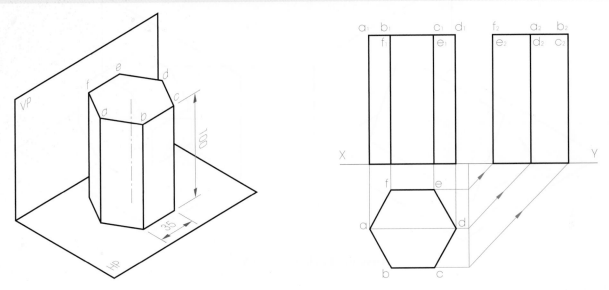

1. The plan, a regular hexagon of side 35 mm, is drawn first.

2. The elevation, having a height of 100 mm, is then projected. This allows the end elevation to be completed as shown above, right.

3. The upper end face is indexed using lower-case letters. Where vertices coincide in a view the letter on the outside represents the vertex nearest the observer, whereas the letter inside represents the vertex furthest away.

Exercises

1. A pictorial view of a **rectangular prism** and a **regular pentagonal prism** are shown below. In each case:

(a) Draw the plan of the solid and project an elevation.

(b) Draw an end elevation of the solid.

(c) Index all vertices on the upper end face of the solid in each view.

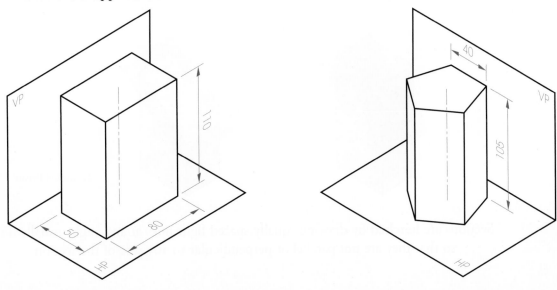

2. The pictorial views below show an **equilateral triangular prism** and a **regular octagonal prism**. In each case:

(a)   Draw the elevation of the solid and project a plan.

(b)   Draw an end elevation of the solid.

(c)   Index all vertices on the front end face of the solid in each view.

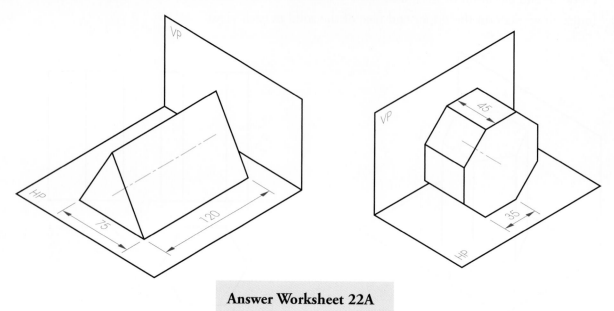

Answer Worksheet 22A

Cross-sections

If a cutting plane passes through a solid the actual part of the solid cut by the plane is called a **section**.

If a cutting plane is perpendicular to the axis of a prism the resulting section is called a **cross-section**. All cross-sections of a prism are identical.

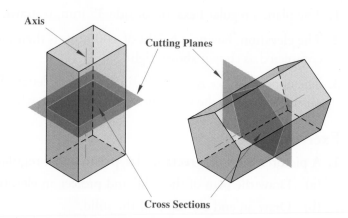

Truncated Prisms

If a prism is cut by a cutting plane inclined to its axis and one portion removed, the result is a **truncated prism**.

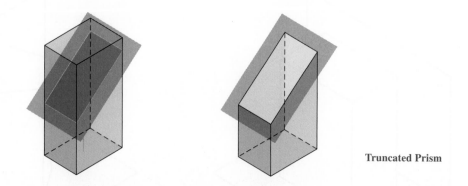

Truncated Prism

Sections are **hatched** by drawing equally spaced light lines at any angle, usually 45°, so that they are not parallel or perpendicular to any side of the section.

Example

The plan and elevation (drawn using light lines) of a **regular pentagonal prism** are shown over. The solid is to be cut by the cutting plane which is represented by the lines VTH.

(a) Draw the plan and elevation of the **truncated prism**.

(b) Draw an end elevation of the **truncated prism**.

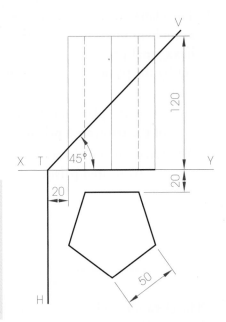

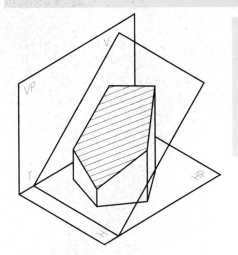

The **vertical trace** (VT) of a plane is the line where it meets the vertical plane.

The **horizontal trace** (HT) of a plane is the line where it meets the horizontal plane.

1. The plan and elevation are drawn as given.

2. The cutting plane appears as an edge in elevation which means that the portion of the prism above the cutting plane is removed, as illustrated above. Accordingly, the elevation can be completed by lining in the portion of the prism below the cutting plane.

3. It is useful to index the section in plan and elevation to help complete the side elevation as shown over.

4. The section is hatched in plan and end elevation with lines at 45°.

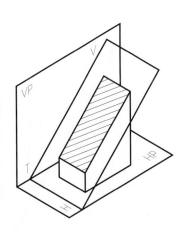

Exercises

1. The plan and elevation (drawn using light lines) of a **rectangular prism** which is to be cut by the plane VTH is shown over.

   (a) Draw the plan and elevation of the **truncated prism**.

   (b) Draw an end elevation of the **truncated prism**.

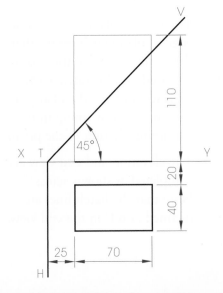

2. The plan and elevation (drawn using light lines) of a **regular hexagonal prism** which is to be cut by the plane VTH is shown over.

   (a) Draw the plan and elevation of the **truncated prism**.

   (b) Draw an end elevation of the **truncated prism**.

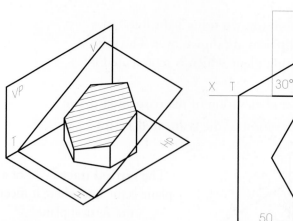

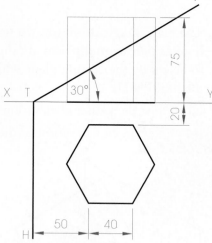

Example

The elevation and plan (drawn using light lines) of a **regular hexagonal prism** are shown over. The solid is to be cut by the cutting plane VTH.

(a) Draw the elevation and plan of the **truncated prism**.

(b) Draw an end view of the **truncated prism**.

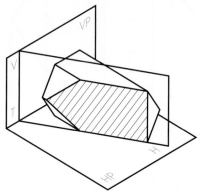

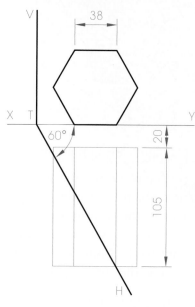

1. The elevation and plan are drawn as given.

2. The cutting plane appears as an edge in plan which means that the front portion of the prism is removed, as illustrated above, left. Accordingly, the plan can be completed by lining in the remaining portion of the prism.

3. The elevation and end view are completed as shown across. Note that the hatch lines are inclined at 60° in the end view.

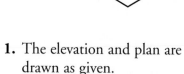

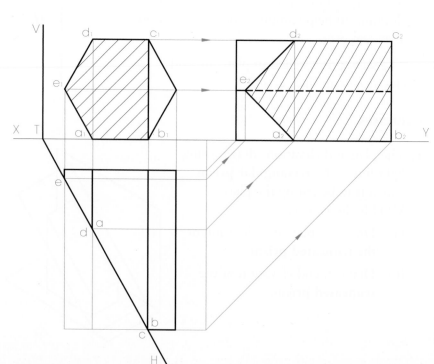

Exercise

The figure below shows the elevation and plan (drawn using light lines) of an **equilateral triangular prism** and a **regular pentagonal prism**. Each solid is to be cut by a plane VTH as indicated. In each case:

(a) Draw the elevation and plan of the **truncated prism**.

(b) Draw an end elevation of the **truncated prism**.

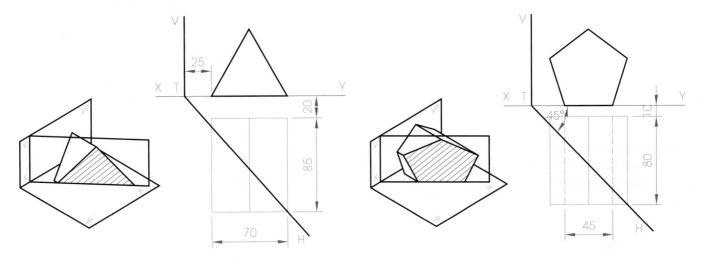

Pyramids

> A **pyramid** has a polygon as base, with triangular side faces meeting at a common point called the **apex**.
>
> The **axis** is an imaginary line which passes through the apex and the centre of the base of a pyramid.

Pyramids are named according to the shape of their bases. Accordingly, the pyramid over is a rectangular pyramid because its base is a rectangle.

> A **pyramid** is regular if its base is a regular polygon.
>
> A **right pyramid** is a pyramid whose axis is perpendicular to its base.

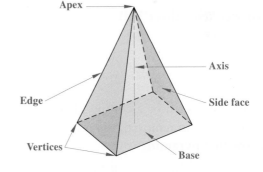

The figure below shows some right regular pyramids.

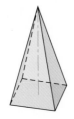
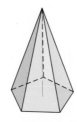
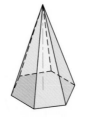

| Equilateral triangular pyramid | Square pyramid | Regular pentagonal pyramid | Regular hexagonal pyramid | Cone – circular pyramid |

The right circular pyramid (cone) is also included. This is the limiting case which results if we imagine that the number of sides of the regular polygon base are increased to infinity. The base is now circular and the side faces are straight lines.

All pyramids referred to in this text are **right** unless otherwise stated.

The figure over shows a pictorial view of a **rectangular pyramid**. The plan and elevation of the pyramid are also shown. Note the **altitude** of the pyramid, which is the distance from the apex at right angles to the base.

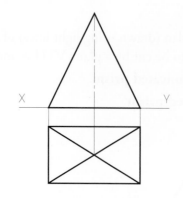

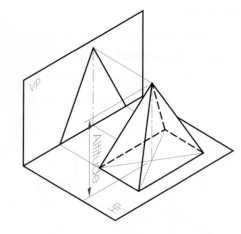

Exercise

A pictorial view of a **rectangular pyramid** and a **regular pentagonal pyramid** are shown over. In each case:

(a) Draw the plan of the pyramid and project an elevation.

(b) Draw an end elevation of the solid.

(c) Index all vertices of the solid in each view.

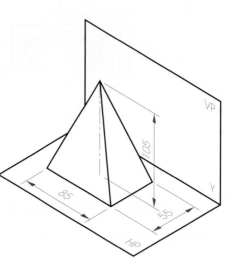

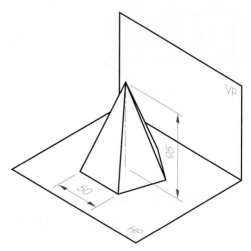

Answer Worksheet 22B

Truncated Pyramids

If a pyramid is cut by a cutting plane and one portion removed, the result is a **truncated pyramid**.

If the cutting plane is parallel to the base of the pyramid the portion containing the base is called a **frustum**.

The figure over shows a pictorial view of a frustum of a rectangular pyramid. The resulting elevation and plan are also shown.

All sections resulting from cutting planes parallel to the base of a pyramid are similar to the base of that pyramid.

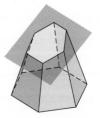

Truncated pyramid

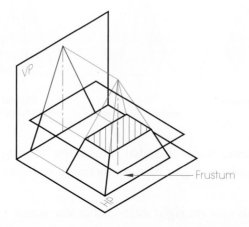

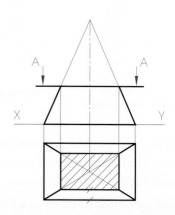

Example

The incomplete elevation and plan of a **rectangular pyramid**, which is to be cut by the plane VTH are shown over.

(a) Draw the elevation and plan of the **truncated pyramid**.

(b) Draw an end view of the **truncated pyramid**.

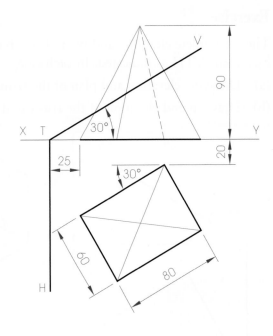

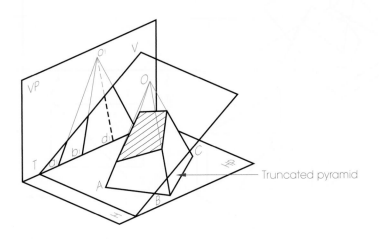

Truncated pyramid

1. The incomplete plan and elevation are drawn as given.

2. The cutting plane appears as an edge in elevation which means that the portion of the pyramid above the cutting plane is removed, as illustrated above. Accordingly, the elevation is completed as shown below.

3. The points where the plane VTH cuts the edges OA, OB, OC and OD are then projected to plan of the respective edges allowing the drawing to be completed as shown below.

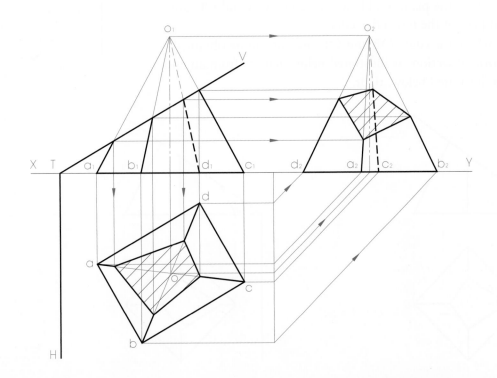

Exercise

The incomplete elevation and plan of two **rectangular pyramids** are shown below. Each solid is to be cut by a plane VTH as indicated. In each case:

(a) Draw the elevation and plan of the **truncated pyramid**.

(b) Draw an end elevation of the **truncated pyramid**.

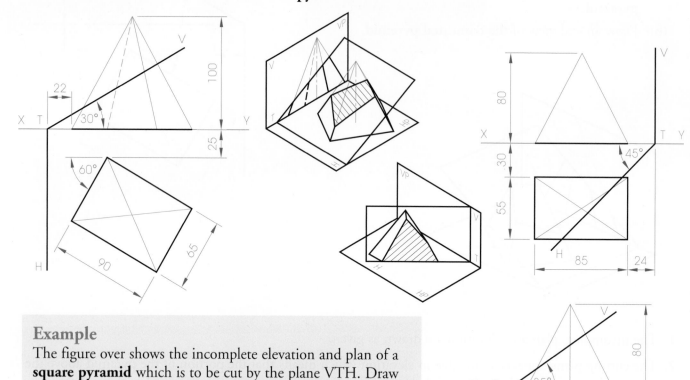

Example

The figure over shows the incomplete elevation and plan of a **square pyramid** which is to be cut by the plane VTH. Draw the elevation and plan of the **truncated pyramid**.

1. The elevation is readily completed as the cutting plane appears as an edge in this view.
2. The points where the plane VTH cuts the edges OA and OC are projected to plan of the respective edges.
3. The points where the edges OB and OD are cut can be obtained from a horizontal section, as illustrated below, left, or from an end elevation as illustrated below, right.

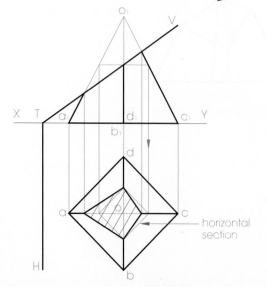

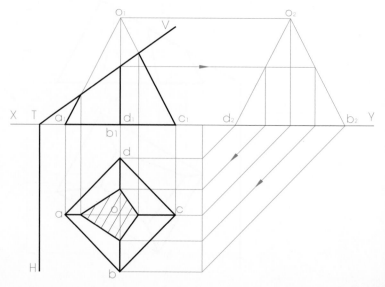

Exercise

The incomplete elevation and plan of a **regular pentagonal pyramid** which is to be cut by the plane VTH are shown over. Draw the elevation and plan of the **truncated pyramid**.

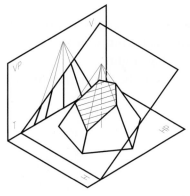

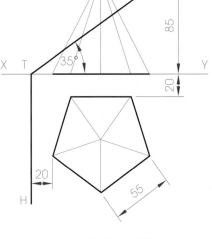

True Shape of Sections

A section will appear in **true shape** in a view in which the viewing direction is perpendicular to that section.

Example

The elevation and plan of a **truncated regular hexagonal prism** are shown over. Determine the **true shape** of the cut section of the solid.

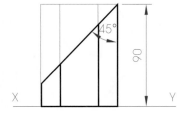

1. The true shape of the section can be obtained by rotating it into the horizontal plane using the HT as the axis of rotation as illustrated below, right. Accordingly, it is useful to draw the traces VTH of the cutting plane as shown below, left.

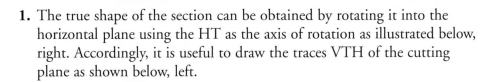

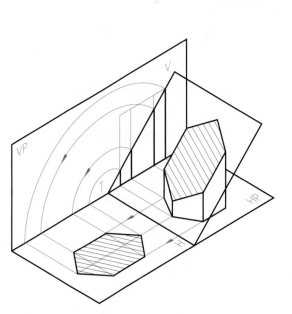

2. The axis of rotation appears as a point in elevation which means that points on the section will rotate in an arc of a circle in this view.

3. Points on the section will move at right angles to the axis of rotation in plan allowing the true shape to be completed as shown above, left.

Rotating a surface into the horizontal plane (or vertical plane) is known as **rabatment**.

Alternative solution

1. The true shape of the cut section can also be determined by rabatting the cutting plane into the vertical plane about its VT as illustrated below, left. Points on the section will move at right angles to the axis of rotation (VT) in elevation as shown below, right.
2. For convenience the appropriate widths can be transferred on either side of a centre line from the plan as indicated.

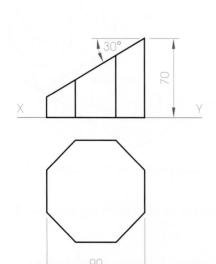

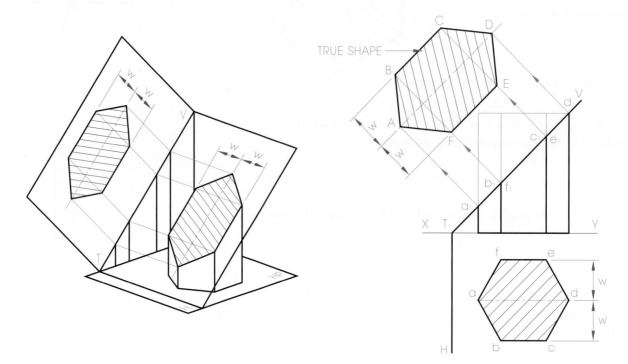

Exercise

The figure below shows the elevation and incomplete plan of a **truncated regular octagonal prism** and a **truncated regular hexagonal pyramid**. In each case:

(a) Draw the **elevation** and **plan** of the solid.

(b) Draw an end elevation of the solid.

(c) Determine the **true shape** of the cut section of the solid.

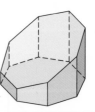
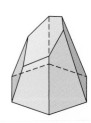

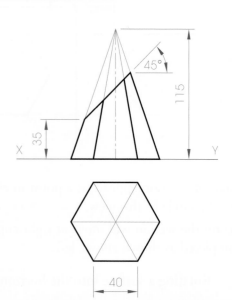

Example

The figure over shows the elevation, plan (both drawn lightly) and end view of a **regular pentagonal prism** which is to be cut by the plane VTH.

(a) Draw the end view and plan of the **truncated prism**.

(b) Project the elevation of the **truncated prism**.

(c) Determine the **true shape** of the cut section of the solid.

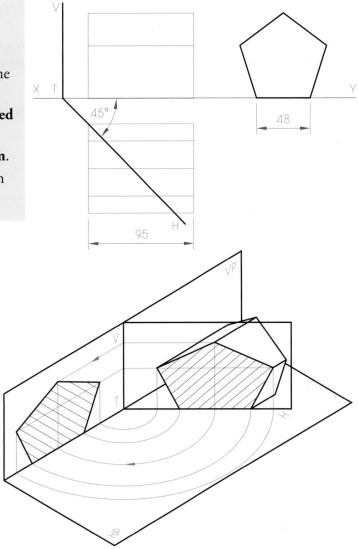

1. The end view, plan and elevation of the truncated prism are drawn in the normal manner.

2. The true shape of the section can be determined by **rabatting** the cutting plane into the vertical plane as illustrated over. The axis of rotation, which is the VT, appears as a point in plan which means that points on the section will rotate in an arc of a circle in this view.

3. Points on the section will move at right angles to the axis of rotation (VT) in elevation allowing the true shape to be completed as shown below.

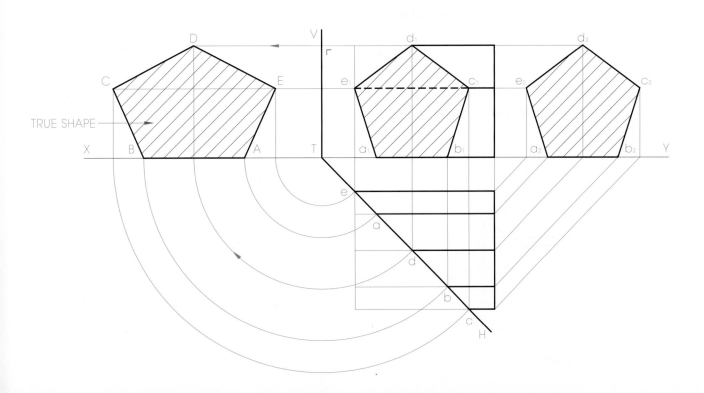

Alternative Method of Determining the True Shape

The true shape of the section can also be determined by drawing an auxiliary elevation of the section in which the viewing direction is perpendicular to the plane of the section as shown below.

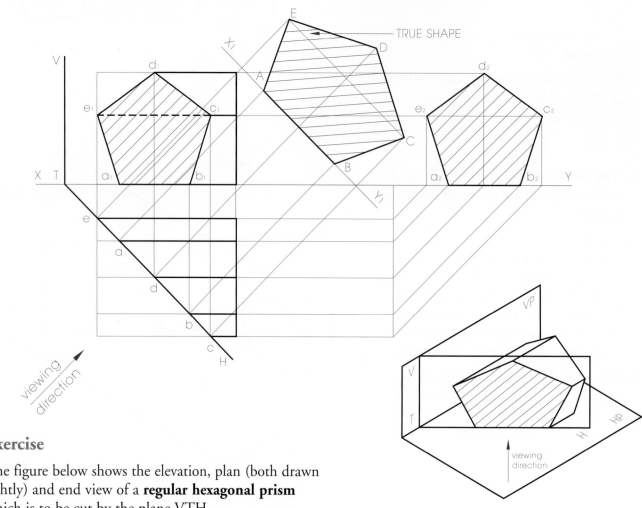

Exercise

The figure below shows the elevation, plan (both drawn lightly) and end view of a **regular hexagonal prism** which is to be cut by the plane VTH.

(a) Draw the end view and plan of the **truncated prism**.

(b) Project the elevation of the **truncated prism**.

(c) Determine the **true shape** of the cut section of the solid.

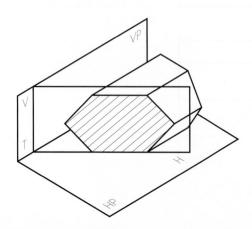

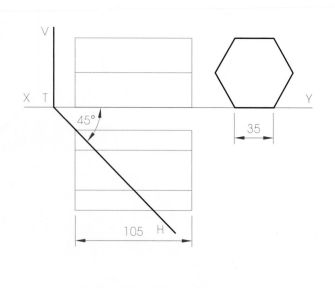

Cylinders

The curved surface of a cylinder can be generated by rotating a straight line about its axis as illustrated across. This means that the curved surface is made up of an infinite number of straight lines, which are called **elements**.

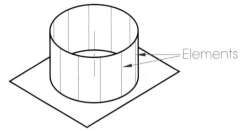

Example

The elevation and incomplete plan of a **truncated cylinder** are shown.

(a) Draw the complete plan, elevation and end view of the truncated cylinder.

(b) Determine the **true shape** of the cut section of the solid.

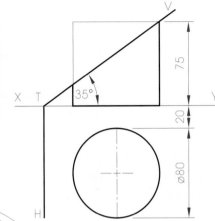

The solution is based on drawing twelve equally spaced elements on the cylinder as shown below and determining the appropriate projections of these truncated elements.

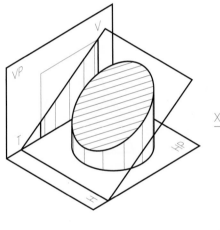

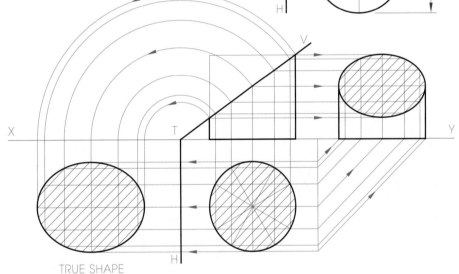

TRUE SHAPE

Exercise

The plan and incomplete elevation and end view of a solid which is to be cut by the plane VTH are shown below.

(a) Draw the end view, plan and elevation of the **truncated solid**.

(b) Determine the **true shape** of the cut section of the solid.

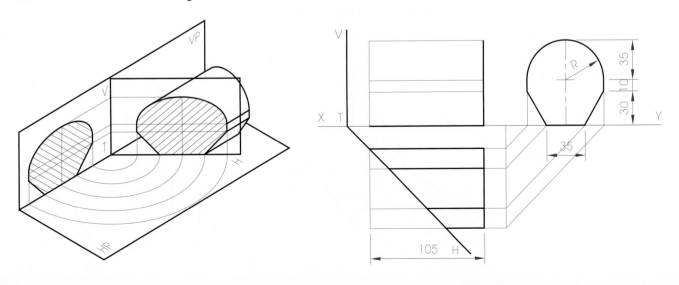

Cones

The curved surface of a cone can be generated by rotating a straight line about its axis as illustrated across. This means that the curved surface is made up of an infinite number of straight lines, which are called **elements**.

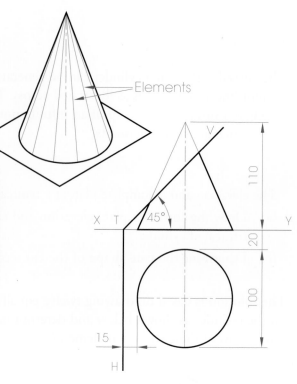

Example

The figure over shows the elevation and incomplete plan of a **truncated cone**. Draw the complete elevation, plan and end view of the **truncated cone** and determine the true shape of the cut section of the solid.

As with the cylinder the solution is based on drawing twelve equally spaced elements on the cone and determining the appropriate projections of these truncated elements.

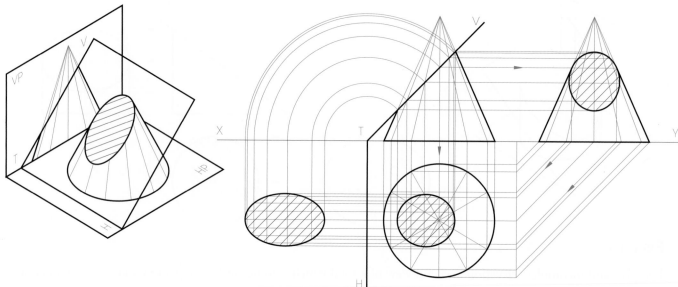

Exercise

The elevation and incomplete plan of a **truncated solid** are shown.

(a) Draw the elevation and plan of the **truncated solid**.

(b) Project an end view of the **truncated solid**.

(c) Determine the **true shape** of the cut section of the solid.

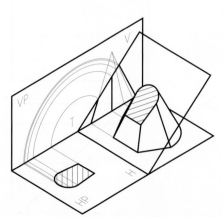

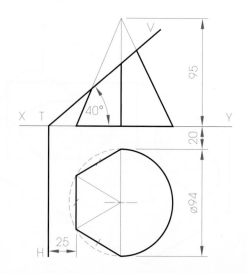

Answer Worksheets 22C, 22D and 22E

True Length using Rotation

A line will appear in true length in an elevation in which the viewing direction is at right angles to the plan of the line.

Consider the cone shown over. The extreme elements, OA and OB, in elevation appear in true length in this view. This is because the viewing direction for the elevation is perpendicular to the plan of these lines. This facilitates a useful method of finding the true length of a line.

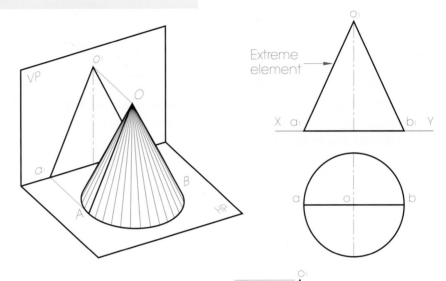

Example

Determine the **true length** of the edge OA of the **square-based pyramid** shown over.

1. Imagine that the line OA is an element of a cone as illustrated below, left.

2. Its true length can be determined by drawing an extreme element of this cone in elevation as shown below, right.

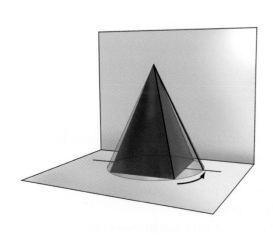

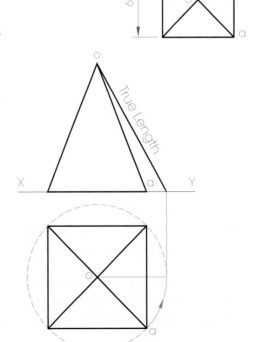

Chapter 23
Rotation of Objects

In this chapter, we will consider **rotations** of two-dimensional objects about a vertical axis and about a horizontal axis.

Example
The figure shows the elevation and plan of a **direction sign**. The sign is pointing in an easterly direction.

(a) Draw the given elevation.

(b) On the same XY line, draw the elevation when the flag is pointing in a south-westerly direction as indicated by the dotted line in the plan.

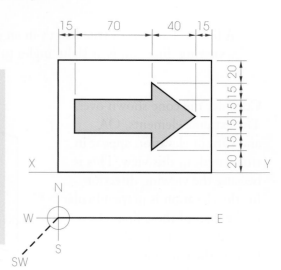

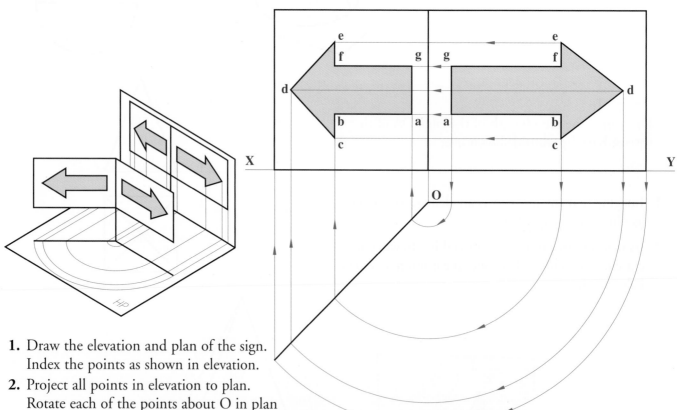

1. **Draw the elevation and plan of the sign.** Index the points as shown in elevation.

2. **Project all points in elevation to plan.** Rotate each of the points about O in plan so that all points lie in a south-westerly direction.

3. **Project the rotated points to elevation.**

4. **The height of each point remains unchanged.** Project the elevation of the points across horizontally to locate points on the image. Join the points in order to complete the solution.

> When the axis of rotation (hinge line) appears as a point in plan:
> • the points will rotate in an arc of a circle in this view.
> • the points will move at right angles to the axis of rotation in elevation.

Exercises

1. The figure below shows the elevation and plan of a **sign** for a **golf course**. The sign is pointing in an easterly direction.

   (a) Draw the given elevation.

   (b) On the same XY line, draw the elevation when the flag is pointing in a south-westerly direction as indicated by the dotted line in the plan.

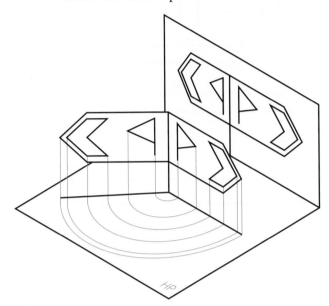

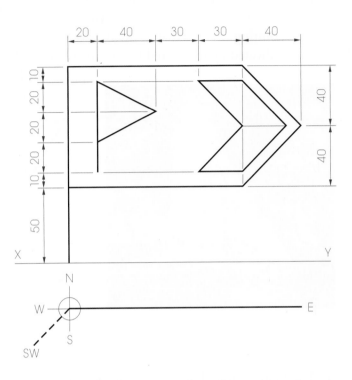

2. The figure shows the elevation and plan of a **road sign.** The sign is pointing in a westerly direction.

   (a) Draw the given elevation.

   (b) On the same XY line, draw the elevation when the flag is pointing in a south-easterly direction as indicated by the dotted line in the plan.

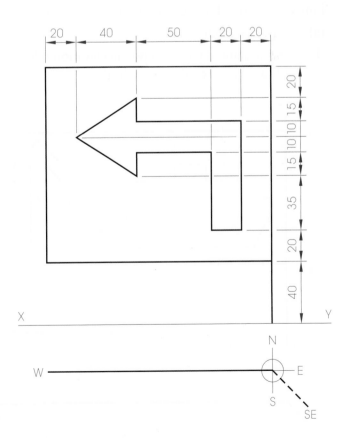

3. The figure across shows the elevation and plan of a **sailboat**. The sail containing the letters 'EI' is pointing in an easterly direction.

    (a) Draw the given plan and elevation.

    (b) On the same XY line, draw the elevation of the sail containing the letters when it is pointing in a south-westerly direction as indicated by the dotted line in the plan.

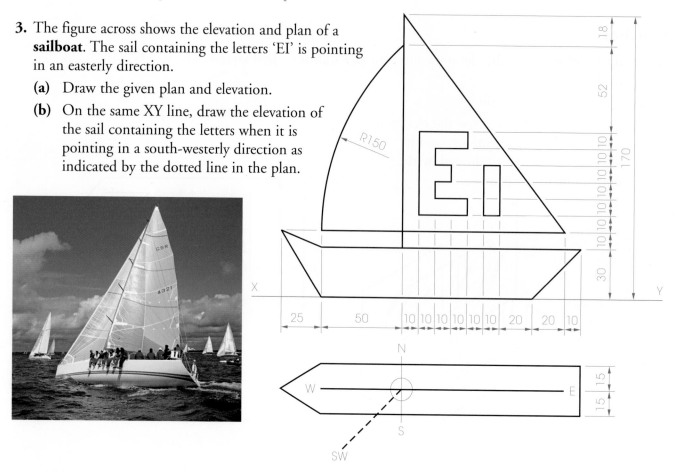

4. The figure below shows the elevation and plan of a **road direction sign** for a **ferry**. It is drawn on a 10 mm square grid. The sign is pointing in an easterly direction.

    (a) Draw the given elevation.

    (b) On the same XY line, draw the elevation when the sign is pointing in a south-westerly direction as indicated by the dotted line in the plan.

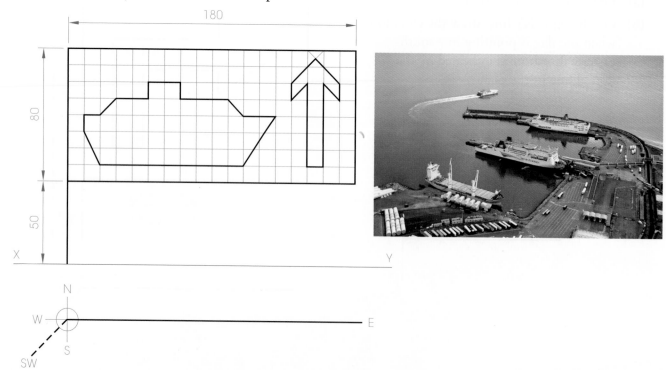

Example

The figure shows the elevation and plan of a flag containing a logo.

The flag is flying in an easterly direction.

(a) Draw the given elevation.

(b) On the same XY line, draw the elevation when the flag is flying in a south-westerly direction as indicated by the dotted line in the plan.

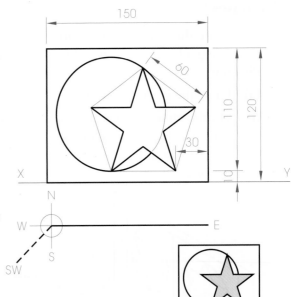

1. Draw the elevation and plan of the flag. Index the points as shown. The chords AF and DF are bisected to locate the centre K of the circle.

2. Project all points in elevation to plan. Rotate each of the points about O in plan so that all points lie in a south-westerly direction.

3. Project the rotated points to elevation. Project the elevation of the points across horizontally to locate points on the required image. Notice that the circle appears as an ellipse.

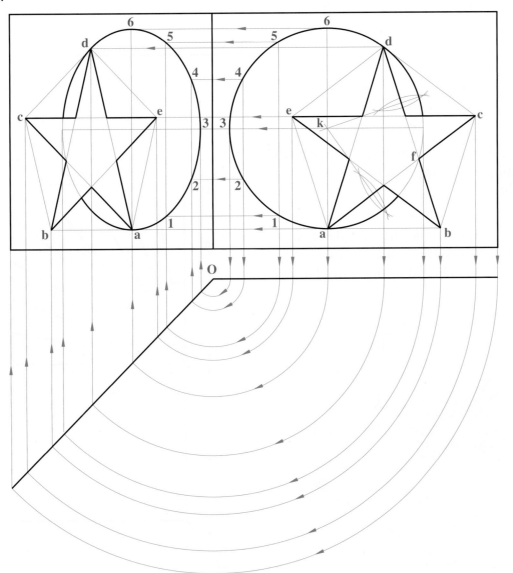

Exercises

1. The figure shows the elevation and plan of a flag containing a logo. The flag is flying in a westerly direction.

   (a) Draw the given elevation.

   (b) On the same XY line, draw the elevation when the flag is flying in a south-easterly direction as indicated by the dotted line in the plan.

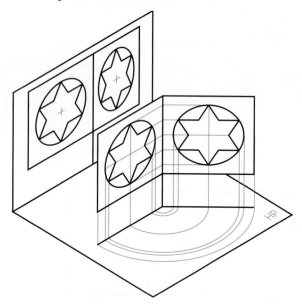

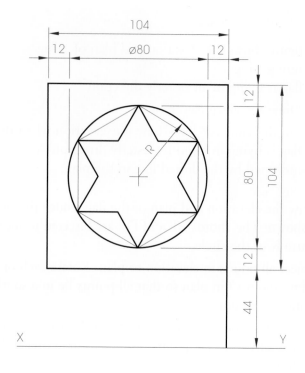

2. The figure shows the elevation and plan of a **GAA county supporters' flag**. The flag is flying in an easterly direction.

   (a) Draw the given elevation.

   (b) On the same XY line, draw the elevation when the flag is flying in a south-westerly direction as indicated by the dotted line in the plan.

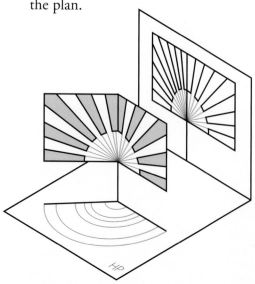

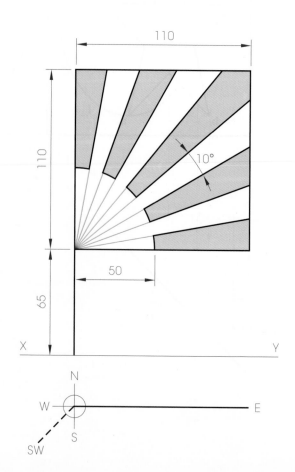

3. The figure across shows the elevation and plan of a flag containing a logo. The design contains an **equilateral triangle**, a **regular hexagon** and a **regular octagon**. The flag is flying in an easterly direction.

(a) Draw the given elevation.

(b) On the same XY line, draw the elevation when the flag is flying in a south-westerly direction as indicated by the dotted line in the plan.

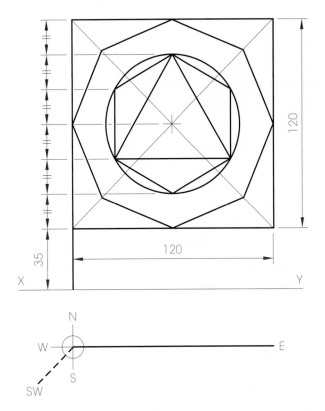

4. The figure shows the elevation and plan of a **stable door**. The door is in two parts, the top part and the bottom part.

(a) Draw the given elevation.

(b) On the same XY line, draw the elevation when the bottom part is opened through an angle of 135° as indicated by the dotted line in the plan.

(c) On the same XY line, draw the elevation when the top part is opened through an angle of 150° as indicated by the dotted line in the plan.

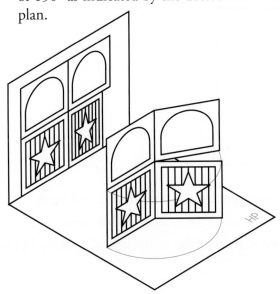

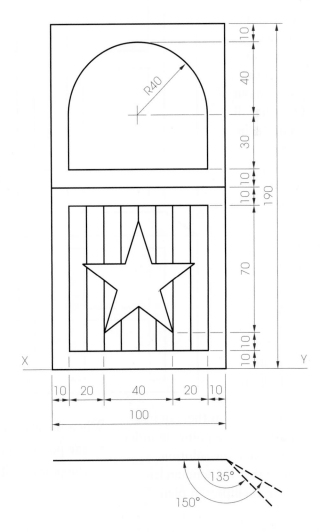

Example

The figure shows the elevation and end view of a sign for a **Hewlett Packard** cartridge box stand. The sign can rotate as shown.

(a) Draw the given views.

(b) Draw the plan of the sign when it has rotated to a position at 45° to the vertical plane as indicated by the dotted line in the end view.

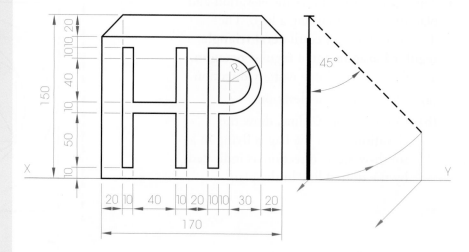

1. Draw the elevation and end view of the sign. Project all points in elevation to end view and rotate each of the points about O so that all points lie in a plane at 45° to the vertical plane as shown.

2. Project the rotated points to plan. Project the elevation of the points vertically to plan to locate points on the required image. Join the points in order to complete the solution. Notice that the semicircles appear as ellipses in plan.

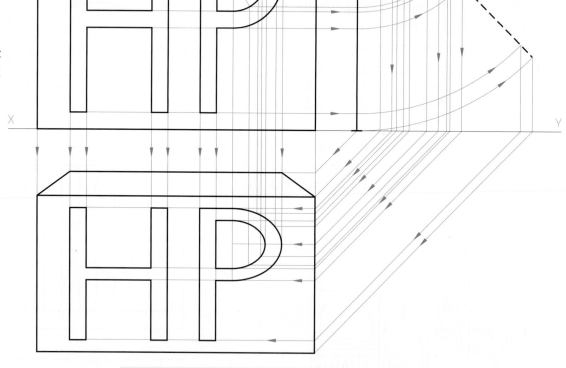

When the axis of rotation appears as a point in the end view:
- the points will rotate in an arc of a circle in this view.
- the points will move at right angles to the axis of rotation in plan.

Exercises

1. The figure shows the elevation and end view of a **hanging sign** which can sway in the wind.

   (a) Draw the given views.

   (b) Draw the plan of the sign when it has blown to a position at 45° to the vertical plane as indicated by the dotted line in the end view.

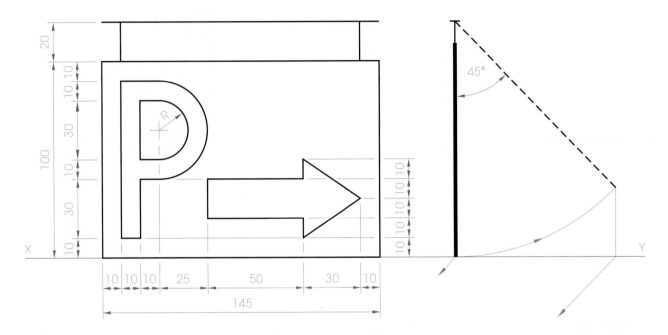

2. The figure below shows the elevation and end view of an **emergency exit sign** which can rotate. The sign is drawn on a grid of 10 mm squares.

   (a) Draw the given views.

   (b) Draw the plan of the sign when it has blown to a position at 45° to the vertical plane as indicated by the dotted line in the end view.

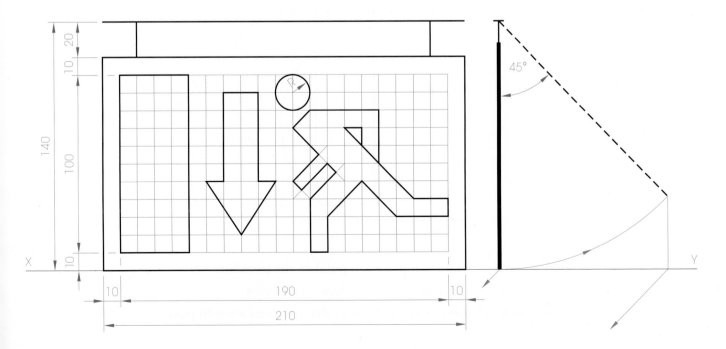

Example

The elevation and plan of a **CD case** are shown in the figure across.

The cover of the case contains a logo based on a regular hexagon.

(a) Draw the given elevation and plan.

(b) Project an end elevation in the direction of arrow A to show the cover of the case in the open position, as indicated by the broken line in elevation.

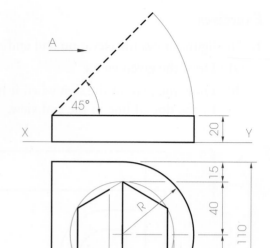

1. Draw the elevation, plan and end view of the CD case. Project all points in plan to elevation and rotate each of the points about O so that all points lie in a plane at 45° to the horizontal plane.

2. Project the rotated points to end view. Project the plan of the points to the end view to locate points on the required image. Join the points in order to complete the solution. The semicircle appears as an ellipse in the end elevation.

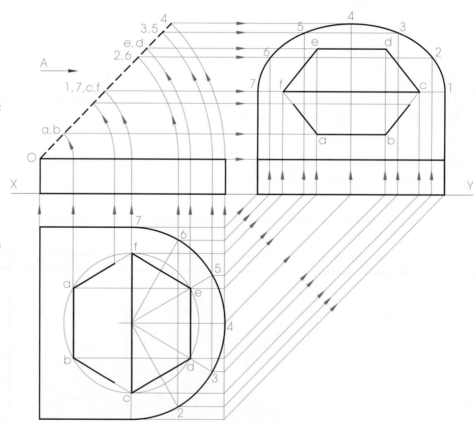

When the axis of rotation appears as a point in the elevation:

• the points will rotate in an arc of a circle in this view.

• the points will move at right angles to the axis of rotation in plan.

Exercises

1. The elevation and plan of a **technical graphics equipment box** are shown across.

The cover of the box contains a logo as shown in the plan.

(a) Draw the given elevation and plan.

(b) Project an end elevation in the direction of arrow A to show the cover of the box in the open position, as indicated by the broken line in elevation.

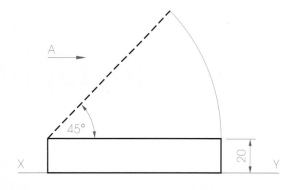

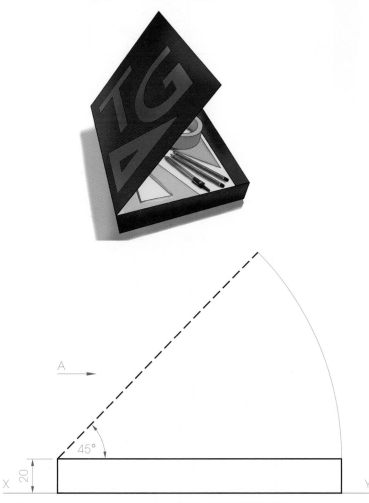

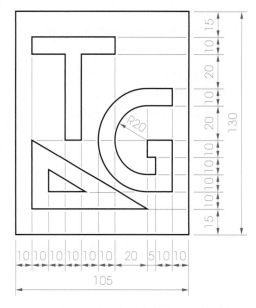

2. The elevation and plan of a **flip mobile phone** are shown.

The cover of the phone contains a logo as shown in the plan.

(a) Draw the given elevation and plan.

(b) Project an end elevation in the direction of arrow A to show the cover of the phone in the open position, as indicated by the broken line in elevation.

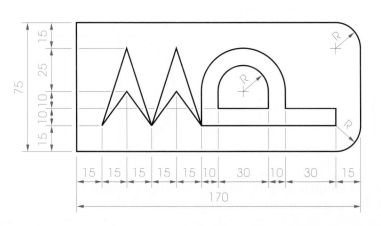

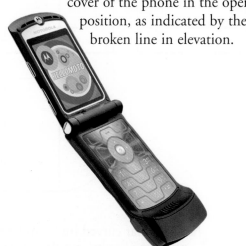

Chapter 24

Orthographic Projection 3

Noncircular curved lines in orthographic views

Example

The figure over shows a pictorial view of an **address platform**.

(a) Draw an **elevation** looking in the direction of arrow **A**.

(b) Draw an **end view** looking in the direction of arrow **B**.

(c) Draw a **plan** projected from (a) above.

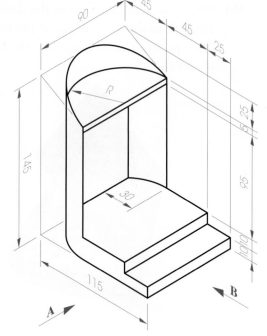

1. The elevation and incomplete end view are drawn as shown below, left.

2. The plan is then projected in the normal manner. Note that the sloped curved line on the platform appears as a semicircle in plan and a straight line in elevation.

3. Locate additional points (2–6) on the semicircle in plan and project them to the elevation.

4. Project these points from the plan and elevation to the end view as shown below, right, and draw a smooth curve to pass through them. Then complete the drawing as shown.

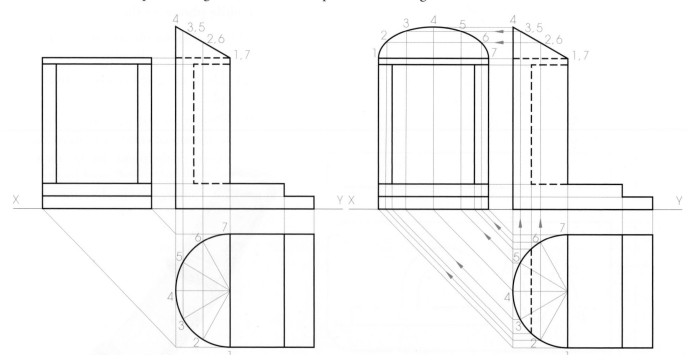

Non-circular curved lines can be drawn in an orthographic view by locating a sufficient number of points on the curve and drawing a smooth curve to pass through them.

Exercises

1. The figure over shows a pictorial view of a **desk-tidy**.

   (a) Draw an **elevation** looking in the direction of arrow **A**.

   (b) Draw an **end view** looking in the direction of arrow **B**.

   (c) Draw a **plan** projected from (a) above.

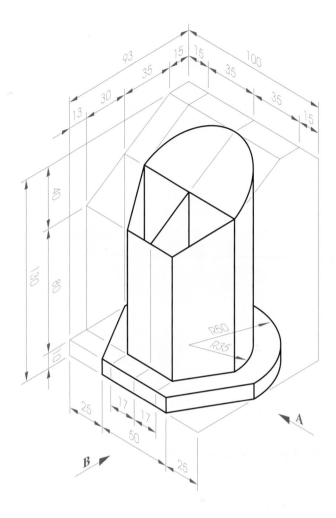

2. A pictorial view of a **hairdryer** is shown below.

   (a) Draw an **elevation** looking in the direction of the arrow **A**.

   (b) Draw an **end view** looking in the direction of the arrow **B**.

   (c) Draw a **plan** projected from (a) above.

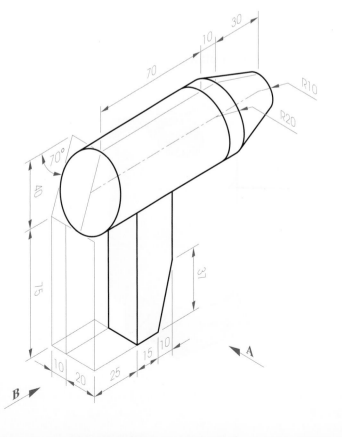

3. The figure over shows a pictorial view of a **solid**.

    (a) Draw an **elevation** looking in the direction of the arrow **A**.

    (b) Draw an **end view** looking in the direction of the arrow **B**.

    (c) Draw a **plan** projected from (a) above.

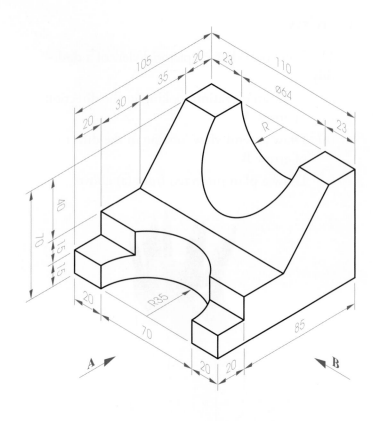

4. A pictorial view of a **hand wash dispenser** is shown over.

    (a) Draw an **elevation** looking in the direction of the arrow **A**.

    (b) Draw an **end view** looking in the direction of the arrow **B**.

    (c) Draw a **plan** projected from (a) above.

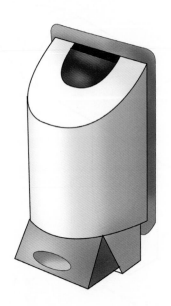

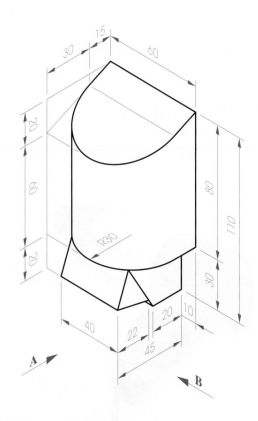

Example

The elevation and end view of a **bread bin** are shown below. Also shown is the direction of a new ground line X₁Y₁.

(a) Draw the given views of the bread bin.

(b) Draw a **plan** projected from the elevation.

(c) Draw an **auxiliary elevation** of the bread bin on the ground line X₁Y₁.

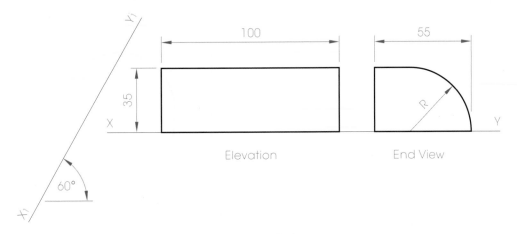

1. The elevation, end view and plan are drawn as shown below.

2. Draw the ground line X₁Y₁ in any convenient position and project points on the object from the plan at right angles to this ground line.

3. Transfer the height of 35 mm from the front elevation and line in the auxiliary elevation omitting the curves.

4. Locate additional points such as 2 and 3 on the end view of the quadrants and project these points to the plan.

5. Project these points from the plan to the auxiliary elevation and locate them by transferring the heights h₁ and h₂ from the end view as indicated below.

6. Complete the auxiliary view as shown.

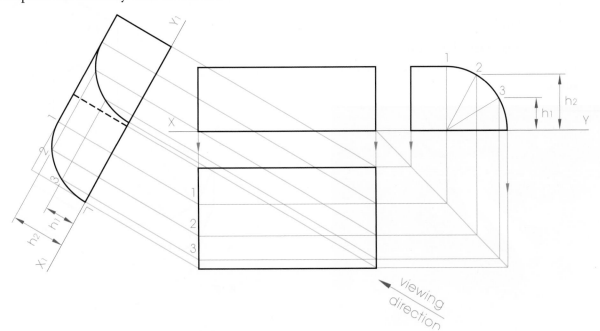

Exercises

1. The elevation and end view of a **treasure chest** are shown below. Also shown is the direction of a ground line X_1Y_1.

(a) Draw the given views of the treasure chest.

(b) Draw a **plan** projected from the elevation.

(c) Draw an **auxiliary elevation** of the treasure chest on the ground line X_1Y_1.

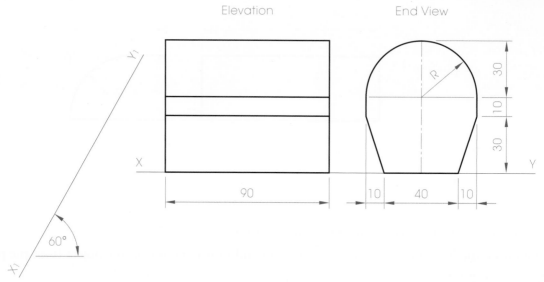

Elevation   End View

90   10 40 10

X_1Y_1 60°

2. The figure over shows a pictorial view of a **solid**.

(a) Draw an **elevation** looking in the direction of the arrow **A**.

(b) Draw an **end view** looking in the direction of the arrow **B**.

(c) Draw a **plan** projected from (a) above.

(d) Draw an **auxiliary elevation** of the *entire solid* which will show the true shape of the surface S.

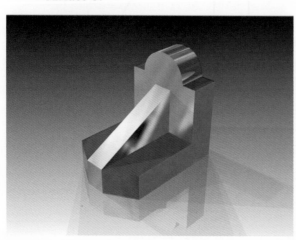

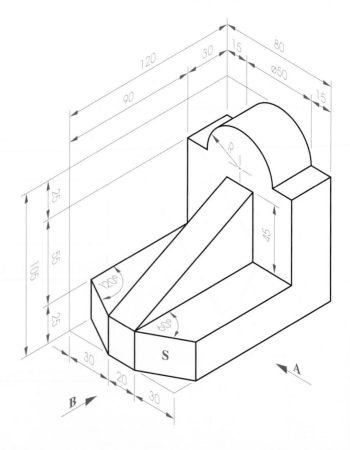

Example

A pictorial view of a **solid** is shown over.

(a)   Draw an **elevation** looking in the direction of the arrow **A**.

(b)   Draw an **end view** looking in the direction of the arrow **B**.

(c)   Draw a **plan** projected from (a) above.

(d)   Draw an **auxiliary elevation** of the *entire solid* which will show the true shape of the surface S.

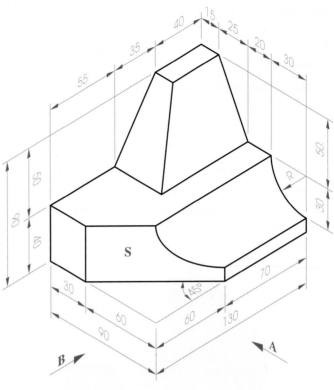

1. The elevation (excluding the curve), end view and plan are drawn in the normal manner.

2. Surface **S** appears as an edge (line) in plan. Therefore points on the curved line on surface **S** can be projected from the end view to meet this edge to locate them in plan.

3. These points can be located in elevation by projecting them from the plan and end view as shown below. Draw a smooth curve to pass through them to complete the elevation.

4. Draw the X_1Y_1 line parallel to the plan of surface **S**. Project points on the object from the plan at right angles to the new ground line.

5. Transfer the heights from the front elevation to the auxiliary elevation and line it in as shown below.

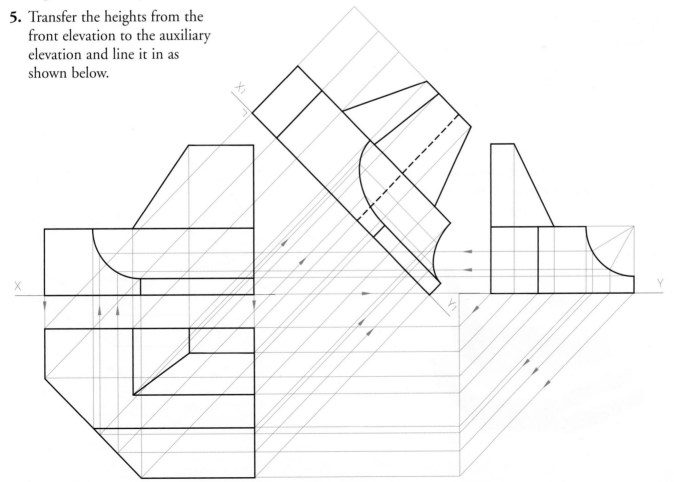

Exercises

1. A pictorial view of a **flight of steps** is shown over.

   (a) Draw an **elevation** looking in the direction of the arrow **A**.

   (b) Draw an **end view** looking in the direction of the arrow **B**.

   (c) Draw a **plan** projected from (a) above.

   (d) Draw an **auxiliary elevation** of the *entire solid* which will show the true shape of the surface S.

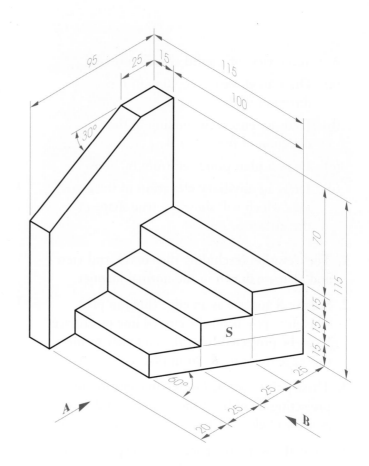

2. The figure over shows a pictorial view of a **solid**.

   (a) Draw an **elevation** looking in the direction of the arrow **A**.

   (b) Draw an **end view** looking in the direction of the arrow **B**.

   (c) Draw a **plan** projected from (a) above.

   (d) Draw an **auxiliary elevation** of the *entire solid* which will show the true shape of the surface S.

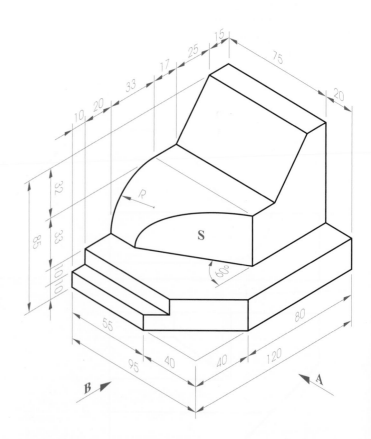

3. A pictorial view of a **solid** is shown below. A photo-realistic image of the solid is also shown.

(a) Draw an **elevation** looking in the direction of the arrow **A**.

(b) Draw an **end view** looking in the direction of the arrow **B**.

(c) Draw a **plan** projected from (a) above.

(d) Draw an **auxiliary elevation** of the *entire solid* which will show the true shape of the surface S.

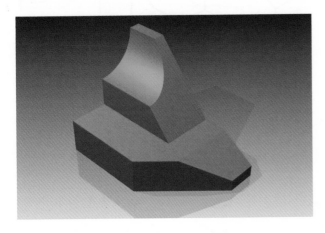

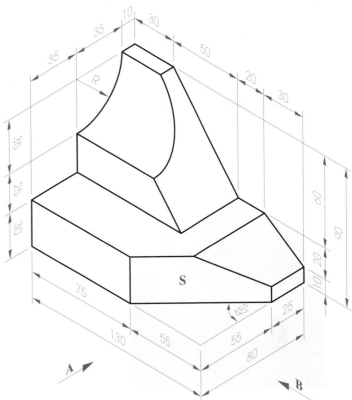

4. The figure over shows a pictorial view of a **structure**. Each step is of *equal height.*

(a) Draw an **elevation** looking in the direction of the arrow **A**.

(b) Draw an **end view** looking in the direction of the arrow **B**.

(c) Draw a **plan** projected from (a) above.

(d) Draw an **auxiliary elevation** of the *surface S* which will show its true shape.

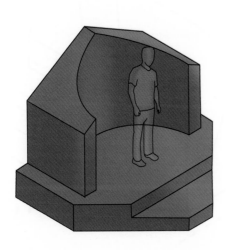

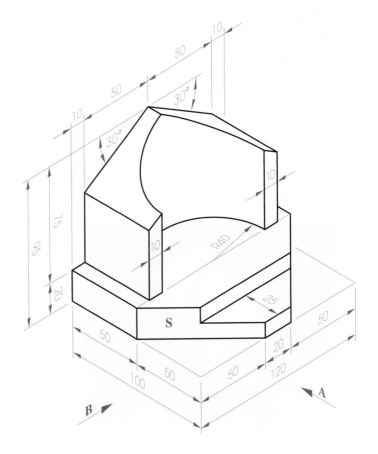

5. A pictorial view of a **coffee machine** is shown over.

  (a) Draw an **elevation** looking in the direction of the arrow **A**.

  (b) Draw an **end view** looking in the direction of the arrow **B**.

  (c) Draw a **plan** projected from (a) above.

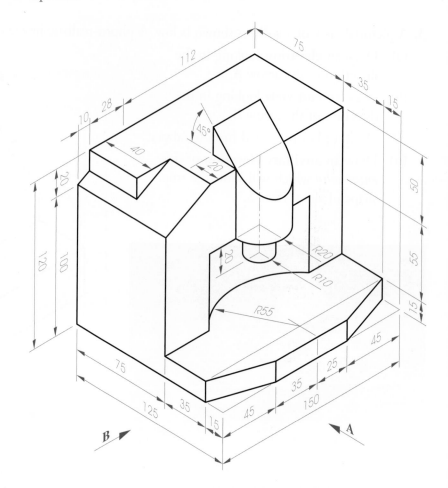

6. The figure below shows a pictorial view of a **solid**. A photo-realistic image of the solid is also shown.

  (a) Draw an **elevation** looking in the direction of the arrow **A**.

  (b) Draw an **end view** looking in the direction of the arrow **B**.

  (c) Draw a **plan** projected from (a) above.

  (d) Draw an **auxiliary elevation** of the *surface S* which will show its true shape.

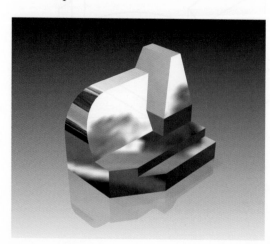

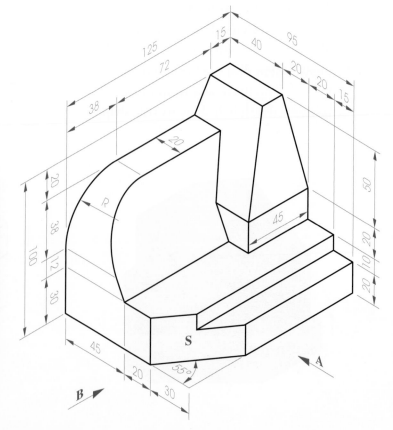

7. A pictorial view of a **digital camera** is shown over.

   (a) Draw an **elevation** looking in the direction of the arrow **A**.

   (b) Draw an **end view** looking in the direction of the arrow **B**.

   (c) Draw a **plan** projected from (a) above.

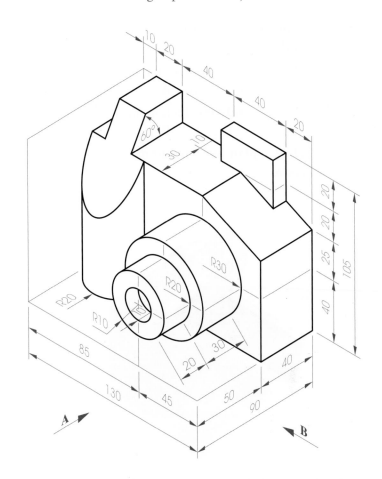

8. The figure below shows a pictorial view of a **solid**. A photo-realistic image of the solid is also shown.

   (a) Draw an **elevation** looking in the direction of the arrow **A**.

   (b) Draw an **end view** looking in the direction of the arrow **B**.

   (c) Draw a **plan** projected from (a) above.

   (d) Draw an **auxiliary elevation** of the *surface S* which will show its true shape.

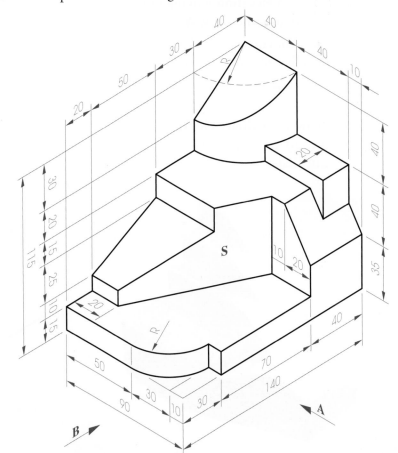

9. The figure over shows a pictorial view of a **camcorder**.

(a) Draw an **elevation** looking in the direction of the arrow **A**.

(b) Draw an **end view** looking in the direction of the arrow **B**.

(c) Draw a **plan** projected from (a) above.

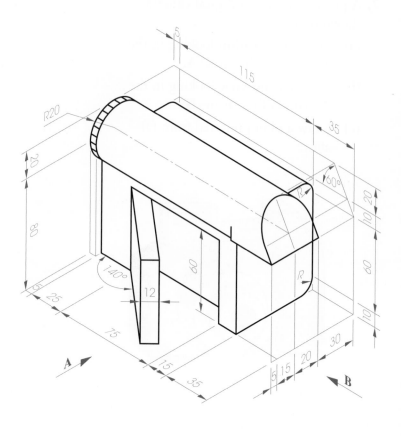

10. The figure below shows a pictorial view of a **solid**. A photo-realistic image of the solid is also shown.

(a) Draw an **elevation** looking in the direction of the arrow **A**.

(b) Draw an **end view** looking in the direction of the arrow **B**.

(c) Draw a **plan** projected from (a) above.

(d) Draw an **auxiliary elevation** of the *surface S* which will show its true shape.

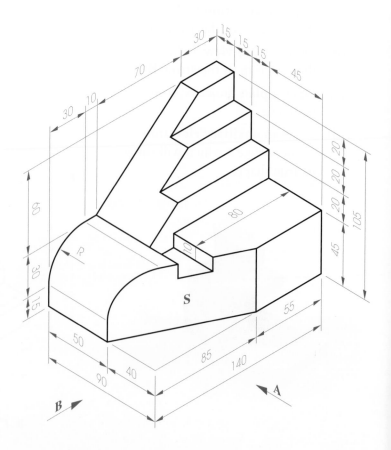

Chapter 25

Pictorial Drawing 3

Circles in Isometric Projection

In chapter 14 we used axonometric projection as an efficient means of producing an isometric projection of objects comprising plane surfaces. Now we shall turn our attention to objects which contain circular parts and curved surfaces.

> Circles appear elliptical in isometric projection.

Example

The incomplete isometric projection of a **printer** using the axonometric axes method is shown over. The elevation and plan are also shown in their required positions.

  (i) Draw the axonometric axes X, Y and Z.

 (ii) Draw the plan orientated at 45° as shown.

(iii) Draw the side elevation orientated at 15° as shown.

 (iv) Draw the completed axonometric projection.

1. Draw the axes, plan and elevation as shown.

2. Draw the incomplete axonometric projection shown in the normal manner, excluding the curve.

3. Locate two additional points 2 and 3 on the curve in plan as shown over, say offset by 20 mm for convenience.

4. Locate these points in elevation as shown.

5. Now locate points 2 and 3 in the axonometric projection by projecting them from the plan and elevation. Draw a smooth curve through points 1 to 4.

6. Repeat this process for the second curve.

7. Complete the axonometric projection in the normal manner.

> A curve can be determined in axonometric projection by projecting corresponding points on the curve from two given views.

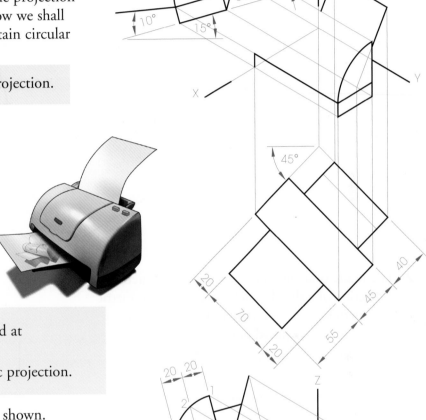

Exercises

1. The incomplete isometric projection of a **bread bin** using the axonometric axes method is shown below. The front and side elevations are also shown in their required positions.

   (i) Draw the axonometric axes X, Y and Z.

   (ii) Draw the elevations orientated at 15° as shown.

   (iii) Draw the completed axonometric projection.

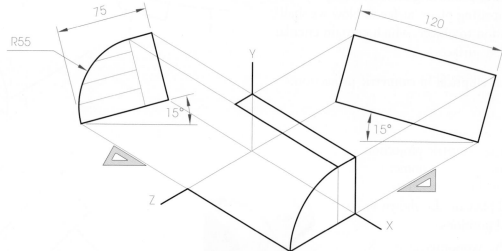

2. The figure over shows the incomplete isometric projection of a **dog kennel** using the axonometric axes method. The elevation and plan are also shown in their required positions.

   (i) Draw the axonometric axes X, Y and Z.

   (ii) Draw the plan orientated at 45° as shown.

   (iii) Draw the elevation orientated at 15° as shown.

   (iv) Draw the completed axonometric projection.

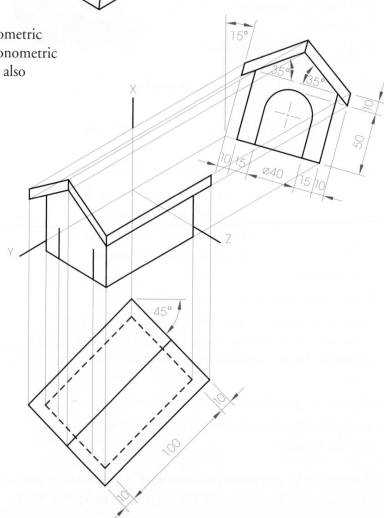

3. The incomplete isometric projection of a **Celebrations box** using the axonometric axes method is shown over. The box is based on a *regular octagonal prism.* The end elevation and plan are also shown in their required positions.

(i) Draw the axonometric axes X, Y and Z.

(ii) Draw the plan orientated at 45° as shown.

(iii) Draw the elevation orientated at 15° as shown.

(iv) Draw the completed axonometric projection.

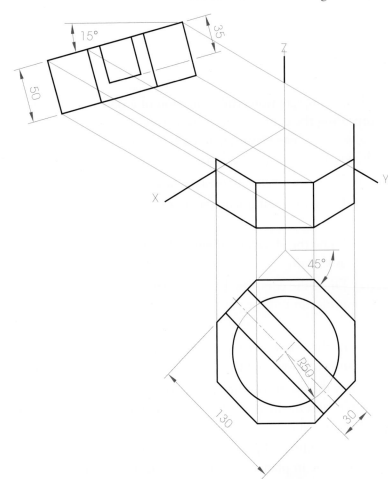

4. The figure below shows the incomplete isometric projection of a **bird feeder** using the axonometric axes method. The front and side elevations, which are identical, are also shown in their required positions.

(i) Draw the axonometric axes X, Y and Z.

(ii) Draw the side elevations orientated at 15° as shown.

(iii) Draw the completed axonometric projection.

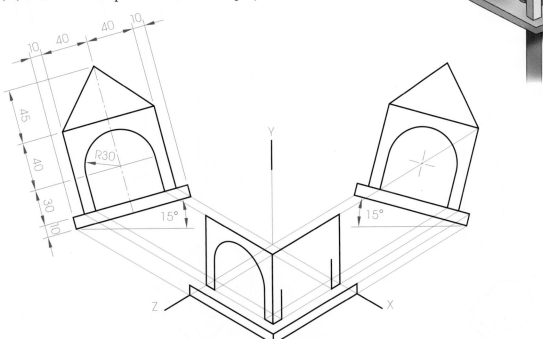

Cylinders in Isometric Projection

Example

The incomplete isometric projection of a **pen top** using the axonometric axes method is shown over. The elevation and plan are also shown in their required positions.

  (i) Draw the axonometric axes X, Y and Z.

  (ii) Draw the plan orientated at 45° as shown.

  (iii) Draw the elevation orientated at 15° as shown.

  (iv) Draw the completed axonometric projection of the pen top.

1. Draw the axonometric axes, plan and elevation as shown below, right.

2. Draw the given incomplete axonometric projection in the normal manner excluding the semi-ellipse.

3. Locate additional points (2 to 6) on the semicircle in plan as shown using, say a 13 mm offset for convenience.

4. Locate these points in elevation as shown.

5. Project these points from the plan and elevation to the axonometric projection and join the points where corresponding lines meet with a smooth curve.

6. Repeat this process for the bottom curve as appropriate.

7. Complete the axonometric projection by locating the tangent as shown below, left.

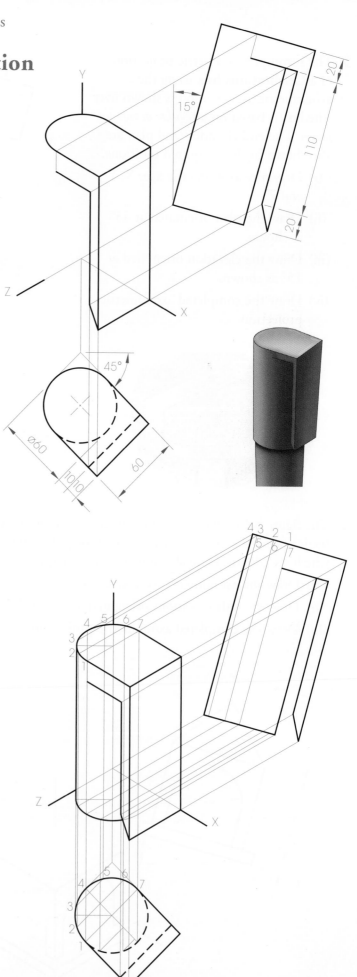

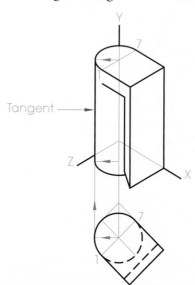

Exercises

1. The figure over shows the incomplete isometric projection of a **component** using the axonometric axes method. The elevation and plan are also shown in their required positions.

  (i) Draw the axonometric axes X, Y and Z.

 (ii) Draw the plan orientated at 45° as shown.

(iii) Draw the elevation orientated at 15° as shown.

(iv) Draw the completed axonometric projection.

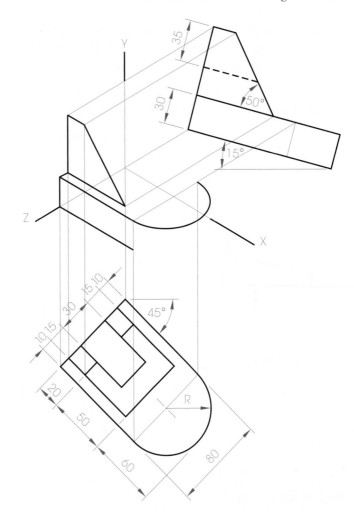

2. The figure below shows the incomplete isometric projection of an **archway** using the axonometric axes method. The front and side elevations are also shown in their required positions.

  (i) Draw the axonometric axes X, Y and Z.

 (ii) Draw the side elevations orientated at 15° as shown.

(iii) Draw the completed axonometric projection.

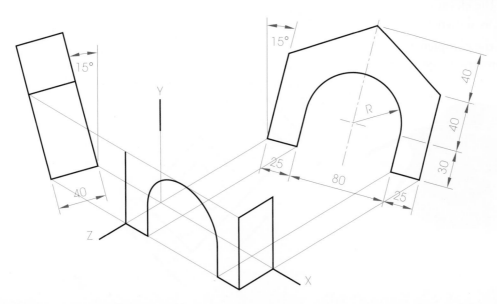

3. The incomplete isometric projection of a **treasure chest** using the axonometric axes method is shown below. The front and side elevations are also shown in their required positions.

   (i) Draw the axonometric axes X, Y and Z.

  (ii) Draw the elevations orientated at 15° as shown.

 (iii) Draw the completed axonometric projection.

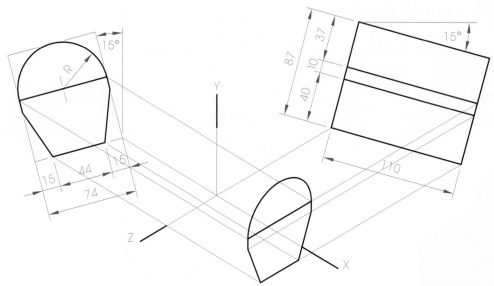

4. The figure over shows the incomplete isometric projection of a **whistle** using the axonometric axes method. The elevation and plan are also shown in their required positions.

   (i) Draw the axonometric axes X, Y and Z.

  (ii) Draw the plan orientated at 45° as shown.

 (iii) Draw the elevation orientated at 15° as shown.

 (iv) Draw the completed axonometric projection.

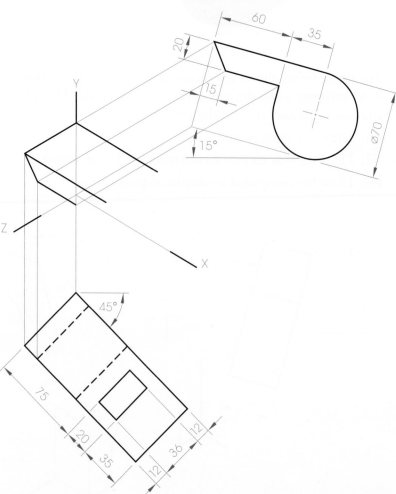

5. The incomplete isometric projection of a **Grandfather clock** using the axonometric axes method is shown over. The elevation and plan are also shown in their required positions.

(i) Draw the axonometric axes X, Y and Z.

(ii) Draw the plan orientated at 45° as shown.

(iii) Draw the elevation orientated at 15° as shown.

(iv) Draw the completed axonometric projection.

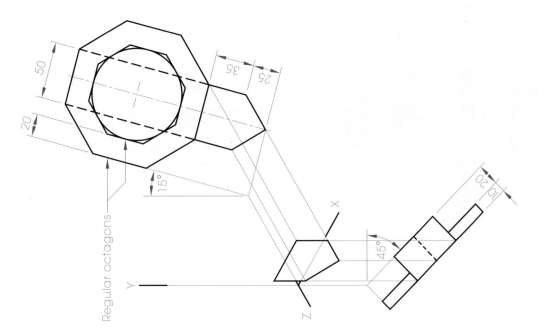

Regular octagons

Spheres in Isometric Projection

A sphere appears as a circle in isometric projection.

This is because the circle that forms the outline of a sphere relative to the relevant viewing direction is parallel to the plane of projection. As a result this circle appears in true shape.

Example 1

The isometric projection of a **fountain** using the axonometric axes method is shown over.

The sphere is determined in the axonometric projection by:

(i) locating the centre of the sphere.

(ii) using this as centre to draw a circle of radius 30 mm.

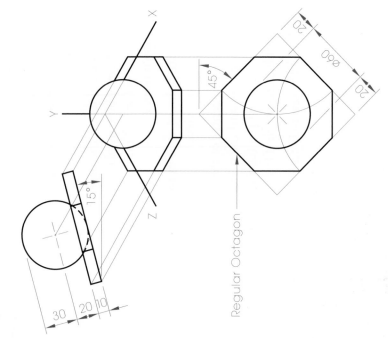

Regular Octagon

Example 2

The incomplete isometric projection of a **stamp** using the axonometric axes method is shown over. The end elevation and plan are also shown in their required positions.

(i) Draw the axonometric axes X, Y and Z.

(ii) Draw the plan orientated at 45° as shown.

(iii) Draw the end elevation orientated at 15° as shown.

(iv) Draw the completed axonometric projection of the stamp.

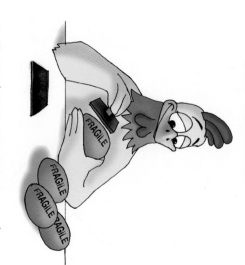

1. Draw the axonometric axes, plan and end elevation in the normal manner.

2. Draw the axonometric projection of the base of the stamp as shown over.

3. Locate points on the base of the hemisphere in plan and end elevation (say 12 mm offset) as shown over.

4. Locate points 1 to 6 in the axonometric view.

5. Locate the centre of the hemisphere and the major axis of the semi-ellipse (construction highlighted overleaf).

6. Draw the semi-ellipse.

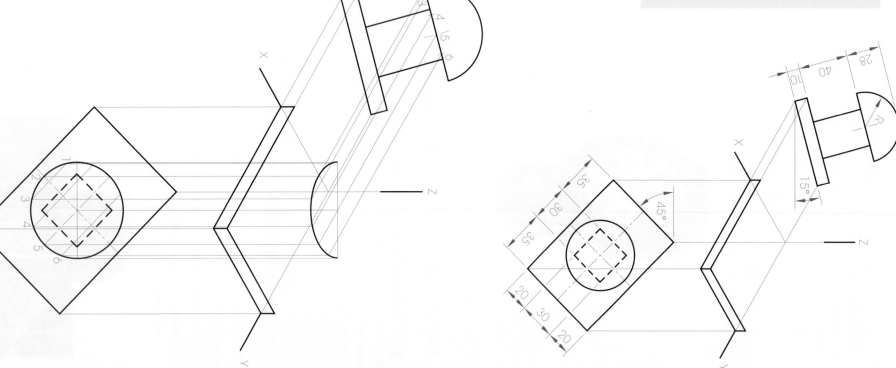

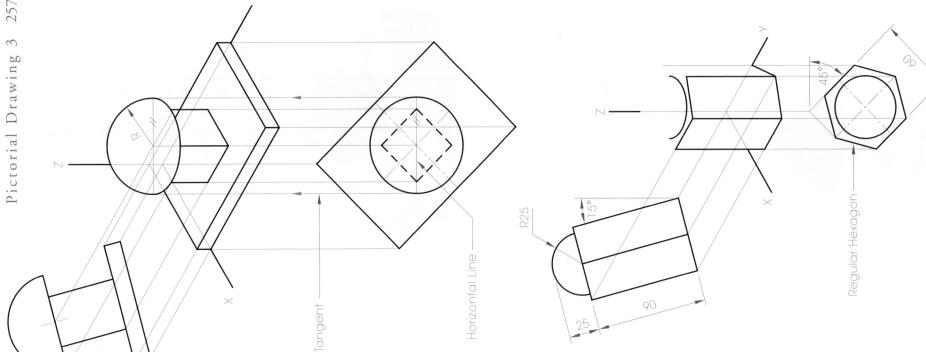

Tangent

Horizontal Line

Regular Hexagon

7. Draw the semicircle of radius 28 mm to complete the hemisphere.

8. Complete the axonometric projection as shown over. Note that some construction lines have been omitted for the purposes of clarity.

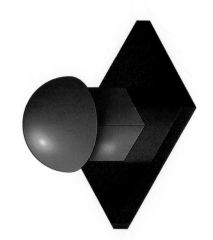

Exercises

1. The figure over shows the incomplete isometric projection of a **salt container** using the axonometric axes method. The side elevation and plan are also shown in their required positions.

   (i) Draw the axonometric axes X, Y and Z.

   (ii) Draw the plan orientated at 45° as shown.

   (iii) Draw the side elevation orientated at 15° as shown.

   (iv) Draw the completed axonometric projection.

2. The axonometric axes required for the
   isometric projection of a **sculpture** are
   shown over. The elevation and plan are
   also shown in their required positions.

   (i) Draw the axonometric axes X, Y
       and Z.

   (ii) Draw the plan orientated at 45°
        as shown.

   (iii) Draw the elevation orientated at
         15° as shown.

   (iv) Draw the axonometric projection
        of the sculpture.

3. The figure over shows the axonometric
   axes required for the isometric projection
   of a **spinning top**. The elevation and
   plan are also shown in their required
   positions.

   (i) Draw the axonometric axes X, Y
       and Z.

   (ii) Draw the plan orientated at 45°
        as shown.

   (iii) Draw the elevation orientated at
         15° as shown.

   (iv) Draw the axonometric projection
        of the spinning top.

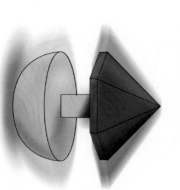

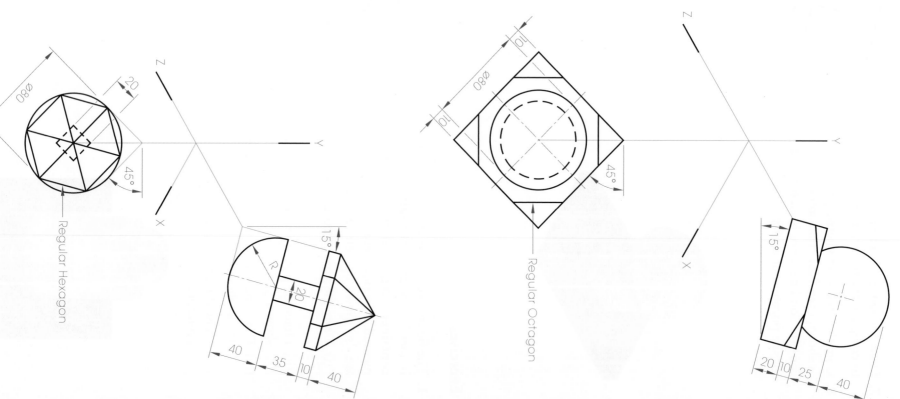

Regular Hexagon

Regular Octagon

4. The figure over shows the isometric projection of a **waste basket** using the axonometric axes method. The elevation and plan are also shown in their required positions.

    (i) Draw the axonometric axes X, Y and Z.

    (ii) Draw the plan orientated at 45° as shown.

    (iii) Draw the elevation orientated at 15° as shown.

    (iv) Draw the completed axonometric projection.

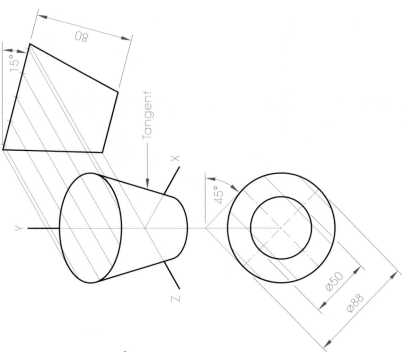

5. The incomplete isometric projection of a **hand basin and mirror** using the axonometric axes method are shown over. The elevation and plan are also shown in their required positions.

    (i) Draw the axonometric axes X, Y and Z.

    (ii) Draw the plan orientated at 45° as shown.

    (iii) Draw the elevation orientated at 15° as shown.

    (iv) Draw the completed axonometric projection.

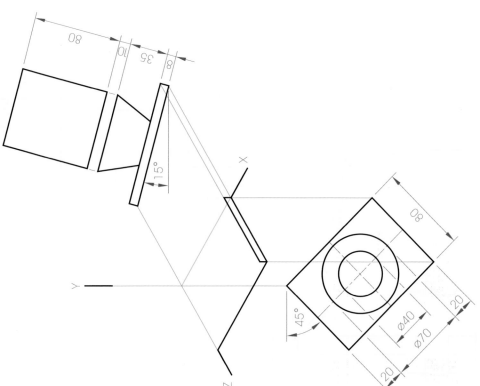

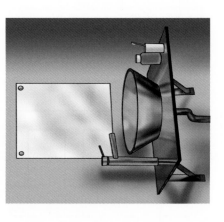

Perspective Drawing

Perspective Drawings closely resemble what you actually see. They do, for example, reflect the following types of observations:

- When strands of wire in a fence are parallel they appear to meet at a point in the distance at eye level, which we call a **vanishing point.**

- Fence posts which are equally spaced appear closer together as they become further away.

- The fence posts which we know to be the same size appear to get smaller as they move away.

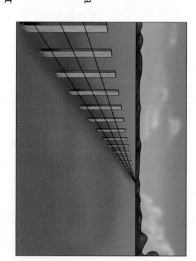

One-point Perspective

Example

The figure over shows an isometric view of a letter **H.** Draw a **one-point perspective view** of the letter:

1. Draw the front face of the letter full-size. Then draw the horizon line which determines the eye level of the observer.
2. Choose and mark a location for the vanishing point (VP) on the horizon line. Then join the corners of the H to the vanishing point lightly as shown below, left.
3. Estimate the depth of the object and draw a line to represent an edge at the back of the letter.
4. Complete the drawing making the edges on the back surface parallel to the corresponding edges on the front surface as shown below, right.

Horizon Line   VP

Horizon Line   VP

Exercise

The elevation and plan of a number **1** and a letter **F** are shown over. Draw a **one-point perspective view** of each separately.

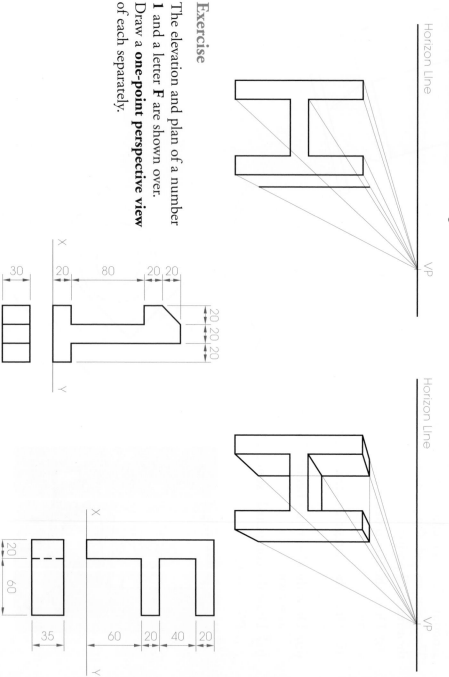

Two-point Perspective

Example 1
Make a **two-point perspective drawing** of the **steps** shown over.

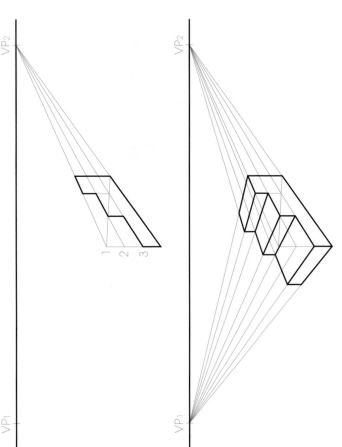

1. Draw the leading edge of the box into which the steps fits lightly and draw the horizon line which determines the eye level of the observer.

2. Choose and mark the location for the vanishing points on the horizon line. Then mark off the height of each step on the leading edge and draw lines from these points to VP_2.

3. Estimate the overall length of the steps and draw a vertical line to represent the rear edge of the steps as shown over, top.

4. The length of the steps will appear to decrease as they become further away. Drawing the diagonal shown to intersect the lines from 2 and 3 gives the correct diminishing lengths. Line in the front face.

5. Draw light lines from each corner of the front face to VP_1 and estimate the width of the steps.

6. Complete the drawing as shown over, bottom.

In two-point perspective vertical lines remain vertical and any set of parallel horizontal lines meet at a vanishing point on the horizon line.

Example 2
Complete the **two-point perspective drawing** of the **dog kennel** shown over, top.

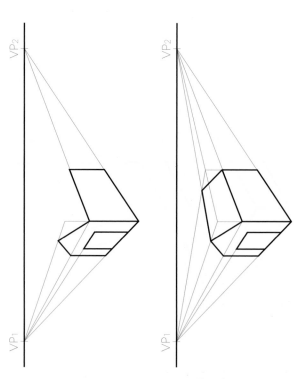

The drawing can be completed by *boxing* it in as shown over, bottom.

Answer Worksheets 25A, 25B and 25C

Exploded Isometric Views

The figure over shows a pictorial view of the parts for a **bread bin** when they have been moved apart. Such a view is known as an **exploded view**. Exploded views are useful to show how objects are assembled from their component parts.

> Objects must be **exploded** parallel to the principal axes.

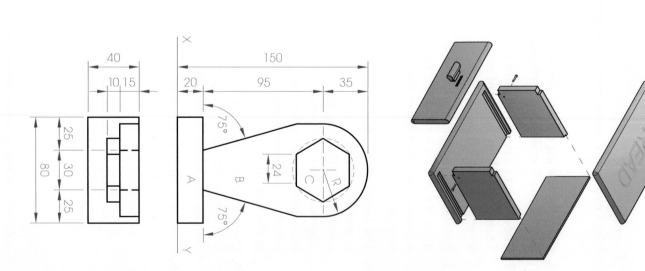

Example

The figure over shows the elevation and plan of a **trophy** which is made up of three parts A, B and C. Draw an **exploded isometric view** of the trophy.

The exploded view simply involves drawing an isometric view of the individual parts when they have been exploded parallel to the isometric axes as shown below.

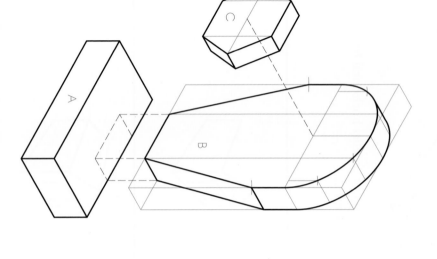

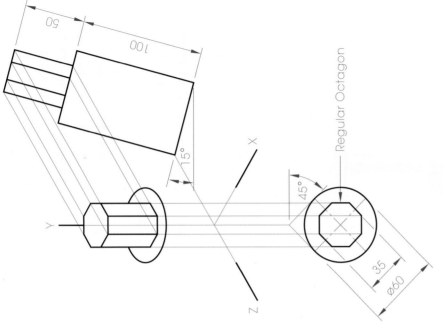

Regular Octagon

50

100

15°

45°

35

Ø60

X

Y

Z

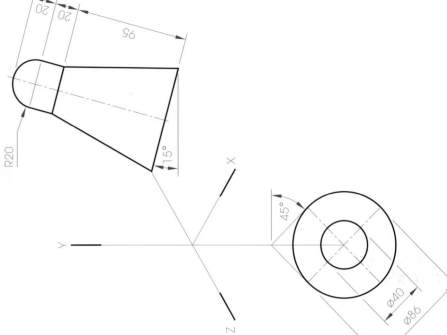

R20

20

20

95

15°

45°

Ø40

Ø86

X

Y

Z

Exercises

1. The incomplete isometric projection of a **Tippex bottle** using the axonometric axes method is shown over. The elevation and plan are also shown in their required positions.

   (i) Draw the axonometric axes X, Y and Z.

   (ii) Draw the plan orientated at 45° as shown.

   (iii) Draw the elevation orientated at 15° as shown.

   (iv) Draw the completed axonometric projection.

2. The figure over shows the axonometric axes required for the isometric projection of the three surfaces of a **badminton shuttle**. The elevation and plan are also shown in their required positions.

   (i) Draw the axonometric axes X, Y and Z.

   (ii) Draw the plan orientated at 45° as shown.

   (iii) Draw the elevation orientated at 15° as shown.

   (iv) Draw the axonometric projection of the three surfaces of the shuttle.

3. The figure over shows the axonometric axes required for the isometric projection of a **table lamp**. The elevation and plan are also shown in their required positions.

(i) Draw the axonometric axes X, Y and Z.

(ii) Draw the plan orientated at 45° as shown.

(iii) Draw the elevation orientated at 15° as shown.

(iv) Draw the axonometric projection of the table lamp.

Regular Octagon

4. The axonometric axes required for the isometric projection of a **plaque** are shown over. The front and side elevations are also shown in their required positions.

(i) Draw the axonometric axes X, Y and Z.

(ii) Draw the elevations orientated at 15° as shown.

(iii) Draw the axonometric projection of the plaque.

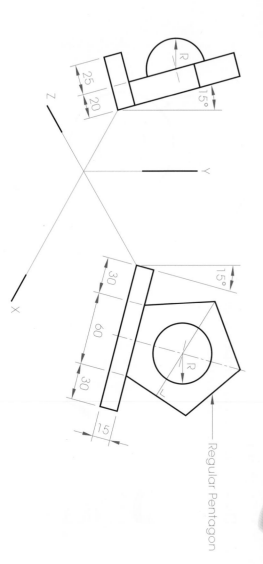

Regular Pentagon

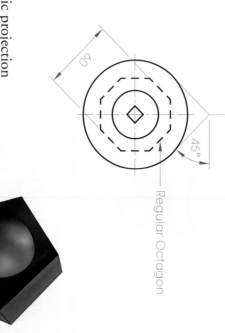

Chapter 26

Transformation Geometry 2

In Chapter 15 you studied the movement of shapes from one position to another under **translations**, **rotations**, **axial symmetries** and **central symmetries**. In this chapter, you will study the same four transformations at a more advanced level.

Example

The figure shown is subjected to transformations in the following order:

(i) Axial symmetry in the line QR.

(ii) Translation equal to QR.

(iii) Central symmetry in the point S.

Draw the given figure and determine the image figures in each of the transformations.

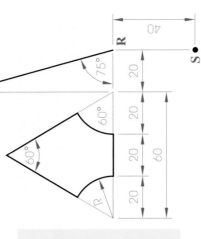

1. Draw the given figure and the line QR. Index the points of the figure as shown.

Draw lines from each of the points A, B and C perpendicular to QR and extend as shown. Locate A_1 so that A_1 is the same distance from QR as A. A_1 is the image of A under **axial symmetry** in the line QR.

Repeat the procedure for each of the points B and C. Join the points and complete the image figure.

2. Draw lines parallel to QR through each of the points A_1, B_1 and C_1. Locate A_2 so that the distance from A_1 to A_2 is equal to the length of QR. A_2 is the image of A_1 under the translation QR.

Repeat the procedure for each of the points B_1 and C_1. Join the points and draw the image figure on the right (bottom).

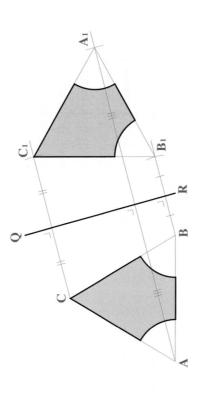

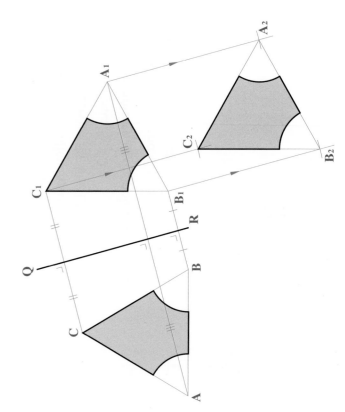

3. Locate the point S. Join A₂ to S and extend. Locate A₃ so that the distance from A₃ to S is equal to the distance from A₂ to S. A₃ is the image of A₂ under **central symmetry** in the point S.

Repeat the procedure for each of the points B₂ and C₂.

Join the points in order and complete the image of the figure under the central symmetry in the point S.

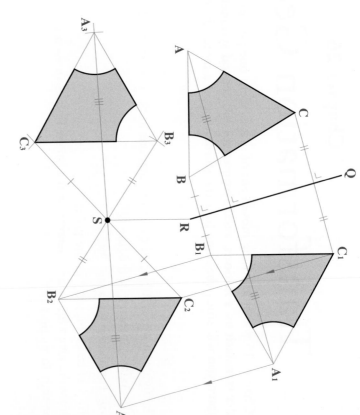

Exercises

1. The figure shown across is subjected to transformations in the following order:

(i) **Axial symmetry** in the line QR.

(ii) **Translation** equal to QR.

(iii) **Central symmetry** in the point R.

Draw the given figure and determine the image figures in each of the transformations.

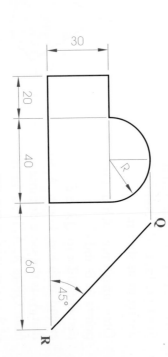

2. The figure shown over is subjected to transformations in the following order:

(i) **Axial symmetry** in the line LM.

(ii) **Translation** equal to LM.

(iii) **Central symmetry** in the point N.

Draw the given figure and determine the image figures in each of the transformations.

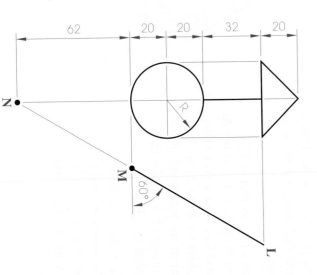

3. The figure of the rosette shown over is subjected to transformations in the following order:

   (i) **Axial symmetry** in the line QR.
   (ii) **Translation** equal to QR.
   (iii) **Central symmetry** in the point S.

   Draw the given figure and determine the image figures in each of the transformations.

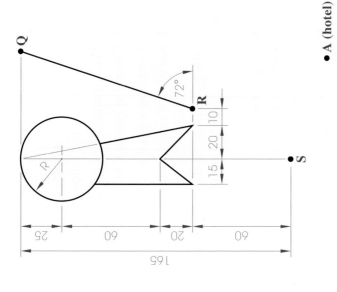

More on Translations and Axial Symmetries

Example 1

A pedestrian crossing is to be provided in order to facilitate hotel guests walking between the hotel (position A) and a leisure centre on the other side of the road (position B). Determine the position of the crossing that will minimise the journey involved.

The method of solution used involves *moving* the position of the leisure centre towards the road a distance equal to the width of the road (i.e. a **translation** from B).

The image point B_1 is then joined to A by the shortest path. B_1X of this path is then translated to position BY so that the road reaches B. XY is the position for the pedestrian crossing.

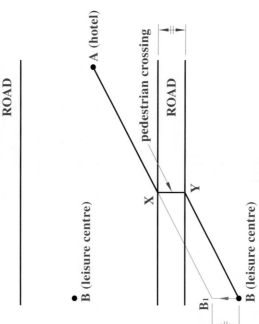

Example 2

Plot the path of the black ball if it is to enter the pocket marked P after being struck by the white ball.

The method of solution involves finding the image of the black ball B under an **axial symmetry** in the side MN (below, right). The image B_1 is joined to P intersecting the line MN at C. Join CB and CP. BCP is the path of the black ball.

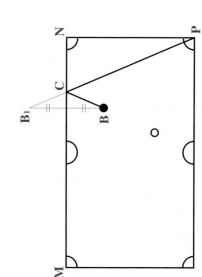

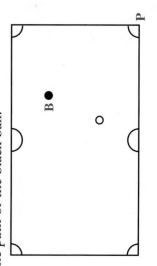

Example 3

The figure shown is subjected to transformations in the following order:

(i) **Axial symmetry** in the line QR.

(ii) **Central symmetry** in the point S.

(iii) **Translation** equal to ST.

(iv) **Rotation** clockwise about point R through an angle of 50°.

Draw the given figure and determine the image figures in each of the transformations.

1. Draw the given figure and the line QR. Index the points of the figure as shown.

   Draw lines from each of the points A, B and D perpendicular to QR and extend as shown. Locate A_1 so that A_1 is the same distance from QR as A. A_1 is the image of A under **axial symmetry** in the line QR.

   Repeat the procedure for each of the points B and D. Locate C_1, the midpoint of A_1D_1. Join the points and complete the image figure.

2. Locate the point S. Join A_1 to S and extend. Locate A_2 so that the distance from A_2 to S is equal to the distance from A_1 to S. A_2 is the image of A_1 under **central symmetry** in the point S.

   Repeat the procedure for each of the points B_1 and D_1. Locate C_2. Join the points in order and complete the image of the figure.

3. Locate the line ST. Draw lines parallel to ST through each of the points A_2, B_2 and D_2. Locate A_3 so that the distance from A_2 to A_3 is equal to the length of ST. A_3 is the image of A_2 under the **translation** ST.

   Repeat the procedure for each of the points B_2 and D_2. Locate C_3. Join the points and draw the image figure.

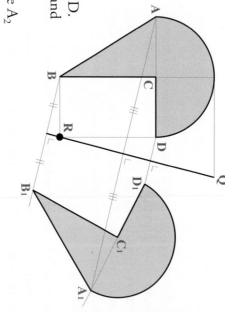

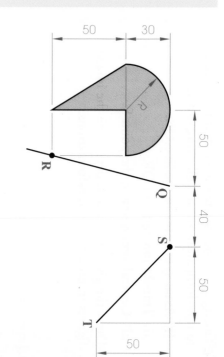

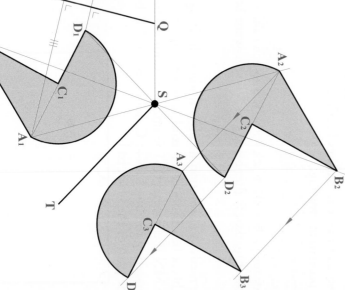

4. With R as centre and RA$_3$ as radius, draw an arc in a clockwise direction.

Join RA$_3$. Draw a line from R at an angle of 50° to RA$_3$ to locate A$_4$, the image of A$_3$.

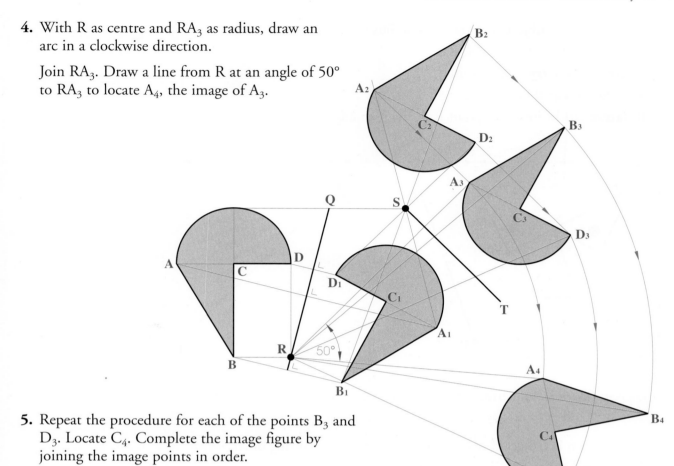

5. Repeat the procedure for each of the points B$_3$ and D$_3$. Locate C$_4$. Complete the image figure by joining the image points in order.

Exercises

1. The figure shown is subjected to transformations in the following order:
  (i) **Axial symmetry** in the line QR.
  (ii) **Central symmetry** in the point S.
  (iii) **Translation** equal to ST.
  (iv) **Rotation** clockwise about point R through an angle of 45°.

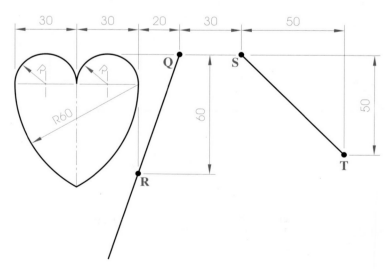

Draw the given figure and determine the image figures in each of the transformations.

2. The figure shown is subjected to transformations in the following order:

(i) **Axial symmetry** in the line QR.
(ii) **Central symmetry** in the point S.
(iii) **Translation** equal to ST.
(iv) **Rotation** clockwise about point R through an angle of 40°.

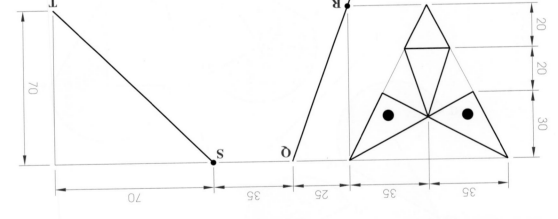

Draw the given figure and determine the image figures in each of the transformations.

3. The figure shown is subjected to transformations in the following order:

(i) **Axial symmetry** in the line QR.
(ii) **Central symmetry** in the point S.
(iii) **Translation** equal to ST.
(iv) **Rotation** clockwise about point S through an angle of 60°.

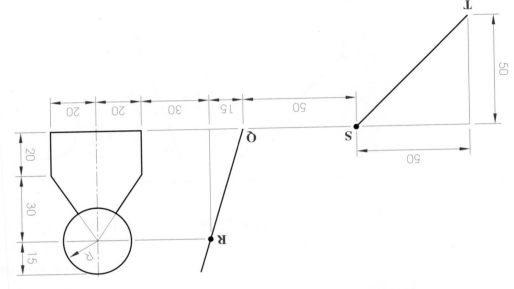

Draw the given figure and determine the image figures in each of the transformations.

Example

The figure (below, left) shows a rectangle ABCD and a line RM. The rectangle ABCD is rotated anti-clockwise about the point R until the vertex A reaches the line RM. Draw the given figure and determine the image figure under the transformation.

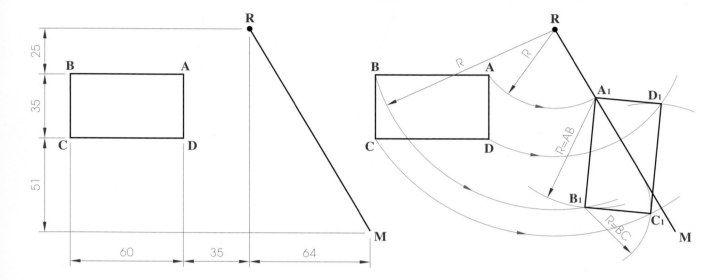

1. With R as centre and RA as radius, draw an arc in an anti-clockwise direction to locate A_1 on the line RM.

2. With R as centre and RB as radius, draw an arc in an anti-clockwise direction. With A_1 as centre and AB as radius, draw an arc to locate B_1 on the arc drawn from B.

3. With R as centre and RC as radius, draw an arc in an anti-clockwise direction. With B_1 as centre and BC as radius, draw an arc to locate C_1 on the arc drawn from C.

4. Repeat the procedure for point D. Join the points in order to obtain the required image $A_1B_1C_1D_1$.

Exercises

1. The figure shown is subjected to transformations in the following order:
    (i) **Axial symmetry** in the line LQ.
   (ii) **Central symmetry** in the point Q.
  (iii) **Translation** equal to QR.
  (iv) **Rotation** anti-clockwise about point R until the vertex P reaches the line RM.

Draw the given figure and determine the image figures in each of the transformations.

2. The figure shown is subjected to transformations in the following order:

(i) **Translation** equal to QR.

(ii) **Axial symmetry** in the line LQ.

(iii) **Central symmetry** in the point R.

(iv) **Rotation** anti-clockwise about point R until the vertex A reaches the line RM.

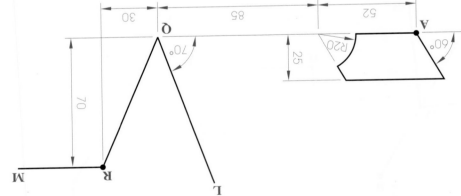

Draw the given figure and determine the image figures in each of the transformations.

Example

The figure PABCD (below, left) is based on a square and an equilateral triangle. It is subjected to **a rotation** clockwise through an angle of 120°. P_1 shows the position of the vertex P under this transformation.

Draw the given figure and determine the image figure under the rotation.

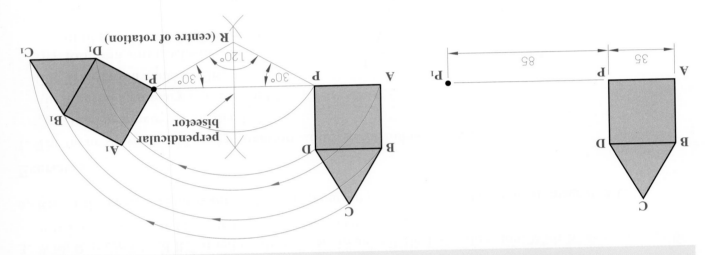

1. Join P to P_1 and construct the perpendicular bisector of this line. The **centre of rotation** lies on the perpendicular bisector as every point on the bisector is equidistant from P and P_1.

2. The centre of rotation will lie on the lower side of the line PP_1 in order to allow for a clockwise rotation. If the centre of rotation were on the upper side of the line, this would allow for an anti-clockwise rotation. Draw lines at 30° to PP_1 to locate R, the centre of rotation. Complete the rotation as shown, and draw the image figure $P_1A_1B_1C_1D_1$.

$\triangle PRP_1$ is isosceles. As $\angle PRP_1$ is 120°, then $\angle RPP_1 = \angle RP_1P = 30°$ ($180° - 120° = 60° \div 2 = 30°$).

Exercises

1. The figure shown is subjected to transformations in the following order:

   (i) **Axial symmetry** in the line L.

   (ii) **Translation** equal to QR.

   (iii) **Central symmetry** in the point Q.

   (iv) **Rotation** anti-clockwise through an angle of 110° so that R will be the image of vertex P.

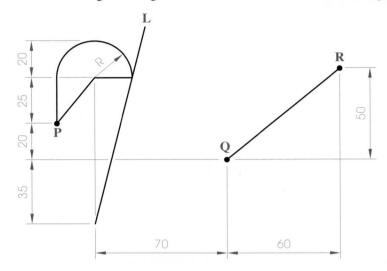

Draw the given figure and determine the image figures in each of the transformations.

2. The figure shown is subjected to transformations in the following order:

   (i) **Axial symmetry** in the line L.

   (ii) **Translation** equal to QR.

   (iii) **Central symmetry** in the point R.

   (iv) **Rotation** anti-clockwise through an angle of 100° so that Q will be the image of vertex P.

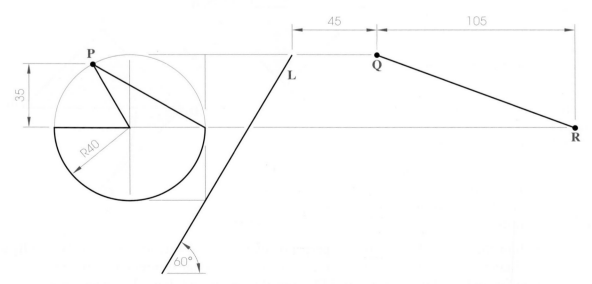

Draw the given figure and determine the image figures in each of the transformations.

Example

The figure shown is subjected to transformations in the following order:

(i) **Central symmetry** in a point.
(ii) **Axial symmetry.**
(iii) **Rotation** clockwise through 120°.
(iv) **Translation.**

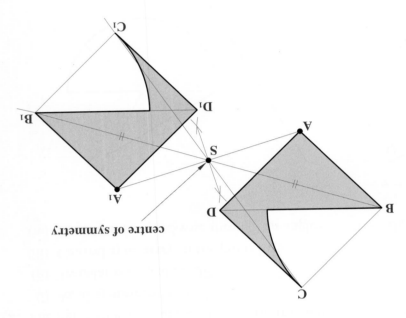

A1, A2, A3 and A4 show the positions of the vertex A under these transformations. Draw the given figure and determine the image figures in each of the transformations.

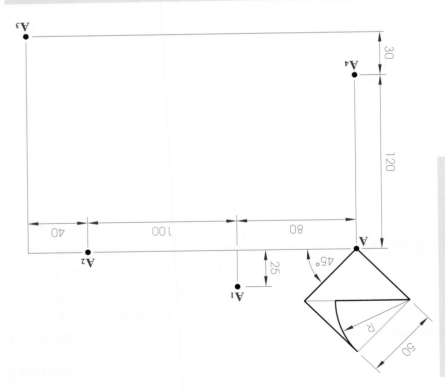

centre of symmetry

1. Draw the given figure and locate the point A_1. Index the points of the given figure as shown. Join A to A_1 and bisect this line at S. S is the **centre of symmetry** for the transformation.

   Join B to S and extend. Locate B_1 so that the distance from B_1 to S is equal to the distance from B to S. B_1 is the image of B under **central symmetry** in the point S.

   Repeat the procedure for each of the points C and D. Join the points in order and complete the image of the figure.

2. Locate the point A_2 (page 275, top). Join A_1 to A_2 and construct the perpendicular bisector L of this line. L is the **axis of reflection** for the transformation.

   Draw lines from each of the points B_1, C_1, and D_1, perpendicular to L and extend as shown. Locate B_2 so that B_2 is the same distance from L as B_1. B_2 is the image of B_1 under **axial symmetry** in the line L.

   Repeat the procedure for each of the points C_1 and D_1. Join the points and draw the image figure.

3. Locate the point A_3 (below). Join A_2 to A_3 and construct the perpendicular of this line. The **centre of rotation** will lie on the left of the line A_2A_3 in order to allow for a clockwise rotation. If the centre of rotation were on the right side of the line, this would allow for an anti-clockwise rotation. Draw a line at 30° to A_2A_2 to locate R, the centre of rotation. Draw the image of the figure under a **rotation** clockwise about the point R through an angle of 120°.

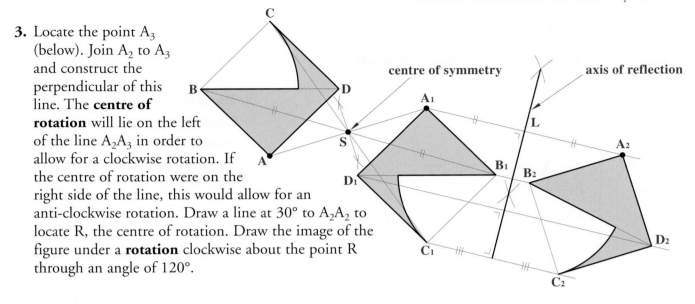

$\triangle A_2RA_3$ is isosceles. $\angle A_2RA_3$ is 120°. Thus, $\angle RA_2A_3 = \angle RA_3A_2 = 30°$ (180° − 120° = 60° ÷ 2 = 30°).

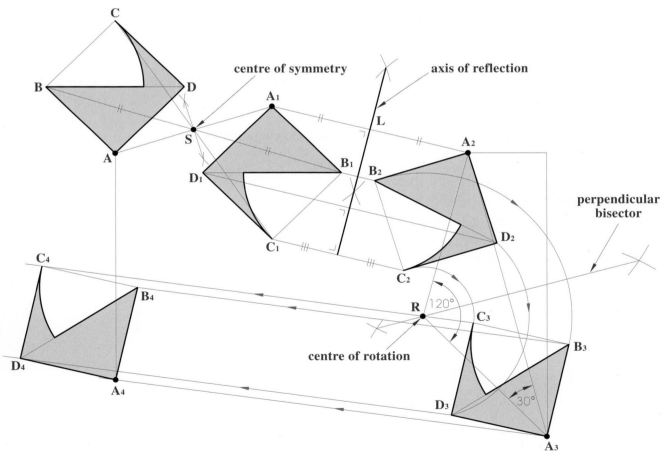

4. Locate the point A_4. Join A_3 to A_4. Draw lines parallel to A_3A_4 through each of the points B_3, C_3 and D_3. Locate B_4 so that the distance from B_3 to B_4 is equal to the length of A_3A_4. B_4 is the image of B_3 under the **translation**.

Repeat the procedure for each of the points C_3 and D_3. Join the points and draw the image figure.

Exercises

1. The figure shown is based on an **equilateral triangle.** It is subjected to transformations in the following order:

  (i) **Translation**

  (ii) **Central symmetry**

  (iii) **Axial symmetry**

  (iv) **Rotation** clockwise through an angle of 120°.

P_1, P_2, P_3 and P_4 show the positions of point P under these transformations. Draw the given figure and determine the image figures in each of the transformations.

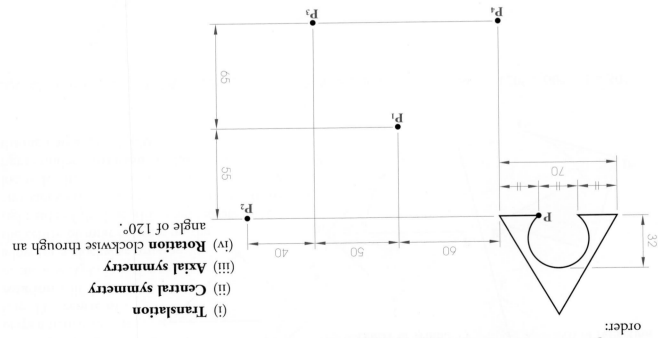

2. The figure shown is subjected to transformations in the following order:

  (i) **Translation**

  (ii) **Axial symmetry**

  (iii) **Central symmetry**

  (iv) **Rotation** clockwise through 90°.

P_1, P_2, P_3 and P_4 show the positions of the vertex P under these transformations. Draw the given figure and determine the image figure in each the transformations.

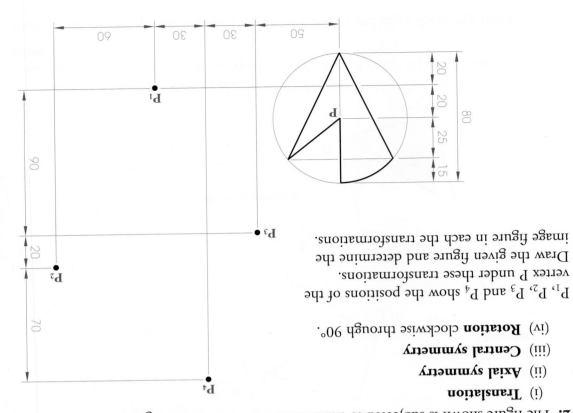

Chapter 27

Solids in Contact

In this chapter we shall start by considering how to determine the **projections** (elevation and plan) of points on the cone, sphere and cylinder. Then we will progress to drawing the projections of these and other solids in contact.

The Cone

We saw on page 266 that the curved surface of a cone is made up of an infinite number of straight lines called *elements*. Imagine moving along the elements OA and OB as illustrated over.

The **elevation** of the path is represented by the elements denoted o_1a_1 and o_1b_1.

The **plan** of the path is represented by the same elements denoted oa and ob.

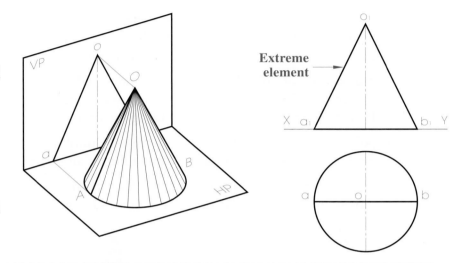

The extreme elements of a cone in elevation are represented by the diameter parallel to the XY line in plan.

Example 1

The elevation and plan of a **cone** are shown over. The location of two points **P** and **Q** on the curved surface of the cone are also shown in the **elevation** and **plan** respectively.

(a) Locate point **P** in the **plan**.

(b) Locate point **Q** in the **elevation**.

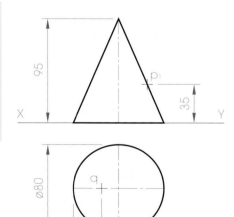

1. Point **P** is on an extreme element of the cone in elevation. As a result, it will be located on the diameter parallel to the XY line in plan and can be projected to the plan as shown over.

2. Point **Q** is on the diameter parallel to the XY line in plan. Accordingly, it will lie on an extreme element of the cone in elevation and can be projected to the elevation as shown.

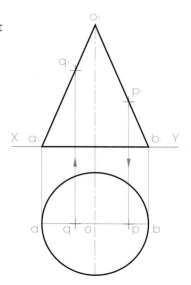

Example 2

The elevation and plan of a **cone** are shown over. The location of two points **P** and **Q** on the curved surface of the cone are also shown in plan and elevation respectively.

(a) Show the position of point **P** in **elevation**.

(b) Show the position of point **Q** in **plan**.

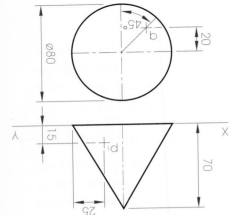

1. Point **P** can be rotated about the axis of the cone until it lies on an extreme element as illustrated below, middle. In doing so, point **P** will move in an arc of a circle in plan as shown below, left.

2. This rotated position of point **P** in plan can be projected to the extreme element in elevation as shown. This determines the height of point **P** as its height remains the same during rotation.

3. Imagine point **Q** is rotated about the axis of the cone until it lies on an extreme element. As point **Q** rotates it moves horizontally in elevation until it lies on an extreme element as shown below, left.

4. In this rotated position point **Q** will lie on the diameter parallel to the XY line in plan. This point can be rotated in an arc of a circle to give the plan of point **Q** as shown.

> If a point rotates about the axis of an upright cone:
> It moves horizontally in elevation.
> It travels in a circular path in plan.

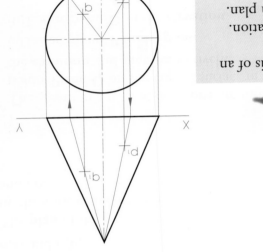

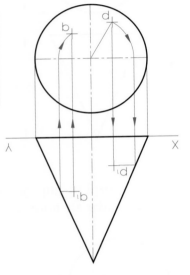

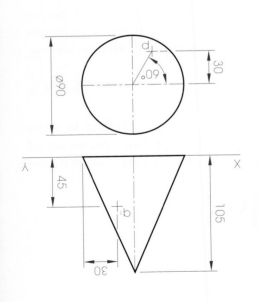

Alternative solution

Determining the projections of elements that contain points P and Q as shown above, right can also solve this problem.

Exercise

The elevation and plan of **two cones** are shown over. In each case:

(a) Locate point **P** in the **plan**.

(b) Locate point **Q** in the **elevation**.

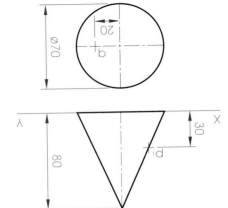

The Sphere

> A sphere appears as a circle in all orthographic views.

Imagine a person moving on the sphere, over along the circle highlighted.

The **elevation** of a person's path is represented by the outline of the sphere in elevation, shown far right.

The **plan** of a person's path is represented by the diameter parallel to the XY line.

> Points on the outline of a sphere in elevation are represented by the diameter parallel to the XY line in plan.

By considering the illustration of the ball shown over, it can be appreciated that:

> If a point moves horizontally on the surface of a sphere:
>
> It moves horizontally in elevation.
>
> It travels in a circular path in plan.

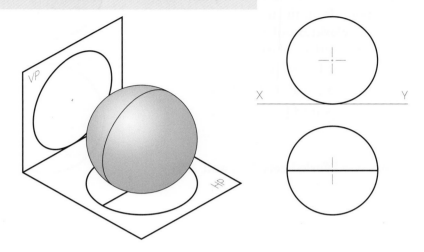

Example

The elevation and plan of a **sphere** are shown across. The **elevation** of a point **P** and the **plan** of a point **Q** on the upper surface of the sphere are also shown.

(a) Locate point **P** in the **plan**.

(b) Locate point **Q** in the **elevation**.

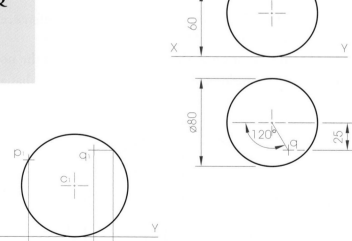

1. Point **P** is on the outline of the sphere in elevation. As a result it will be located on the diameter parallel to the XY line in plan.

2. It can be projected to the plan as shown over.

3. In plan point **Q** can be rotated about C until it lies on the diameter parallel to the XY. This rotated position of point **Q** will lie on the outline of the sphere in elevation as shown.

4. This establishes the height of point **Q** as it will have moved horizontally in elevation. As a result the original position of point **Q** in elevation can be located as shown across.

The Cylinder

Example

The elevation and plan of a **cylinder** are shown over. The location of a point **P** on the front part of the curved surface of the cylinder is also shown.

(a) Draw the given views and locate point **P** in elevation and plan.

(b) Draw an end elevation of the cylinder showing the location of point **P**.

1. The given views are drawn as shown and point **P** is located in elevation.

2. Point **P** can be projected to lie on the circumference of the circle in plan as the circumference represents the curved surface of the cylinder in this view.

3. The end elevation of the cylinder is drawn in the normal manner, as shown below, right.

4. Point **P** can be located in this view as its location has already been established in two orthographic views.

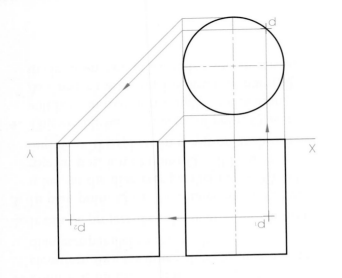

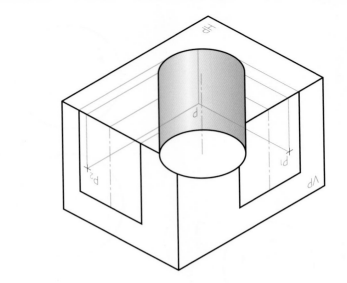

Exercises

The elevation and plan of **two spheres** are shown over. The plan of a point **P** on the upper surface and the **elevation** of a point Q on the lower surface of each sphere are also shown. In each case:

(a) Locate point **P** in the **elevation**.

(b) Locate point Q in the **plan**.

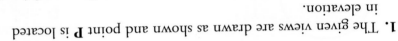

The Cone and Sphere in Mutual Contact

Example
The elevation and incomplete plan of a **cone** and **sphere** in mutual contact are shown across.

(a) Draw the elevation and complete the plan.

(b) Show the point of contact in both views.

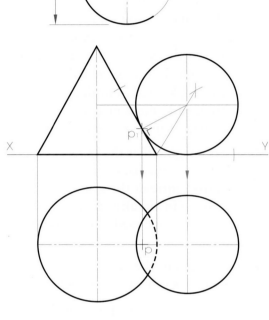

1. The plan of the cone can be drawn lightly and its elevation projected in the normal manner.

2. The sphere has a radius of 30 mm and is resting on the HP. As a result its centre will lie on a horizontal line 30 mm from the XY line in elevation.

3. The sphere will be tangential to an extreme element of the cone and the XY line in the elevation. Accordingly, its centre will also lie on the bisector of the angle shown. The point where these lines meet gives the location of the centre of the sphere, allowing the sphere to be drawn in elevation.

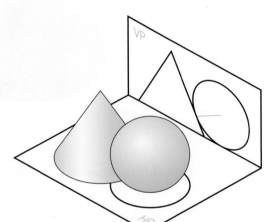

4. The centre of the sphere can then be projected to lie on the extended diameter parallel to the XY line in plan as shown over. The plan of both solids can then be completed.

5. In elevation the point of contact between the solids (P) will lie on an extreme element of the cone and on the outline of the sphere. Therefore it can be located by constructing the normal shown. Point P can be located in plan by considering it as a point on the cone or sphere.

Exercise

The elevation and incomplete plan of a **cone** and **sphere** in mutual contact are shown over.

(a) Draw the complete elevation and plan of the solids.

(b) Locate the point of contact in both views.

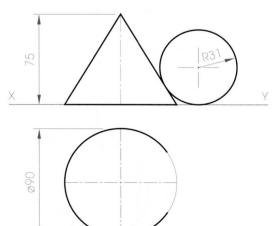

Example

The elevation and plan of a **cone** and **sphere** in mutual contact are shown across.

(a) Draw the given views.
(b) Locate the point of contact in both views.

1. First, the plan and elevation of the cone are drawn as shown below, left. Imagine that the required sphere has been rotated about the axis of the cone until its centre lies on the diameter parallel to the XY line in plan as illustrated pictorially over.

2. In this rotated position the elevation of the sphere will be tangential to an extreme element of the cone and the XY line. The elevation of the sphere can be drawn in this rotated position and the point of contact located as in the previous example. Subsequently the centre of the sphere and the point of contact can be projected to the plan as shown.

3. Then imagine that the sphere is rotated about the axis of the cone back into the original position. In plan the centre of the sphere and the point of contact will rotate in circular arcs about the axis of the cone to lie on the inclined line. This allows the plan to be completed.

4. The height of the centre of the sphere remains the same during rotation allowing it to be located in elevation as shown below, right.

5. The elevation of the point of contact (P) can be located by treating it as a point on the curved surface of the cone. Then the solids are lined in as appropriate.

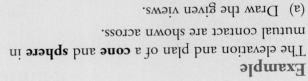

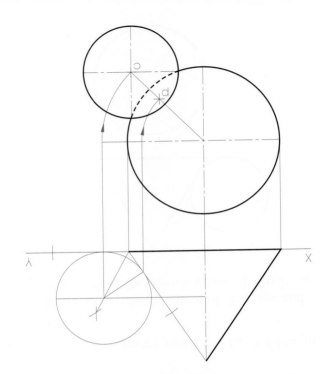

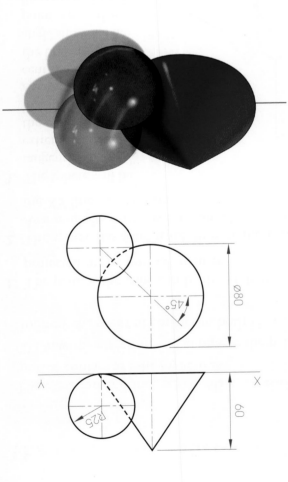

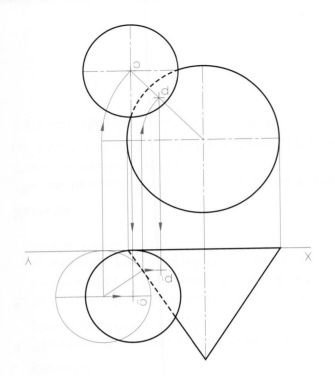

Exercise

The elevation and plan of a **cone** and **sphere** in mutual contact are shown over.

(a) Draw the elevation and plan of the solids.

(b) Locate the point of contact in both views.

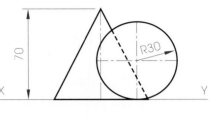

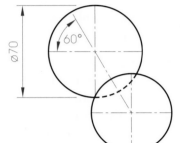

Example 1

The elevation and incomplete plan of **two spheres** in mutual contact are shown over.

(a) Draw the complete elevation and plan of the solids.

(b) Locate the point of contact in both views.

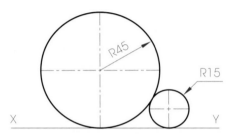

1. First draw the plan and elevation of the sphere of radius 45 mm as given.

2. The elevation of the second sphere will be tangential to the XY line and the first circle in elevation. Therefore its centre will lie on a horizontal line 15 mm from the XY line in elevation.

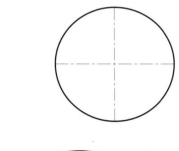

3. Its centre will also lie on an arc of radius 60 mm (45 + 15) drawn from the centre of the first circle. The resulting point of intersection is the centre for the second sphere in elevation, allowing it to be drawn, as shown over.

4. The centre of the second sphere can be projected to lie on the extended diameter parallel to the XY line in plan allowing both solids to be lined in as appropriate.

5. The point of contact between the two spheres (P) will lie on the line joining their centres. It can be located in elevation and projected to plan as shown.

The point of contact between two spheres lies on the line joining their centres.

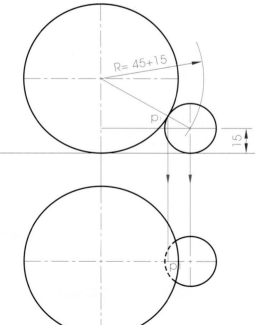

Example 2

The elevation and plan of **two spheres** in mutual contact are shown over.

(a) Draw the elevation and plan of the solids.

(b) Show the position of the point of contact in both views.

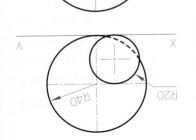

1. First draw the plan and elevation of the sphere of radius 40 mm lightly.

2. Imagine that the second sphere has been rotated along the HP about the centre of the first sphere until it appears tangential to the first sphere in elevation as illustrated pictorially over. The elevation and plan of the second sphere can be drawn lightly in this rotated position as in the previous example. The point of contact (P) can also be located.

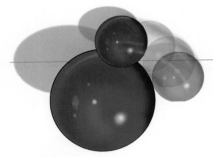

3. Then imagine that the second sphere is rotated back into its original position. In plan the centre of the sphere and the point of contact will rotate in circular arcs about the centre of the first sphere until they lie on the line inclined at 75°. This allows the plan to be completed.

4. The final resting position of the centre and point of contact can be projected to elevation where their heights have already been established as shown over. The elevation can then be lined in as appropriate. Note that the point of contact lies on the line joining the centres of the spheres in elevation also.

Exercise

The elevation and plan of **two spheres** in mutual contact are shown over.

(a) Draw the elevation and plan of the solids.

(b) Locate the point of contact in both views.

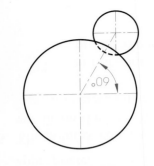

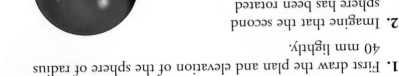

The point of contact between a plane and a sphere can be located in a view showing the plane as an edge.

Example

The incomplete elevation and plan of an **equilateral triangular pyramid** and **two spheres**, **A** and **B**, are shown across. Each sphere is in contact with the HP and a sloping surface of the pyramid.

(a) Draw the complete plan and elevation of the solids.

(b) Show the position of the points of contact between the pyramid and the spheres in both views.

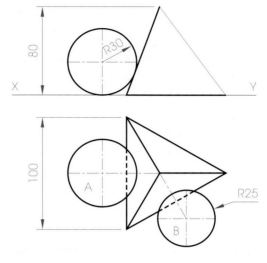

1. The plan and elevation of the pyramid are drawn lightly.

2. The centre of sphere **A** can be located in elevation by drawing a horizontal line 30 mm from the XY line and bisecting the angle as shown across.

3. The sphere can now be drawn in elevation and the point of contact located by constructing the normal to the edge view of the sloping surface as shown. The sphere and point of contact **P** can then be projected to the plan.

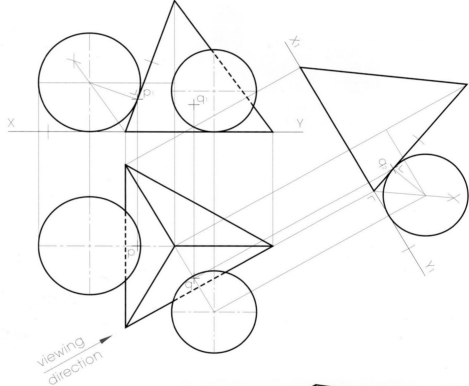

4. Sphere **B** can be located by constructing an auxiliary elevation in which the sloping surface it is in contact with appears as an edge. The required viewing direction is shown above and the X_1Y_1 line will be perpendicular to this viewing direction.

5. The centre of sphere **B** can be located in this view by first drawing a line parallel to the X_1Y_1 line and 25 mm from it and then bisecting the angle as shown.

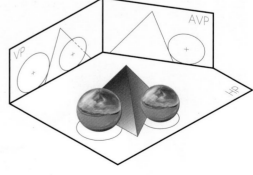

6. The point of contact **Q** can be located in this view by constructing the normal to the edge view of the sloping surface. The sphere and point of contact can then be projected to the plan.

7. The sphere and point of contact can be located in elevation by transferring the appropriate heights from the auxiliary elevation allowing the drawing to be completed.

Exercises

1. The elevation and plan of a **regular pentagonal pyramid** and **two spheres** are shown over. Each sphere is in contact with the HP and a sloping surface of the pyramid.

   (a) Draw the plan and elevation of the solids.

   (b) Show the position of the points of contact between the spheres and the pyramid in both views.

2. The elevation and plan of **two spheres** in contact with a **truncated regular hexagonal pyramid** are shown below. The pyramid is cut by a plane tangential to the two spheres as shown.

   (a) Draw the plan and elevation of the solids in contact.

   (b) Project an end elevation of the solids.

   (c) Locate the points of contact between the spheres and the pyramid in *all* views.

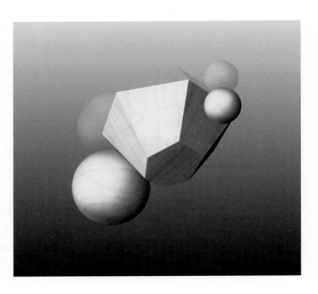

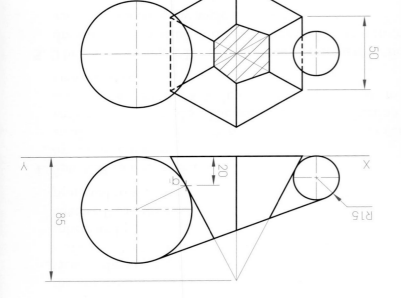

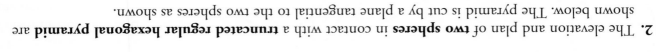

Example

The figure over shows the elevation and plan of a **cylinder A** in contact with a **cone B**.

(a) Draw the plan and elevation of the solids.

(b) A **sphere** of diameter 60 mm rests on the horizontal plane in position S so that it is in contact with cylinder **A** and cone **B**. Determine the plan and elevation of the sphere.

(c) Show all points of contact in plan and elevation.

1. The given plan and elevation are drawn in the normal manner.

2. The required sphere can be located by drawing a sphere of radius 30 mm in contact with the extreme element of the cylinder in elevation as shown below. Project the centre of this sphere to the plan and rotate it about the axis of the cylinder.

3. Then draw a sphere of radius 30 mm in contact with the extreme element of the cone in elevation as shown. Project the centre of this sphere to the plan and rotate it about the axis of the cone.

4. The centre of the required sphere is the point where the centres of the rotating spheres intersect in plan. This allows the plan and elevation of the sphere to be drawn. This process is illustrated over.

5. Locate the points of contact as in previous examples.

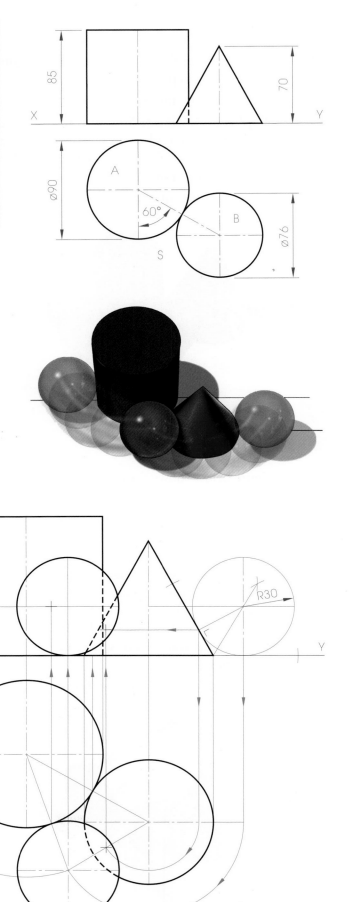

Exercises

1. The elevation and plan of a **cone A** and a **cylinder B** are shown below. Both solids rest on the horizontal plane and are in contact.

(a) Draw the plan and elevation of the solids in the given position.

(b) A **sphere** of diameter 50 mm is to be placed on the horizontal plane in position C so that it is in contact with cone **A** and cylinder **B**. Draw the plan and elevation of this sphere.

(c) Show all points of contact in both views.

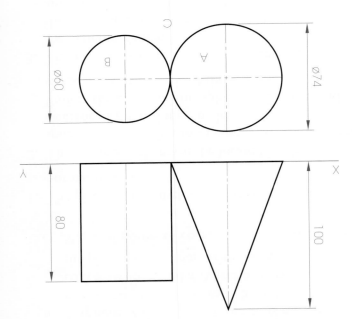

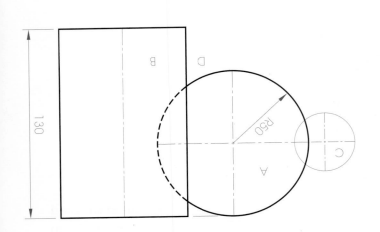

2. The figure below shows the elevation and plan of a **cone A** in contact with a **cylinder B**. Both solids rest on the horizontal plane.

(a) Draw the plan and elevation of the solids.

(b) **Sphere C** (shown using construction lines) is to be rotated along the horizontal plane to position D so that it is in contact with cone **A** and cylinder **B**. Draw the elevation and plan of sphere C in this position.

(c) Show all points of contact in both views.

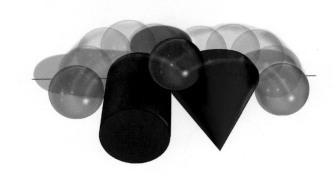

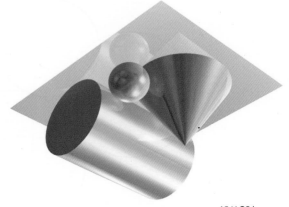

3. The elevation and plan of a **cone A** in contact with a **sphere B** are shown below. Both solids rest on the horizontal plane.

(a) Draw the plan and elevation of the solids in contact.

(b) Another **sphere** of diameter 30 mm is placed on the horizontal plane in position C so that it is in contact with cone **A** and sphere **B**. Determine the projections of this sphere.

(c) Locate all points of contact in both views.

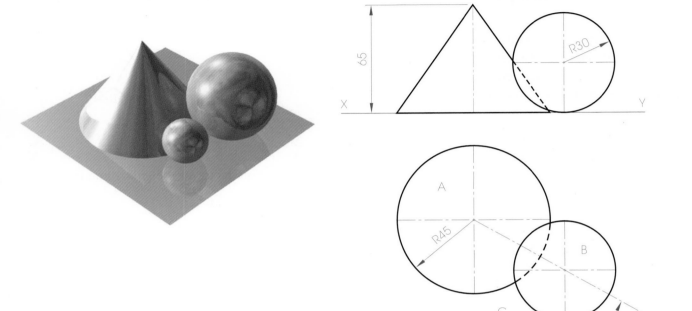

4. The elevation and plan of a box for a **sliotar** of radius 35 mm are shown below. All surfaces of the box are *tangential* to the sliotar.

(a) Draw the given plan and elevation.

(b) Draw an end elevation of the box and sliotar.

(c) Locate the *nine* points of contact in all views.

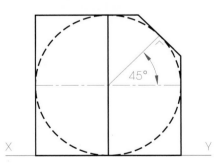

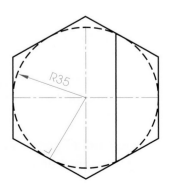

Chapter 28

Enlargement and Reduction

Very often in design, the size of a figure has to be enlarged or reduced proportionally. The easiest way to do this is by means of an **enlargement**. An enlargement changes the size of an object but does not change its shape.

In the figure across, the quadrilateral $A_1B_1C_1D_1$ is an enlargement of the quadrilateral ABCD. Lines are drawn passing through the vertices of the original figure from a point O called the **centre of enlargement**. This point may be set in any convenient position.

The lengths of the enlarged shape are twice the corresponding lengths of the original. The ratio of enlarged length to original length is called the scale factor of the enlargement. The **scale factor** of the enlargement in the figure above is 2.

To be able to construct the image under an enlargement, we need to know:

The **centre of enlargement**: this is the point from where you start measuring.

The **scale factor** = $\dfrac{\text{distance of image point from centre of enlargement}}{\text{distance of corresponding object point from centre of enlargement}}$

In the figure above, the scale factor = $\dfrac{OA_1}{OA} = \dfrac{OB_1}{OB} = 2$

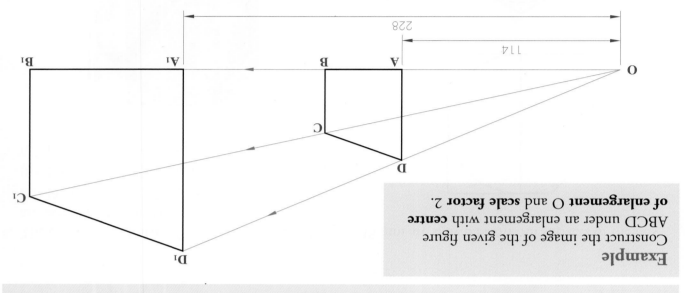

Example

Construct the image of the given figure ABCD under an enlargement with **centre** O and **scale factor 2**.

1. Draw radiating lines from O to pass through the vertices A, B, C and D.
2. Measure the distance from O to A. Locate A_1 so that the distance from O to A_1 is twice the distance from O to A. A_1 is the image of A under the enlargement.
3. Repeat this procedure for each of the points B, C and D_1. Join B_1, C_1 and D_1 giving $A_1B_1C_1D_1$ to obtain the required image.

Under an **enlargement**, a figure is mapped onto a similar figure, and a line is mapped onto a parallel line.

Example 1
Draw a rectangle similar to the given rectangle ABCD but having sides twice the length of those in the given rectangle.

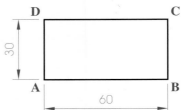

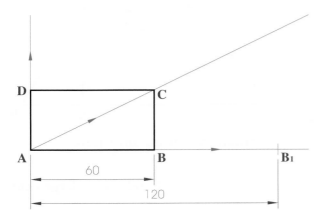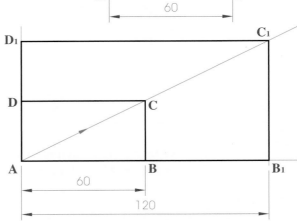

1. Using the vertex A as the centre of enlargement, draw radiating lines to pass through the vertices B, C and D (above, left).
2. Locate the point B_1 so that the length of AB_1 is twice the length of AB.
3. Draw a line through B_1 parallel to BC to locate the point C_1 (above, right).
4. Draw a line through C_1 parallel to DC to locate D_1. $AB_1C_1D_1$ is the required enlarged rectangle.

Example 2
Draw a polygon similar to the given polygon ABCDE (below, left) and having sides two-thirds of the length of those of ABCDE.

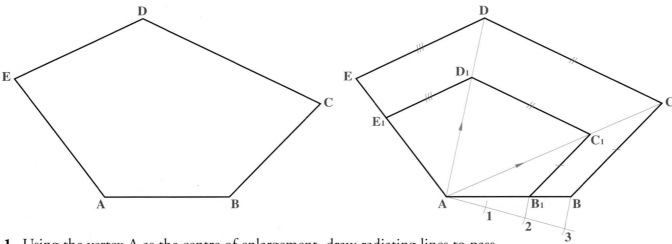

1. Using the vertex A as the centre of enlargement, draw radiating lines to pass through the vertices C and D (above, right).
2. Divide AB in the ratio 2:1. Then AB_1 is two-thirds the length of AB.
3. Draw a line through B_1 parallel to BC to locate the point C_1.
4. Similarly, draw lines through C_1 parallel to CD to locate D_1, and through D_1 parallel to DE to locate E_1.
5. $AB_1C_1D_1E_1$ is the required reduced polygon.

Answer Worksheet 28B

Example

Inscribe a square in the given triangle ABC (below, left).

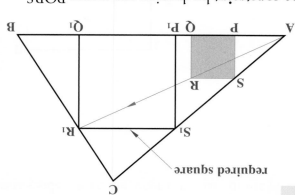

Answer Worksheet 28C

1. The solution involves using the principle of **relaxing one constraint** by drawing any square PQRS having two of its vertices on AB and another vertex on AC.

2. Join AR and extend to meet the side BC in R₁. R₁ is the image of the vertex R under an **enlargement** with **centre of enlargement** A and **scale factor** AR₁/AR. R₁ is a point on the required square.

3. Complete the required square as shown.

Exercises

1. The figure below shows a **triangle**, a **quadrilateral**, a **regular pentagon** and a **regular hexagon**. Also shown is a **square** inscribed in each of the shapes.
   Draw each of the given shapes.

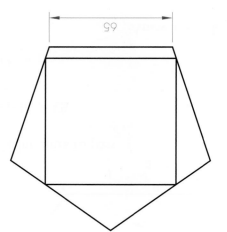

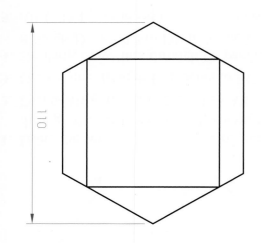

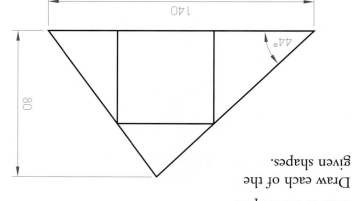

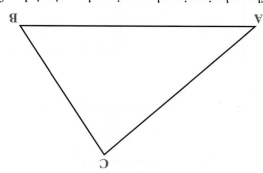

Example
The figure (below, left) is based on a square and an equilateral triangle. Draw the given figure.

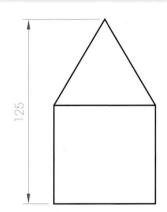

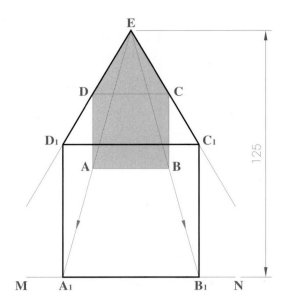

1. The principle of **relaxing one constraint** is used here. Draw any square ABCD and equilateral triangle CDE as shown. This shape is similar to the given figure.

2. Under an **enlargement** with **centre of enlargement** E, this shape may be mapped onto the required shape. Draw radiating lines from E passing through each of the vertices of the square ABCD.

3. Draw the line MN parallel to the side AB and a distance 125 mm from E, to cut the line EA at A_1, and the line EB at B_1. A_1B_1 is one side of the image figure.

4. Draw a line from A_1 parallel to AD to cut the line ED at D_1, thus obtaining another vertex D_1. Locate C_1 in the same manner and draw the required figure.

Exercises

1. The figure shown (below, left) is based on a **square** and a **regular pentagon**. Draw this figure.

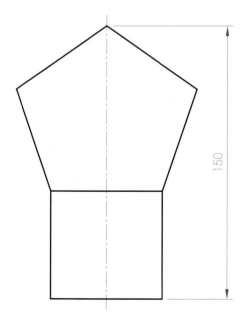

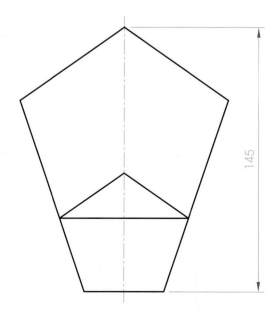

2. Draw the figure above, right. It is based on two interlocking **regular pentagons**.

3. Use an **enlargement** to construct the three **regular hexagons** as shown below given that the sides of successive hexagons are in the ratio 2:3.

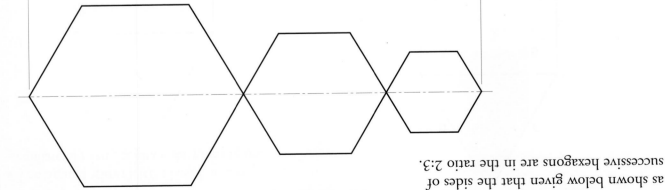

265

Enlarging and Reducing using an External Centre of Enlargement

The centre of enlargement may be positioned in any convenient position as shown in the following example.

Example

Draw a figure similar to the **table lamp** (shown below, right) having an overall height of 110 mm.

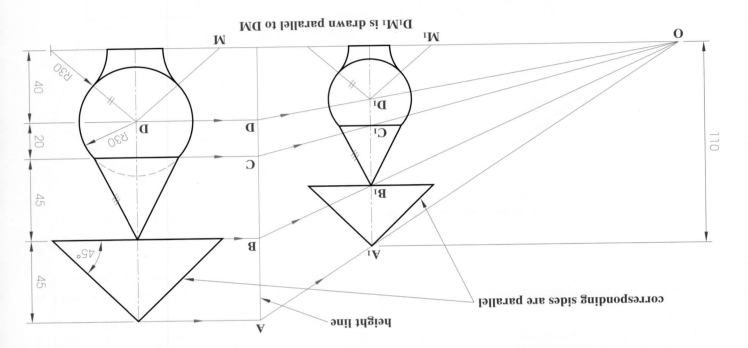

D₁M₁ is drawn parallel to DM

corresponding sides are parallel

height line

110

1. Select a suitable position for the centre of enlargement O on the base extended. Draw a height line and project the heights of the original lamp onto this line. Index the points as shown.

2. Draw a line parallel to the base and a distance of 110 mm from it. Draw a line from O to the point A to intersect this line at A₁.

3. Draw a vertical line from A₁ as shown. Draw lines from O to the points B, C, and D to locate B₁, C₁, and D₁ respectively. Draw horizontal lines through B₁ and C₁.

4. The reduced lamp can be completed because the corresponding sides of the original figure and the image figure are parallel.

Exercises

1. The figure across shows the **road sign** for a camp site. It contains two **equilateral triangles**.

(a) Draw the figure full-size.

(b) Draw a similar figure to the given figure having an overall height of 85 mm.

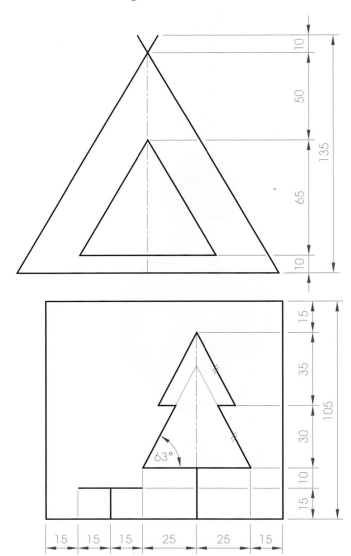

2. The figure across shows a **road sign** for a forestry and picnic area.

(a) Draw the given figure to the given dimensions.

(b) Draw a similar figure to the given figure having an overall height of 170 mm.

3. The figure over shows the outline of a **Celebrations** sweet box.

(a) Draw the figure to the given dimensions.

(b) Draw a similar figure to the given figure having an overall height of 130 mm.

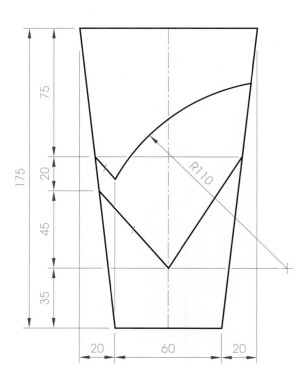

4. The figure over shows the outline of a **bottle** including a label based on a six-pointed star.

(a) Draw the figure to the given dimensions showing all constructions clearly.

(b) On a separate diagram draw a similar figure having an overall height of 140 mm.

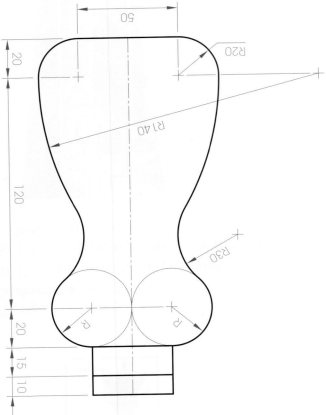

5. The figure across shows the outline of a **Fairy washing up liquid bottle.**

(a) Draw the figure to the given dimensions showing all constructions clearly.

(b) On a separate diagram draw a similar figure having an overall height of 130 mm.

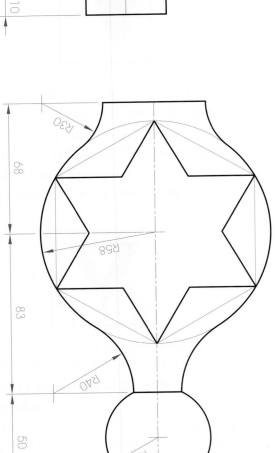

Chapter 29
Developments 2

Parallel-line Developments

In chapter 10 we considered developments of a range of objects. We saw that:

Every face or surface in a development represents the true shape of that face or surface of the object.

Example 1

1. The elevation and plan of a **regular hexagonal prism** are shown over.
   (a) Draw the given views.
   (b) Draw a complete **development** of the prism.

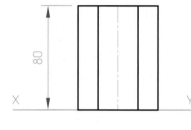

1. The plan and elevation are drawn in the normal manner.

2. The base edges of the prism develop as a straight line which is known as the **stretch-out line**. It will be 6 × 30 = 180 mm long.

3. The lateral edges develop as lines perpendicular to the stretch-out line. It can be seen from the plan that these edges will be 30 mm apart. Their true lengths can be transferred from the elevation, as shown below.

4. The end faces, which appear in true shape in plan, can be redrawn in the development.

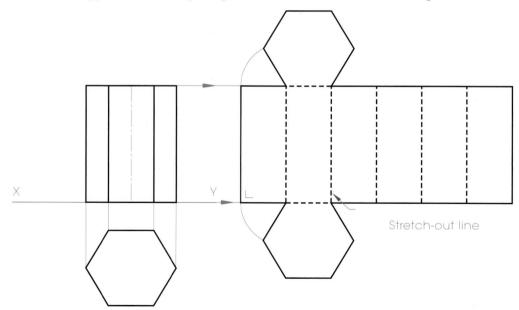

Stretch-out line

The base or end face edges of a prism develop as a straight line known as the **stretch-out line**.
Its lateral edges develop as lines **perpendicular to the stretch-out line**.
The result is known as a **parallel-line development**.

Example 2

1. The elevation and end view of a box **for tennis balls** are shown over.
   (a) Draw the given views.
   (b) Draw a **complete development** of the box.

1. The end view and elevation are drawn in the normal manner.

2. In this case the stretch-out line will be
   6 × 40 = 240 mm long
   and can be drawn as shown below.

3. The lateral edges will be perpendicular to the stretch-out line and 40 mm apart. Their true lengths can be transferred from the elevation.

4. The true length and width of the opening can be transferred from the elevation and end view respectively, allowing the development to be completed as shown.

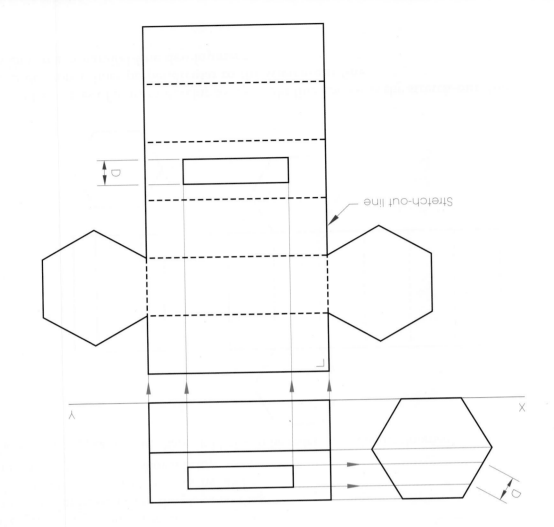

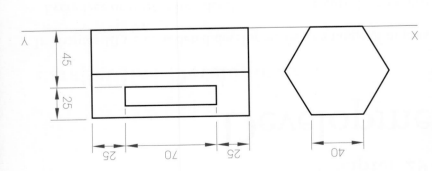

Stretch-out line

Exercise

The elevation and end view of a package for **two golf balls** are shown below. The box is based on a **regular pentagonal prism.**

(a) Draw the given views.

(b) Draw a complete **development** of the box.

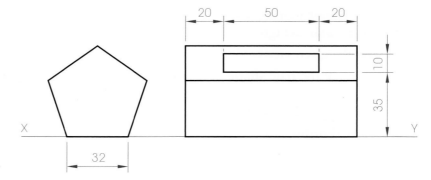

Example
The figure over shows the elevation and plan of a **truncated regular hexagonal prism**.

(a) Draw the given views.

(b) Determine the **true shape** of the cut section of the solid.

(c) Draw a complete **development** of the truncated prism.

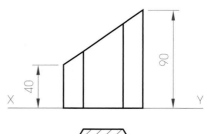

1. The given views and the true shape of the cut section are drawn as shown below (refer to page 222).

2. The stretch-out line will be 210 mm long.

3. The lateral edges will be perpendicular to the stretch-out line and 35 mm apart. Their true lengths can be transferred from the elevation as shown over.

4. The development can be completed by redrawing the base (which appears in true shape in plan) and the true shape of the cut section of the solid.

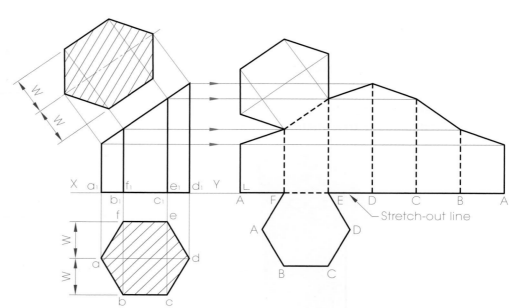

> The seam is normally at the shortest lateral edge.

Exercises

1. The figure below shows the elevation and plan of a truncated **equilateral triangular prism**, a truncated **regular pentagonal prism** and a truncated **regular octagonal prism**. In each case:

   (a) Draw the given views.

   (b) Determine the **true shape** of the cut section of the solid.

   (c) Draw a complete **development** of the truncated prism.

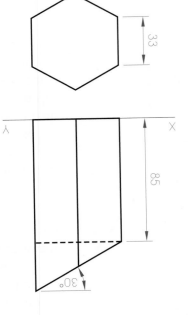

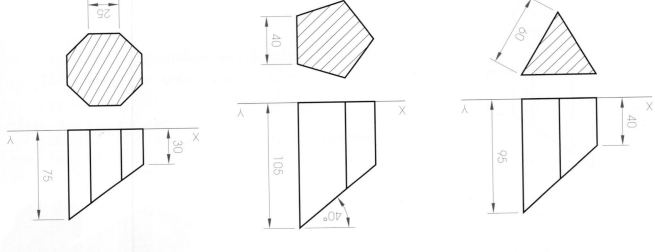

2. The elevation and plan of a **display box** are shown below. The box is based on a **truncated regular hexagonal prism.**

   (a) Draw the given views.

   (b) Draw a complete **development** of the display box.

   (c) A cover is to be used to close the box. Determine the **true shape** of the cover.

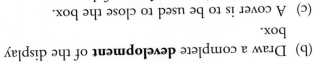

Example

The figure over shows the elevation and end view of a **box**, which is based on a **truncated regular pentagonal prism**.

(a) Draw the given views.

(b) Draw a complete **development** of the box.

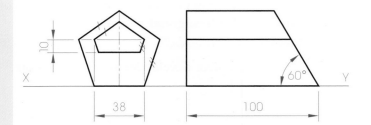

1. The given views are drawn in the normal manner.

2. The stretch-out line will be 5 × 38 = 190 mm long.

3. The lateral edges will be perpendicular to the stretch-out line and 38 mm apart. Their true lengths can be transferred from the elevation as shown over.

4. The left face, a regular pentagon of side 38 mm, can be drawn.

5. The true shape of the cut surface of the prism can be determined by rabatting it into the horizontal plane as shown across.

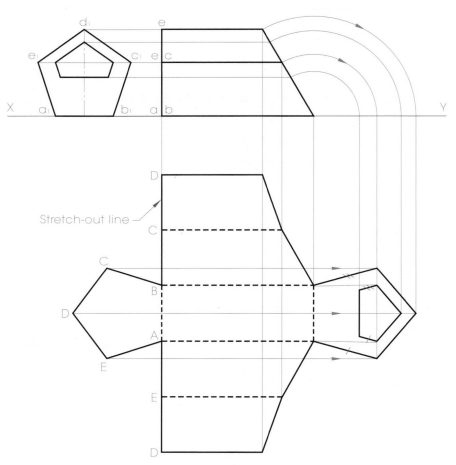

Exercises

1. The elevation and end view of a truncated **equilateral triangular prism** are shown below.

   (a) Draw the given views.

   (b) Draw a complete **development** of the truncated prism.

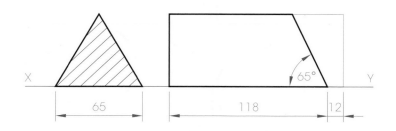

2. The figure below shows the elevation and end view of a package for **two tennis balls.** It is based on a **truncated regular hexagonal prism.**

(a) Draw the given views.

(b) Draw a complete **development** of the package.

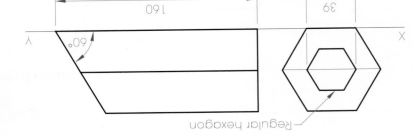

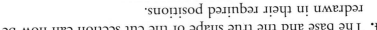

Regular hexagon

160

39

X

Y

60°

Example

The elevation and plan of a **truncated cylinder** are shown over.

(a) Draw the given views.

(b) Determine the **true shape** of the cut section of the solid.

(c) Draw the complete **development** of the solid.

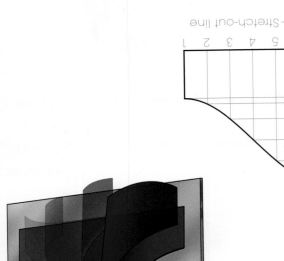

Ø70

X

Y

110

45°

1. The required plan, elevation and true shape are drawn in the normal manner.

2. Consider the projections of twelve equally spaced elements on the surface of the cylinder as shown below. The stretch-out line can be determined by setting out the resulting chord distance twelve times as shown.

3. The elements will develop as lines perpendicular to the stretch-out line. Their true lengths can be transferred from the elevation. Then draw a smooth curve to pass through their endpoints as shown.

4. The base and the true shape of the cut section can now be redrawn in their required positions.

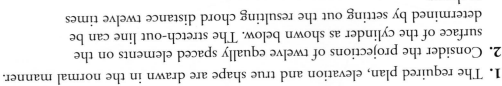

Stretch-out line

Exercises

1. The elevation and plan of a **collection box** are shown over.

   (a) Draw the given views.

   (b) Draw the complete **development** of the box.

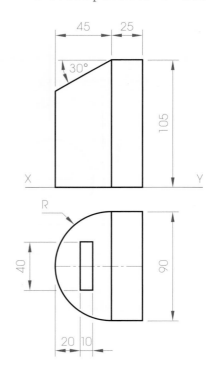

2. The figure over shows the elevation and plan of a **bin**.

   (a) Draw the given views.

   (b) Project an **end elevation** of the bin.

   (c) Draw the **development** of the *curved surface* of the bin.

   (d) Determine the **true shape** of *one* of the sloping surfaces of the bin.

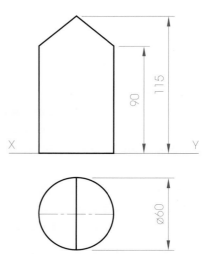

3. The elevation and plan of a **display box** are shown over.

   (a) Draw the given views.

   (b) Draw the complete **development** of the box.

   (c) A lid is to be used to cover the display. Determine the **true shape** of the lid.

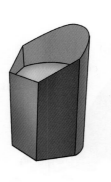

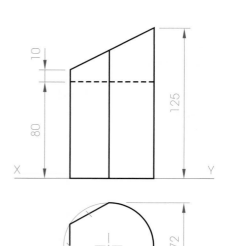

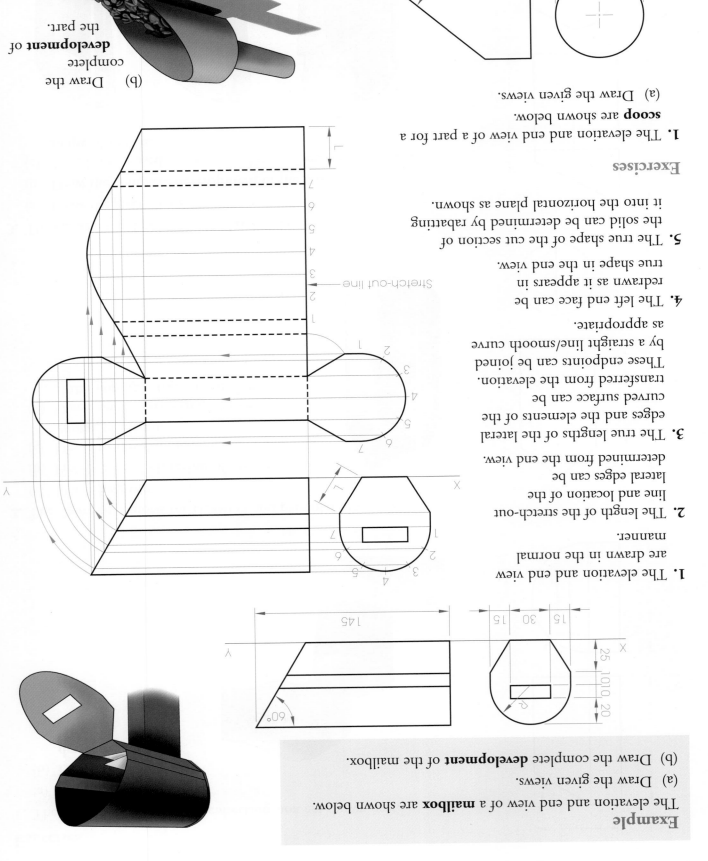

Example

The elevation and end view of a **mailbox** are shown below.

(a) Draw the given views.

(b) Draw the complete **development** of the mailbox.

145   60°

15 30 15

25 10 10 20   R

1. The elevation and end view are drawn in the normal manner.

2. The length of the stretch-out line and location of the lateral edges can be determined from the end view.

3. The true lengths of the lateral edges and the elements of the curved surface can be transferred from the elevation. These endpoints can be joined by a straight line/smooth curve as appropriate.

4. The left end face can be redrawn as it appears in true shape in the end view.

5. The true shape of the cut section of the solid can be determined by rabatting it into the horizontal plane as shown.

Stretch-out line

Exercises

1. The elevation and end view of a part for a **scoop** are shown below.

(a) Draw the given views.

(b) Draw the complete **development** of the part.

120   40°   ⌀70

2. The elevation and end view of a **tunnel** are shown below.

(a) Draw the given views.

(b) Draw the complete **development** of the tunnel.

(c) Determine the **true shape** of the surface ABCDE.

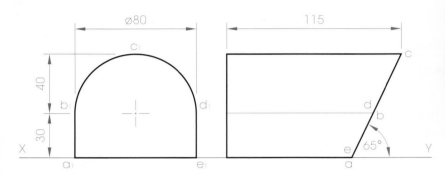

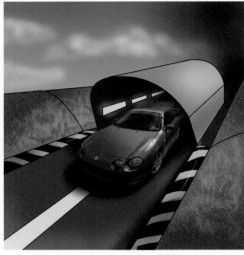

3. The elevation and end view of a package for **two handballs** are shown below.

(a) Draw the given views.

(b) Draw the complete **development** of the package.

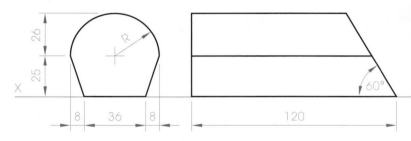

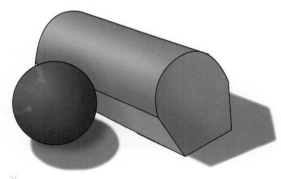

4. The elevation and plan of a **bunker** are shown below.

(a) Draw the given views.

(b) Determine the **true shape** of the door of the bunker.

(c) Draw the complete **development** of the bunker.

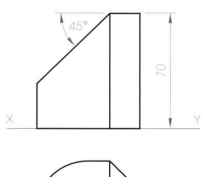

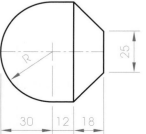

Answer Worksheets 29A, 29B and 29C

Radial-line Developments

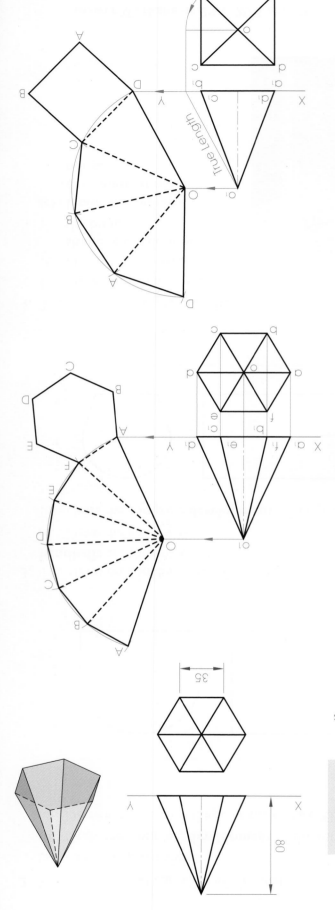

Example 1

The elevation and plan of a **regular hexagonal pyramid** are shown across. Draw the given views and determine the complete **development** of the pyramid.

1. The plan and elevation are drawn as shown.

2. The development will consist of six congruent isosceles triangles and a regular hexagon.

3. The edge OD appears in true length in elevation and can be translated to the development as shown. The lateral edges will radiate from O along an arc with radius equal to the true length of OD.

4. The base of each triangle will be 35 mm long i.e. equal to the length of the base edges of the pyramid.

5. The base of the pyramid appears in true shape in plan and can be redrawn in the development.

Example 2

The elevation and plan of a **square pyramid** are shown below. Draw the given views and determine the complete **development** of the pyramid.

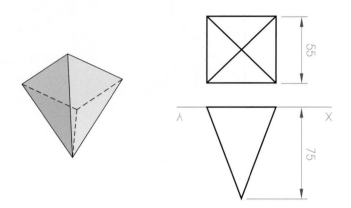

1. The plan and elevation are drawn as shown over.

2. The development will consist of four congruent isosceles triangles and a square.

3. The true length of the edge OB can be determined by rotating it until it is parallel to the vertical plane as shown. This true length gives the radius of the arc for the lateral edges.

4. The true length of the base of each triangle will be 55 mm long allowing the development to be completed as shown.

Exercise

The elevation and plan of a **two regular pyramids** are shown over. In each case:
(a) Draw the given views.
(b) Draw the complete **development** of the pyramid.

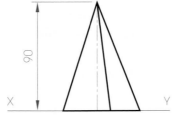
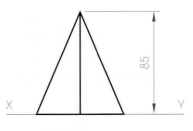

Example

The elevation and plan of a **truncated rectangular pyramid** are shown over.
(a) Draw the given views.
(b) Determine the **true shape** of the cut section of the solid.
(c) Draw the complete **development** of the truncated pyramid.

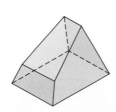
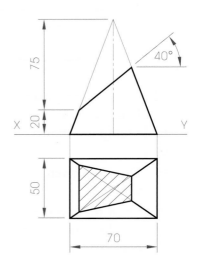

1. The elevation, plan and true shape are drawn as shown over.

2. The development of the truncated pyramid is constructed by first developing the whole pyramid. This is done using the procedure that was used in the previous example but the lateral edges must be drawn lightly.

3. Then the portion containing the apex is removed. This is achieved by locating the points where the cutting plane meets the lateral edges in the true length view and transferring these points to the development.

4. The base and true shape of the cut section are redrawn in the development allowing it to be completed as shown.

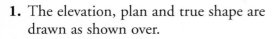
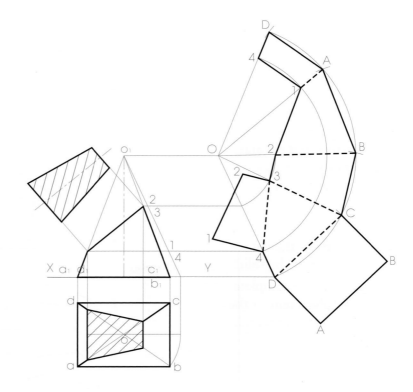

Exercises

1. The figure below shows the elevation and plan of two **light shades.**
Each shade is based on a frustum of a **regular pyramid.** In each case:

(a) Draw the given views.

(b) Draw the complete **development** of the shade.

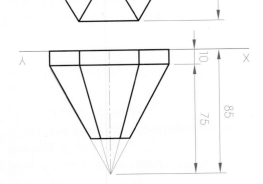

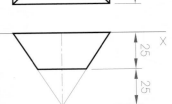

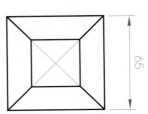

2. The elevation and plan
of a light shade for a
table lamp are shown
over.

(a) Draw the given
views.

(b) Draw the complete
development of the
light shade.

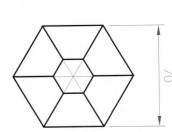

Regular hexagon

3. The figure over shows
the elevation and plan of
two **truncated regular
pyramids.** In each case:

(a) Draw the given
views.

(b) Determine the **true
shape** of the cut
section of the solid.

(c) Draw the complete
development of the
truncated pyramid.

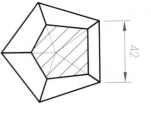

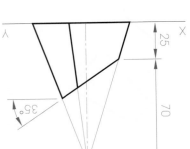

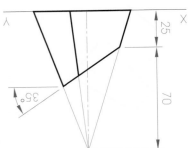

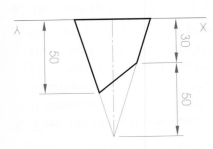

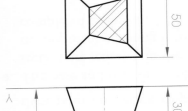

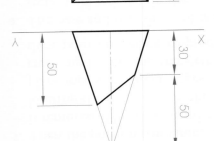

Example 1

The elevation and plan of a **cone** are shown over. A **development** of the cone is also shown.

1. From the illustration, far right, it can be seen that the development of the curved surface of a cone is a sector of a circle. The radius for the sector will be equal to the true length of the elements of the cone, which can be transferred from the elevation.

2. The length of the arc can be approximated by dividing the plan of the cone into twelve equal parts and setting out the resulting chord distance twelve times as shown.

3. The base, which appears in true shape in plan, can be redrawn to complete the development.

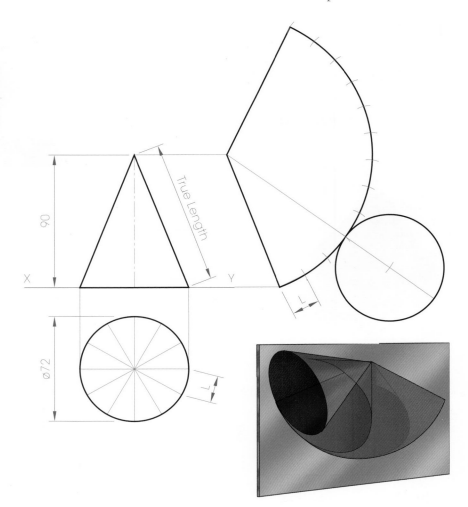

The development of the curved surface of a cone is a sector of a circle.

Example 2

The elevation and plan of a **shade** for a table lamp, which is based on a **frustum of a cone** are shown over. A **development** of the shade is also shown.

1. The development is constructed by first developing the complete curved surface of the cone as in the previous example.

2. Then the portion containing the apex is removed as shown.

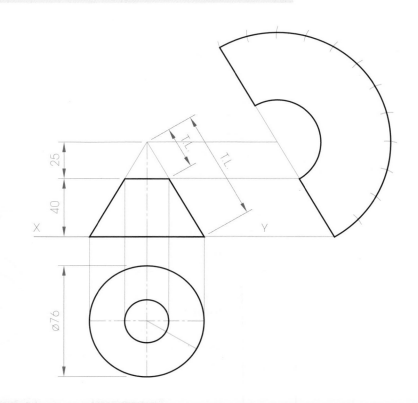

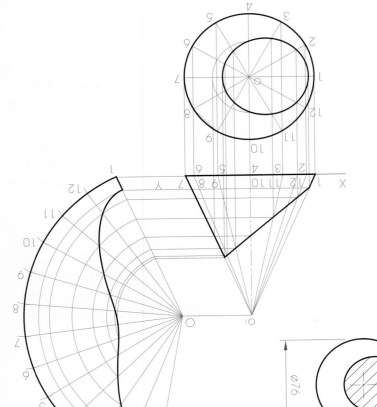

Example

The figure over shows the elevation and plan of a **truncated cone**.

(a) Draw the given views.

(b) Determine the **development** of the curved surface of the truncated cone.

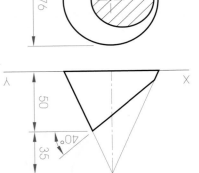

1. The outline plan and elevation are drawn in the normal manner.

2. The plan of the cut section is drawn by determining the plan of twelve equally spaced truncated elements on the cone as shown over. The truncation of elements O–4 and O–10 are determined in plan using a horizontal section.

3. The development of the truncated cone is constructed by first developing the whole cone and drawing in the elements as shown.

4. The portion containing the apex is then removed. This is done by locating the relevant points on the truncated elements in the true length as shown and transferring them to the development.

Ø76

50

35

40°

Exercise

The elevation and plan of a **canopy** and a shade for a **wall light** are shown below. In each case:

(a) Draw the given views.

(b) Draw the complete **development** of the object.

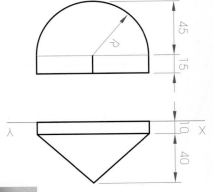

R

45

15

10

40

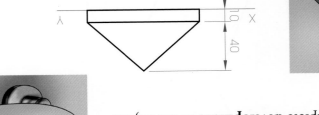

R

50

80

60

Exercises

1. The elevation and plan of the body of a **coal scuttle** are shown over.

  (a) Draw the given views.

  (b) Draw the complete **development** of the body of the coal scuttle.

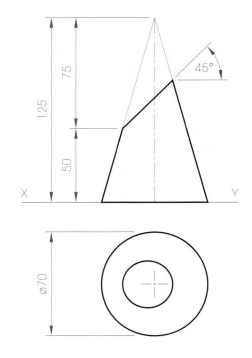

2. The figure below shows the elevation and plan of a **truncated solid**.

  (a) Draw the given views.

  (b) Determine the **true shape** of the cut section of the solid.

  (c) Draw the complete **development** of the solid.

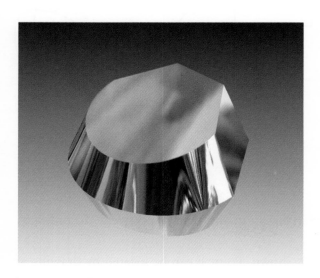

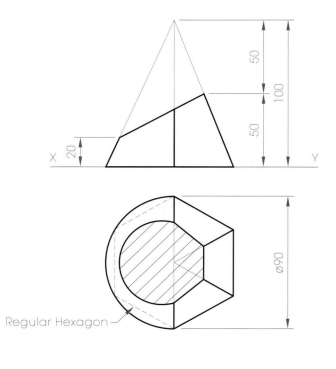

Regular Hexagon

Answer Worksheet 29D

Further Developments

Example
The elevation and plan of a container are shown over.

(a) Draw the given views.

(b) Determine the **true shape** of surfaces **T** and **S** of the container.

(c) Draw the complete **development** of the container.

1. The elevation and plan are drawn in the normal manner.

2. The true shape of surface T can be determined by rabatting it into the horizontal plane about the hinge line CD as shown below.

3. The true shape of surface S can be determined by rabatting it about the hinge line BC. Note that the true length of line CG can be transferred from the true shape of surface T.

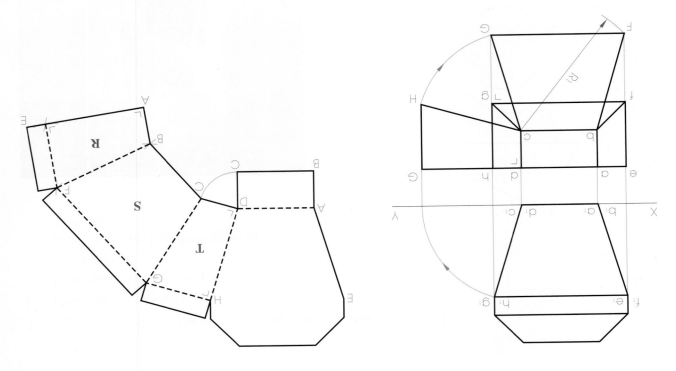

4. The back and base of the container appear in true shape in elevation and plan respectively. Accordingly, they can be redrawn in the development.

5. The true shape of surfaces T and S can then be redrawn as shown. Point F can then be located by drawing an arc of radius 70 mm from G and an arc of radius R_1 from C. Point B can be located in a similar manner.

6. Surface R can then be added to the development as shown.

7. The development is completed by drawing three rectangles having a width of 10 mm as shown.

Exercises

1. The figure over shows the elevation and plan of a **frustum of a rectangular pyramid**, which is based on a **Quality Street** box.

   (a) Draw the given views.

   (b) Determine the **true shape** of the sloping surfaces **A** and **B**.

   (c) Draw the complete **development** of the solid.

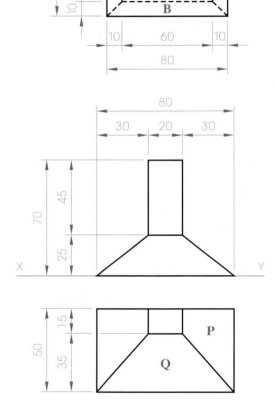

2. The elevation and plan of a solid, which forms the basis for a **cooker hood**, are shown over.

   (a) Draw the given views.

   (b) Determine the **true shape** of the sloping surfaces **P** and **Q** of the solid.

   (c) Draw the complete **development** of the solid.

3. The elevation, plan and end view of a **writing unit** are shown across.

   (a) Draw the **plan** and **elevation** of the unit.

   (b) Determine the **true shape** of the surface **S** of the unit.

   (c) Draw the complete **development** of the unit.

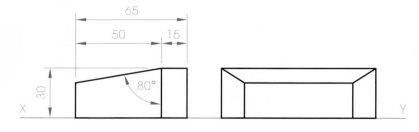

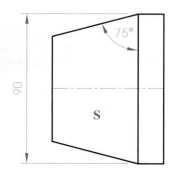

Chapter 30

Computer-aided Drawing

Computer-aided drawing (CAD) is the use of a computer system to produce drawings. It is very productive as computer-aided drawings are easily created, stored, retrieved and modified.

A CAD system is made up of two main components, namely **hardware** and **software**.

Hardware

Hardware refers to the physical parts of a computer system such as a mouse, keyboard or monitor. The hardware used in a CAD system can be divided into four categories:

- The systems box.
- Input devices.
- Output devices.
- Storage devices.

Desktop and Tower cases

The Systems Box

The systems box contains such items as the Central Processing Unit (CPU), Random Access Memory (RAM), sound card, graphics card and disk drives. The central processing unit can be considered to be the 'brain' of the computer and controls its operation.

The systems box can be a **desktop case** or a **tower case** as shown above.

Input Devices

Input devices are a means of giving the computer information by entering information into memory.

Mouse: A mouse is used to control the movement of the pointer (or cursor) on the screen.

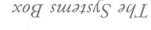

Mouse

Keyboard: A keyboard is used to input typed information.

Keyboard

Digitiser: A digitiser is a device used to enter drawings. It consists of a tablet and a puck. A puck is similar to a mouse with cross-hairs for accurate placement.

Scanner: A scanner can be used to scan a picture or image into a computer and produce a copy on-screen. This copy can be edited and stored for later use.

Scanner

Digital camera

Digital camera: A digital camera can be used to take a digital picture, which is saved onto a memory card. Such pictures can be transferred directly to a computer for a variety of uses.

Output Devices

Monitor: A monitor is used to display information on-screen.

Printer and **Plotter:** A printer or plotter is used to produce a printed copy of a drawing on paper (or other material), known as a **hard copy**. Printers and plotters vary in terms of size of hard copy produced, quality, speed and price.

Monitor

Inkjet Printer

Laser Printer

Plotter

Storage Devices

Storage devices are used to store and retrieve information that can be processed by a computer.

Hard disk: The hard disk is the main data storage device used by a computer. It is normally internal, i.e. housed within the tower/desktop case. It has the capacity to store vast amounts of information (80 GB and more).

Floppy disk

CDs/DVDs

Floppy disk: Floppy disks are used to store small amounts of data. Data can be read from, and written to, these disks by means of a floppy disk drive.

Compact Disk (CD) and Digital Versatile Disk (DVD): CDs and DVDs have a far greater storage capacity than floppy disks (in the region of 700 MB and 9.4 GB respectively). Some CDs/DVDs are read-only, while others can be read from and written to. They are useful for storing large files, software programs and even entire films in the case of DVDs.

CDs/DVDs can be read from/written to using the appropriate **CD/DVD drive**. Such disk drives can be internal or external.

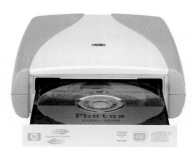

Disk drive

USB memory stick: USB memory sticks have a high capacity (from 128 MB up to 2 GB) and provide a reliable means of transporting files between computers. They are plugged into a port in the computer and are also known as flash drives.

The capacity of storage devices is continually increasing.

Answer Worksheets 30A and 30B

USB Memory Sticks

Software

Software refers to the sets of instructions, which tell the computer what to do and how to do it. There are two main categories of software:

- System software
- Application software

System software controls the internal operations of the computer.

Application software is the programs (sets of instructions) designed to allow you to accomplish specific tasks. Examples are word processors, paint programs, computer games and CAD programs.

Both systems and application software are normally stored on a hard disk.

A CAD Workstation

A CAD workstation is shown over. Some of the main parts have been labelled.

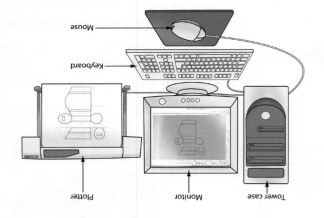

Tower case

Monitor

Plotter

Keyboard

Mouse

CAD Software

There are an extensive range of CAD programs available. CAD software is frequently used for architectural and engineering drawing and for creating any kind of technical illustrations.

AutoCAD is recognised as the standard CAD package for 2-D design. The AutoCAD screen is shown below. You use commands to get AutoCAD (or other CAD programs) to create, modify, store, retrieve and plot drawings. To enter a command you can:

- type a command,
- choose a command from a pull-down menu,
- click an icon in a toolbar.

Then you can respond to the prompts in the command line.

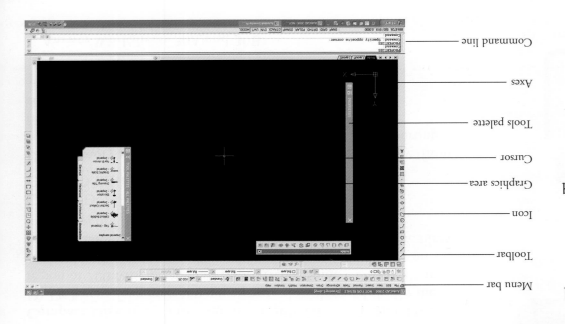

Menu bar

Toolbar

Icon

Graphics area

Cursor

Tools palette

Axes

Command line

Specifying Points in a Drawing

Points can be located in a drawing using the Cartesian coordinate system illustrated below.

The X-axis indicates horizontal distance and the Y-axis indicates vertical distance.

The origin point (0,0) is the point where the two axes meet.

Absolute Coordinates

Absolute coordinates are based on the origin (0,0). You can enter absolute coordinates using:

- Cartesian Coordinates
- Polar Coordinates

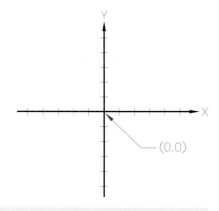

Cartesian coordinates are in the form (**X,Y**).

The X value indicates horizontal distance and the Y value indicates vertical distance in relation to the origin (0,0).

Example
Indicate the position of a point **P** (5,3) and a point **Q** (-4,-2) on the Cartesian coordinate system.

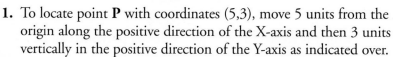

1. To locate point **P** with coordinates (5,3), move 5 units from the origin along the positive direction of the X-axis and then 3 units vertically in the positive direction of the Y-axis as indicated over.
2. To locate point **Q** with coordinates (-4,-2) move 4 units from the origin along the negative direction of the X-axis and then 2 vertically in the negative direction of the Y-axis as indicated over.

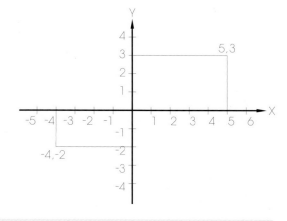

Polar coordinates can be entered in the form **distance<angle**.

Distance indicates the distance of the point from the origin (0,0).

Angle indicates the angle from the origin (0,0) measured from the positive direction of the X-axis.

Example
Indicate the position of a point **R** on a drawing specified by entering the polar coordinates 5<30.

The polar coordinates in the form 5<30 specify the location of a point 5 units from the origin along a line inclined at 30° to the positive direction of the X-axis as shown over.

Angles increase in the counter-clockwise direction and decrease in the clockwise direction.

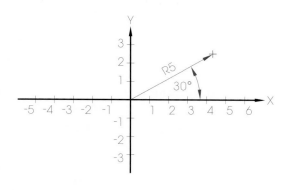

Relative Coordinates

You can enter **relative coordinates** based on the last point entered by preceding the coordinates with a @ sign. They are useful when you know the position of a point in relation to a previous point.

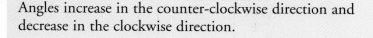

CAD Commands

Line

The line command is used to draw straight line segments by specifying both endpoints of the line.

Example

(a) Draw a **line** from the origin (0,0) to point P (20,30).

(b) Draw a **line** from point Q (40,40) to point R which is 60 units vertically below point Q.

Making the entries shown below in the command line results in the lines being drawn as indicated over.

Command: **line** ↵
Specify first point: **0,0** ↵
Specify next point: **20,30** ↵
Specify next point: ↵

Command: **line** ↵
Specify first point: **40,40** ↵
Specify next point: **@60<270** ↵
Specify next point: ↵

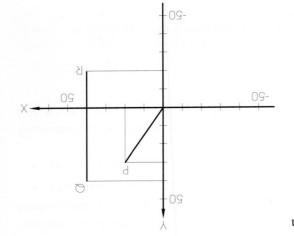

Polyline

A polyline is a connected sequence of line segments which is treated as a single entity. A polyline can be drawn using the polyline command (_pline).

Rectangle

The rectangle command is used to draw rectangles by specifying two opposite vertices of the rectangle.

Example

(a) Draw a **rectangle** with opposite vertices P (-40,-30) and Q (10,20).

(b) Draw a **rectangle** with one vertex at point R (20,10) which has a length of 30 units and a width of 20 units.

Making the entries shown below in the command line results in the rectangles being drawn as indicated over.

Command: **rectangle** ↵
Specify first corner point: **-40,-30** ↵
Specify other corner point: **10,20** ↵

Command: **rectangle** ↵
Specify first corner point: **20,10** ↵
Specify other corner point: **@30,20** ↵

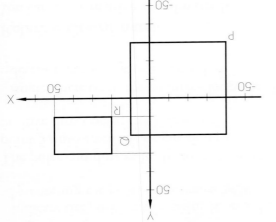

Answer Worksheets 3OC and 3OD

Polygon

The polygon command draws regular polygons. The polygon's size can be specified by the radius of a circle in which it is inscribed, or about which it is circumscribed, or by the length of one edge.

The following command sequences show how to draw a polygon using these three methods.

Pentagon

Command: **polygon** ↵
Enter number of sides: **5** ↵
Specify centre of polygon: **0,0** ↵
Inscribed in/Circumscribed about: **I** ↵
Specify radius of circle: **0,40** ↵

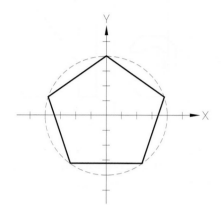

Hexagon

Command: **polygon** ↵
Enter number of sides: **6** ↵
Specify centre of polygon: **0,0** ↵
Inscribed in/Circumscribed about: **C** ↵
Specify radius of circle: **0,30** ↵

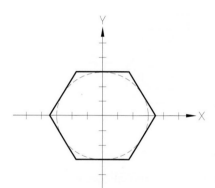

Triangle

Command: **polygon** ↵
Enter number of sides: **3** ↵
Specify centre of polygon: **Edge** ↵
Specify first endpoint of edge: **10,10** ↵
Specify second endpoint of edge: **40,0** ↵

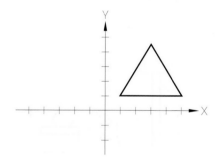

Circle

The circle command can be used to draw a circle by specifying the centre and radius as indicated over.

Command: **circle** ↵
Specify centre point: **10,20** ↵
Specify radius of circle: **30** ↵

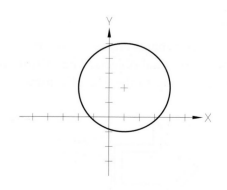

Erase

The erase command allows you to delete objects from a drawing.

Move

The move command lets you move objects a specified distance in a specified direction without changing their orientation or size. It has the same effect as translation.

Copy

The copy command creates a duplicate of objects a specified distance and direction from the original. It leaves the original objects intact.

Rotate

The rotate command allows you to change the position and orientation of objects by rotating them about a specified base point. It has the same effect as rotation with the base point corresponding to the centre of rotation.

Mirror

The mirror command creates a mirror image of objects in relation to a specified mirror line. You can retain or delete the original objects. The mirror command has the same effect as axial symmetry with the mirror line corresponding to the axis of symmetry.

Scale

The scale command changes the size of an object without changing its proportions. Objects can be made larger or smaller. The scale command has the same effect as enlargement and reduction.

Stretch

The stretch command can be used to make objects longer or shorter in one direction.

Trim

The trim command allows you to shorten objects to end precisely at the edges of other objects.

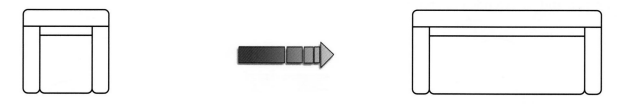

Extend

The extend command allows you to lengthen objects to end precisely at the edges of other objects.

Boundary Hatch

The boundary hatch command allows you to hatch a region. Yon can choose from a variety of patterns. The effect of a solid hatch pattern is shown below.

Chamfer

The chamfer command connects two non-parallel lines with a third line which is a specified distance from their intersection. The two original lines are trimmed and/or extended as appropriate.

Fillet

The fillet command connects two lines with a tangential arc of a specified radius. The two original lines are trimmed and/or extended as appropriate.

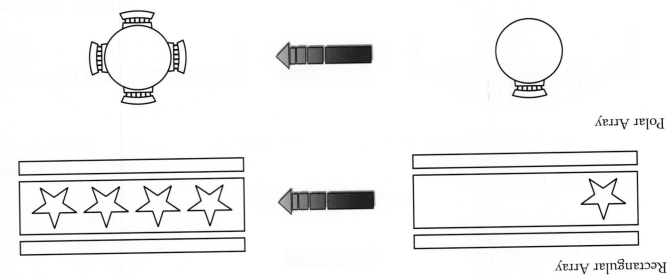

Array

The array command creates multiple copies of objects in a rectangular or polar (circular) pattern.

Rectangular Array

Polar Array

Offset

The offset command constructs an object parallel to another object at a specified distance from it.

Example
List the CAD commands used to modify the figure as shown in the sequence below.

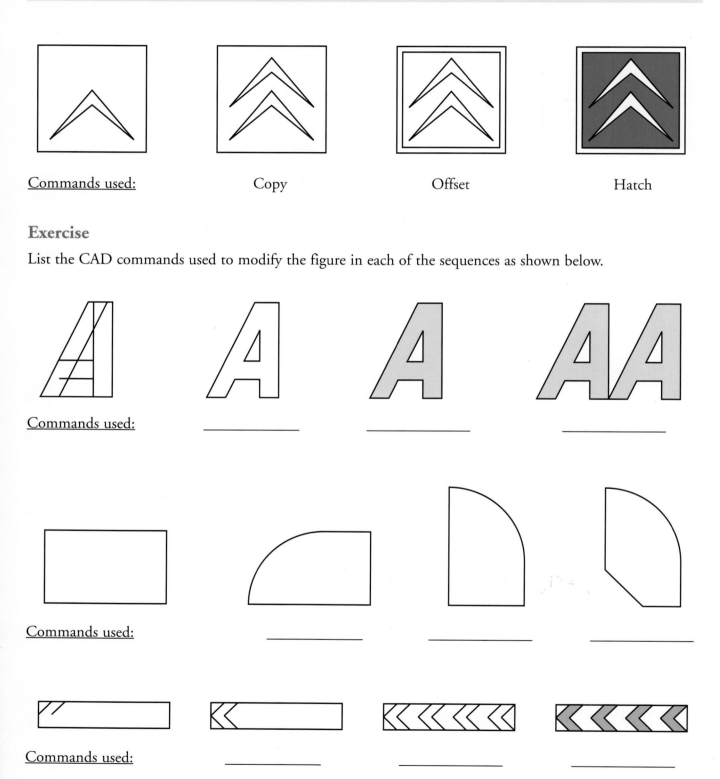

Commands used: Copy   Offset   Hatch

Exercise
List the CAD commands used to modify the figure in each of the sequences as shown below.

Commands used: _____   _____   _____

Commands used: _____   _____   _____

Commands used: _____   _____   _____

Answer Worksheets 30E and 30F

0167235559